Trees

Trees

DAVID FINN

Introduction by Donald Holden

RUDER FINN PRESS

Editorial Director: Susan Slack
Creative Director: Lisa Gabbay
Design Director: Emily Korsmo, Ruder Finn Design
Production Director: Valerie Thompson
Pre-Press: Steve Moss

ISBN 10: 1-932646-25-6
ISBN 13: 978-1-932646-25-2

PRINTED IN THE UNITED STATES OF AMERICA
by Ruder Finn Printing Services, New York
Bryan D'Orazio, Senior Vice President

For Peter
whose idea
it was
to publish this book

For the Love of Trees:
David Finn's Watercolors

DONALD HOLDEN

EUGENE DELACROIX, WHOSE GREAT oil paintings were done in his Paris studio, painted small, charming watercolors on location. He warned artists never to exhibit an oil painting side-by-side with a watercolor. The freshness, spontaneity, transparency, luminosity, intimacy, and sheer simplicity of the watercolor would make the oil painting look dim and heavy-handed by comparison. And with the passage of years, the colors in the oil painting would "come down," while the watercolor would remain as fresh as ever.

Henry Miller, who painted watercolors for sheer joy, wrote an essay the title of which said it all: *To Paint Is to Love Again*.

Those of us who paint watercolors are head-over-heels in love with watercolor—in love with the medium itself. We don't just call ourselves painters. We call ourselves *watercolorists*.

David Finn's delicious watercolors exemplify all the qualities that we love in this delightful—but demanding—medium.

One great attraction of watercolor is that you can make a statement in a brief time with the simplest technical means. I have a happy image of David working with nothing more than a child needs to express his enchantment with his subject: a cup of water, a sheet of paper, one slender brush or perhaps a pen to draw lines, a bigger brush to add color, and a few colors in a pocket-sized painting kit.

Rembrandt (whose monochrome watercolors David has always loved) needed even less: a tiny scrap of paper, a quill or reed pen, a single brush—and no more than a teaspoonful of brown color, diluted with fresh water from the well! And so did all the early masters of watercolor, who made what we now call *wash drawings* in monochrome: Guercino, Tiepolo, Fragonard, and a long list of other great artists.

In his own approach to watercolor, David goes back to these seventeenth and eighteenth century masters—back to the essentials of the medium. He begins with a line drawing: a springy, rhythmic drawing that seems spontaneous, but is actually the product of careful observation and planning. David's great subject is trees, and he strives to capture the unique design, movement, and "personality" of his subject in line before he goes any further and starts to think about color.

When he feels that the line drawing is "right," when he feels that those few simple lines anchor the image solidly on the page, then David is ready to consider adding color.

Selecting just a few colors, he places patches of transparent color between and around the lines. These "color spots" (as the great teacher Charles Hawthorne called them) look spontaneous, as if they're just dashed in. But they're carefully considered and exactly placed. The shape of each "color spot" is designed to complement the nearby lines, and harmonize with an area of bare paper that the lines enclose.

Rather like the colors in Cézanne's watercolors, David's patches of color don't simply fill in the bare paper, but let areas of paper remain untouched. They become passages of pure light, shining between the colors.

The final painting is a free form interplay of lines, patches of color, and patches of bare paper. When I look at David's watercolors, I often think that they're stained glass windows, like fragments of colored glass, limpid and luminous; fragments of clear glass, like brilliant sunlight surrounding the colored shapes; and dark lines, like the leaded structure that holds the entire design together.

For David Finn's many admirers—who know David's achievements as a writer, sculptor, painter, and world-class photographer—this lovely book will reveal a new side of this amazingly versatile man-of-the-arts.

Trees

DAVID FINN

IF I REMEMBER CORRECTLY, I painted my first watercolors when I was about fourteen years old and had become ill with a bad case of pneumonia. When I recovered, my mother took me to Lakewood, New Jersey, to regain my strength. She must have bought a set of watercolors for me, since I remember walking around the lake and painting trees with their reflections in the water.

A couple of years later I found myslef creating sketches on my subway ride to DeWitt Clinton High School in the Bronx. I lived in Manhattan, and the daily trip to school took about 45 minutes each way, which gave me a lot of time to be creative. For a while I made pen and ink sketches of people sitting in the subway. Then I decided to try to do watercolors, and I invented a method of doing so. I filled a small plastic container with brown watercolor paint. Then I attached the container to a Chinese watercolor brush. When I opened the stopper of the container the paint seeped into the hairs of the brush, and I could make quick watercolor sketches of people in the subway. I made quite a few of them and prided myself in thinking they looked a little like Rembrandt's sketches.

On weekends I would walk in Manhattan's Central Park, which I always loved, taking a regular watercolor set with me to paint trees in landscapes. I never got tired of looking at the trees in Central Park. I thought they were magical. At the time I had a teacher who admired the watercolors of George Grosz, and he urged me to learn how to achieve the fluidity of Grosz's technique. But, I developed my own technique to show how the branches of trees created such amazing forms. Henry Moore once told me that he only drew trees in winter; he thought that the foliage in summer looked like cabbage and hid the wonderful forms of branches. I liked to draw and paint trees in all seasons.

I soon began to create oil paintings of other subjects, but I continued to paint watercolors of trees as a way of expressing my love of nature.

After my wife, Laura, and I were married, we lived for a while in Laura's parents' apartment on 111th Street and Broadway in Manhattan, and I painted some watercolors looking out the window of their living room. When we moved to our own apartment in Queens, I painted watercolors looking out of our bedroom window. After our children were born, I painted watercolor portraits of them. When we bought a house in New Rochelle, I painted watercolors of Paine Lake a few blocks away. For a while on weekends I would walk around another lake a little further away from our home and made watercolor sketches of different scenes there. And when we used to vacation at a little house right near the ocean in Florida, at Daytona Beach, I painted watercolors there as well.

Then, for some reason, I stopped painting watercolors. For many years my chosen medium was oil on canvas, and I created a number of series inspired by great works of poetry. Several books of those paintings have been published—one on T.S. Eliot's *Four Quartets*, another on W. B. Yeats's *Byzantium* and *Sailing to Byzantium*, a third on Keats's *Endymion*, and a fourth on Francis Thompson's *The Hound of Heaven*. I also created a series on Milton's *Paradise Lost*, and have been working on a series on Dante's *Paradisio*. I have done a great many of those paintings over the years.

About fifteen years ago, I started painting watercolors again. I remembered the paintings of trees I had made in Central Park and around the lake in New Rochelle, and I found myself focusing on trees on our own property at home. I found that I could always create new compositions looking at the same tree from different angles. My favorite was a Japanese apple tree in the middle of our lawn that had branches going in almost all directions. We called it the "the marrying tree" because all our four children were married under its branches. A few years ago, our "marrying tree" died, and I was devastated. When our gardeners were cutting it apart to take it away, I asked them to leave the trunk and a few branches for me, and I spent a year carving a life-size dancer out if its forms. That sculpture is now is at the entrance of my New York office.

Fortunately there were many other trees on our property, and they gave me an infinite number of images for my watercolors. I felt I could spend my life finding new forms in those trees, and over the years I have never failed to find a different inspiration from a branch here or there. I started painting watercolors every day on weekends, and by now I must have painted hundreds of them. Two more of my favorite trees that were subjects of many paintings have died—which has been painful for me; but there are still plenty of other trees on our property that continue to be inspirations for my watercolors.

When I go outside to select an image of a branch or several branches for a watercolor, I have no idea what I will find. I walk around the grounds—or look through a window if it is raining or snowing—and always find a form that attracts me at that moment. I first make a drawing on the paper of that image, and then I spend some time painting the colors on the paper. Occasionally I don't like what I have done, and when that happens I throw the painting away and start another one immediately, usually of the same subject. The second time it always turns out much better.

I feel a compulsion to do at least a couple of watercolors every week-end, and I sign and date them. This is unusual for me, for I have never signed the oil paintings inspired by poems—somehow I feel they are too close to the lines that inspired them for me to claim them as my own. Instead I write the lines of the poem to which they are related in the margins of the paintings. But signing and dating my watercolors seems right. They are like my diary. They express unconsciously what I feel about life on the day I happen to paint them.

I admire many watercolor paintings created by artists like J.M.W. Turner and Winslow Homer, or more recently, by my friend Donald Holden. They are highly accomplished works. I don't think of my watercolors in that way. I feel they are momentary views of a part of the world I live in. I enjoy creating them as expressions of my love of beauty. My eye becomes inspired as it looks at the wonders of nature that can be seen in that special part of a tree.

Laura used to ask me, "Why do you only paint trees with your watercolors? Why don't you paint something else?" She doesn't ask me that any more, since I never stopped painting trees. The truth is that I don't know the answer to Laura's question. I just know that I love to look at them and paint them. And I am pretty literal about the forms I pick out of trees. If a branch twists to the right, I draw it that way. If it turns up or down, I draw it that way. I feel differently when I put colors on the paper. I like the pools of color to have some resemblance to the tree or the sky or the ground, but I never make them literal images of what I see. In a way, the form of the tree or branch is the skeleton of the painting, and it has to be real. It is the source of my inspiration. But the colors in the painting are abstract. I have no problem choosing or shaping the colors in a way that I find striking. I never make them literal images of what I see, and they may even have little relationship to the scene in front of me. The paintings are a peculiar mixture of what I see and what I feel.

There are dozens of watercolors framed in my firm's offices. Sometimes a friend asks if he or she can have one, and I am glad to present it as a gift. But I have never sold any watercolors. I feel they are simply personal expressions of my inner feelings. Creating them is its own reward.

It was my son, Peter, who suggested that a book be published with my watercolors. I don't know why he suggested it, but I was pleased with the idea. I had never thought of publishing such a book, although I have published so many books over the years. But then the question was—how many watercolors should there be, and how should I select them?

I keep most of my watercolors on racks in my basement, and when Peter talked about creating a book, I decided to take them all out and select those that I thought were the best. I was surprised how many there were that I didn't think were so good and wondered if I should throw them away. But I remembered that friends who have asked for a watercolor often picked one I didn't think was so successful. So I felt I should not trust my own judgment, and just keep them all.

However, this time, for a book of my watercolors, I wanted to choose the ones I thought were my best. Peter thought we might want to publish 200 or 300 of them, but I focused on the ones that meant the most to me, and there were only a few more than 100.

Then Michael Schubert, my friend and colleague, who has worked on so many books with me, suggested that we lay all of them out in a conference room and see if we could figure out categories that would work as separate chapters. This would help us group them appropriately. I pointed out that each of the watercolors was signed and dated, and maybe we should think of putting together the ones that were dated for each month. Michael loved the idea of separating them out into twelve sections, and we were delighted when we found that we could select eleven of my favorite paintings for each month. That's how the plan for this book came about.

As I looked at the paintings dated for different months, I discovered that there was a consistency in each of those periods. I guess it should not be surprising that the watercolors I did in a particular month, no matter what year they were done, had something in common. I had never been aware of that before. Making a selection of paintings by month—regardless of year—then seemed to make a lot of sense.

I wondered what kind of text should be in such a book. I tried several approaches. First I thought of just putting some words together that expressed the feeling of the month. I had done something similar for text in a book on the sculpture of Lynn Chadwick, and that had worked out quite well. But somehow, I wasn't sure that was the right approach for this book. Then, since I had considered these watercolors as a sort of diary, I wondered if I should write something that happened in my life in each particular month, no matter what year it happened, as an accompanying text. Thus, January was my brother, Herbert's, birthday; February was my father's birthday; March was my sister's as well as two of my children's birthdays. I tried writing something about each of them, with confidence that I could find some part of my life that was related to each month of the year. But when I wrote those few examples, I didn't think they made much sense. There was really no relation between the images in the watercolors and the stories of people I would choose to write about for each month.

Then, I went back to the idea of writing words that were inspired by the paintings. This time it seemed to work. It helped a good deal when I came up with the idea of shaping the passages in geometric patterns, which somehow gave an added character to the images.

The way I formed the words seemed to have some relation to the way I painted the watercolors.

And so that's how this book came about. In a way it is a brief story of my life, without any details. I have been doing watercolors for all these years, and although I have kept on painting after making the selections for this book, I think the ones I chose for each month make sense. They are images that tell my story.

Somehow, I hope that these paintings representing each month of the year reflect an important part not only of my life but of other lives as well.

January

The forms of trees
trunks, branches, spaces
against the winter sky (sometimes
casting shadows on the snow)—life
seems far away. Curves, angles, rising upwards,
extending outwards, creating spaces in
between, thin lines and outlines,
images that show the barren
beauty at the height
of winter.

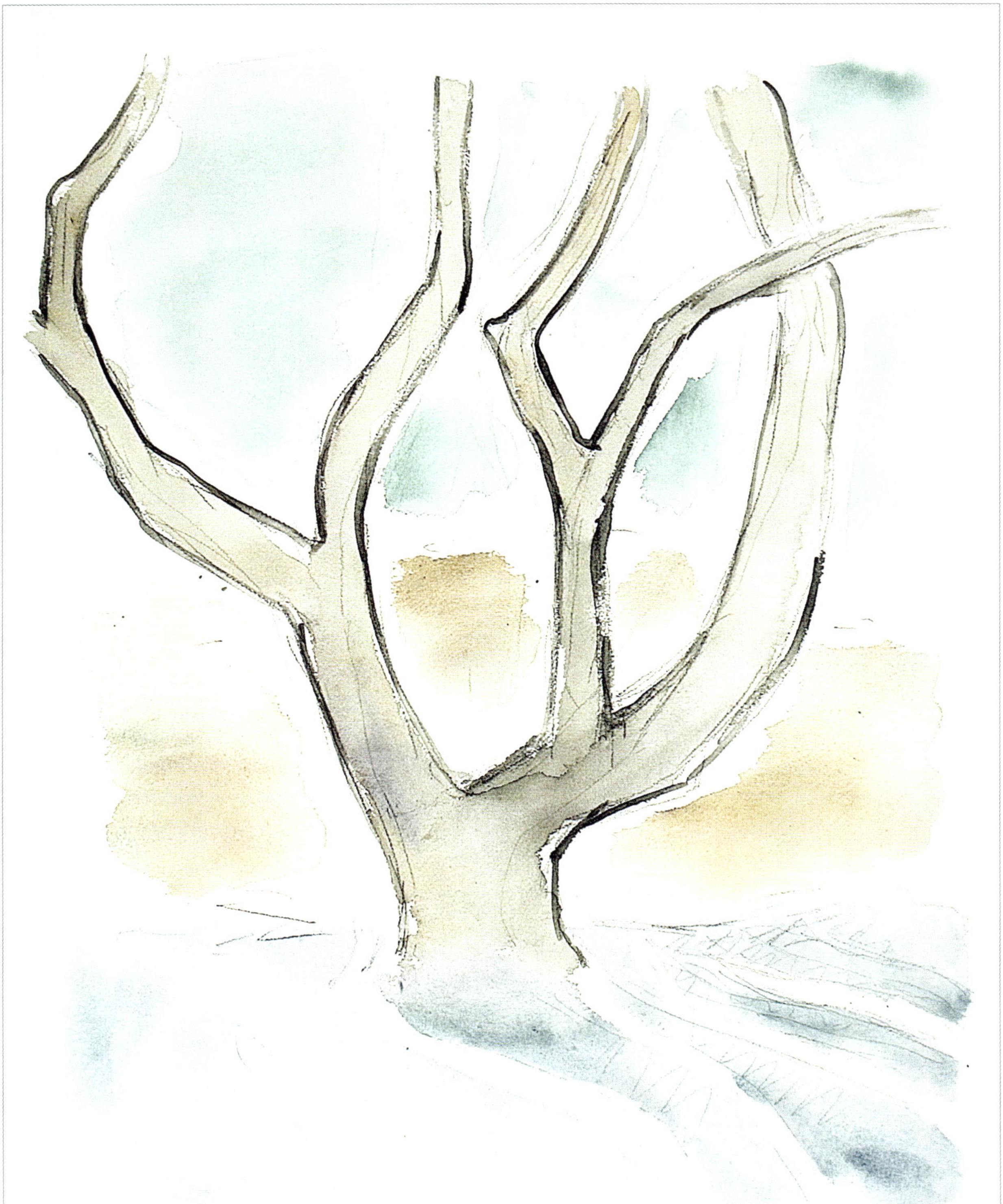

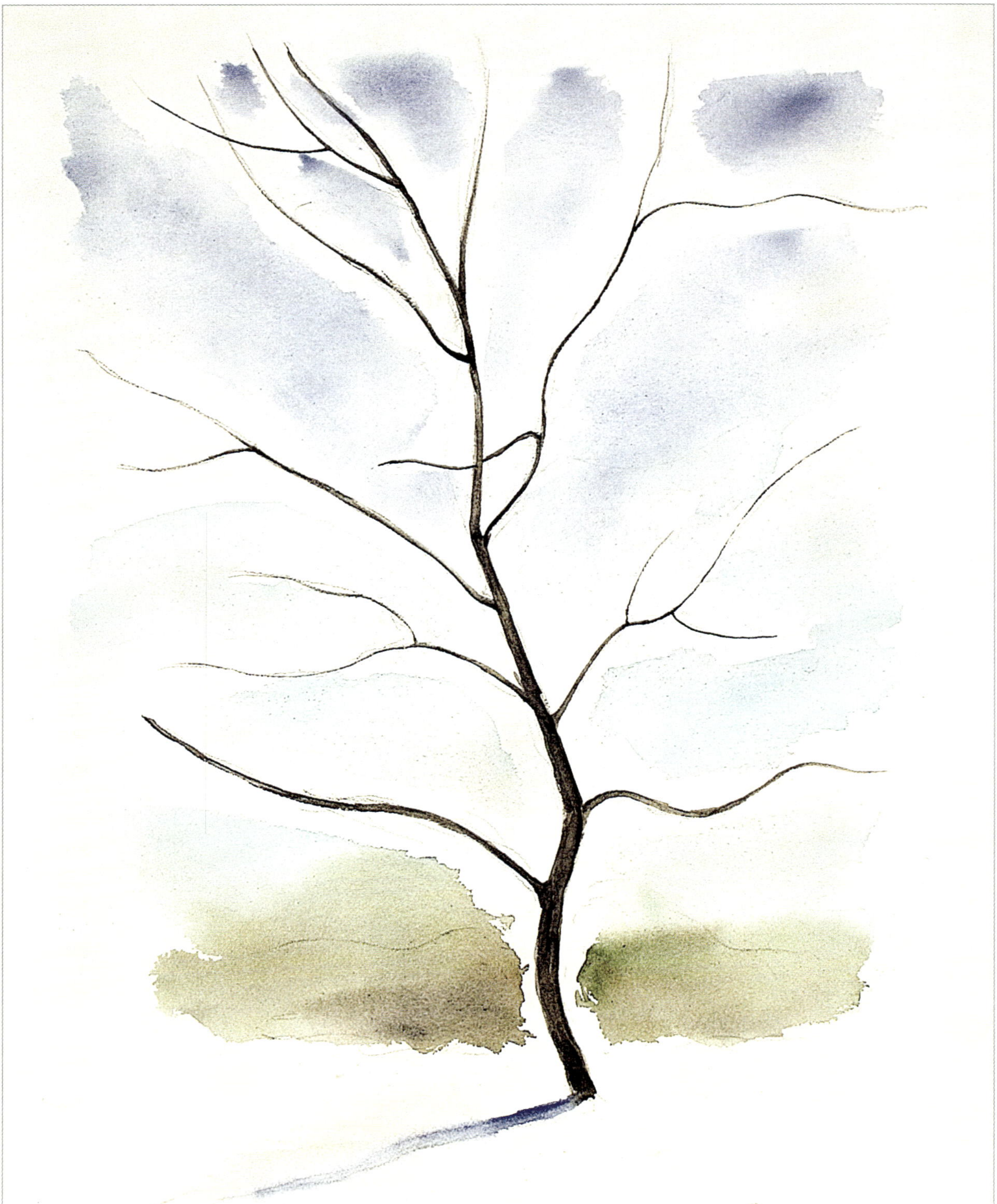

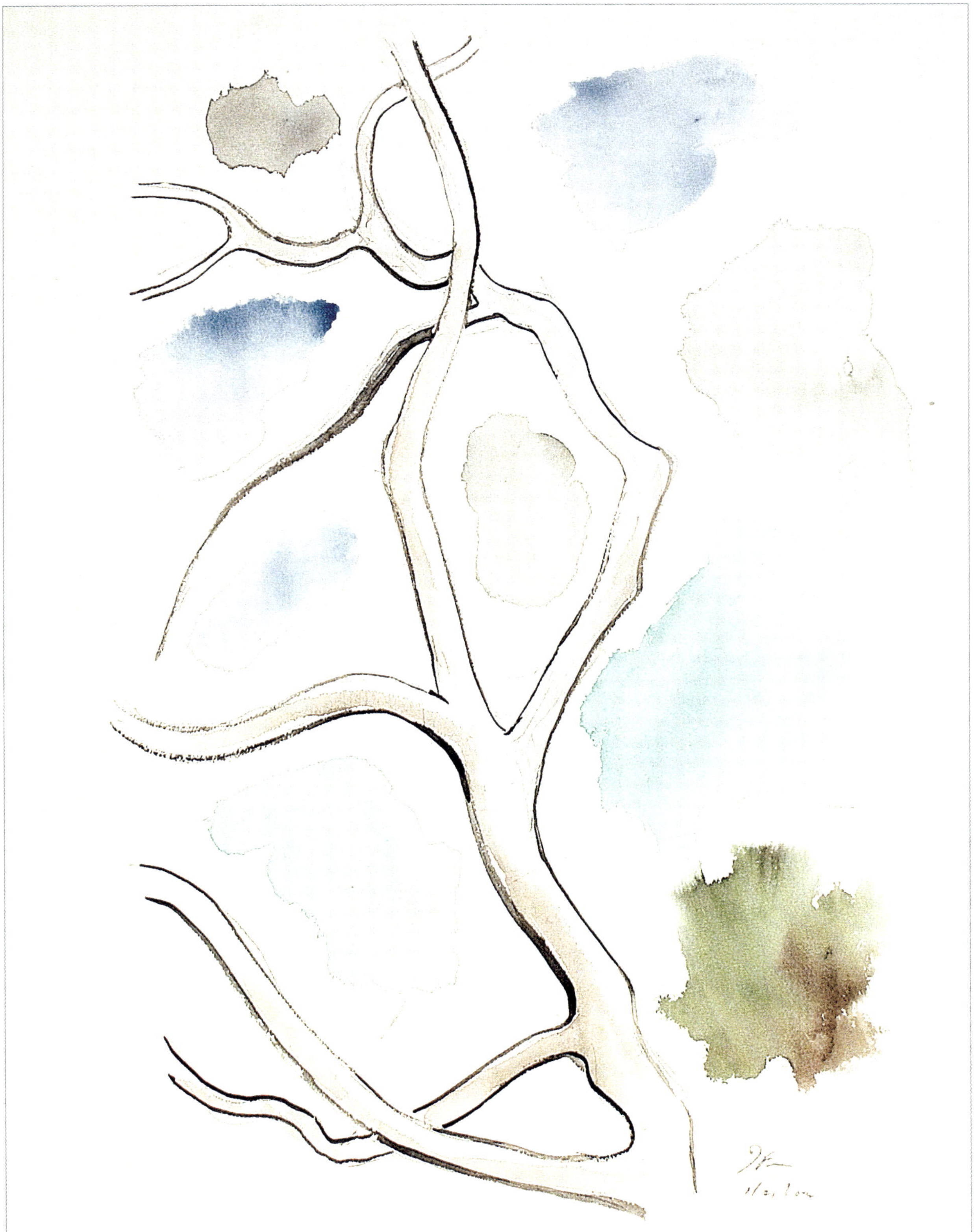

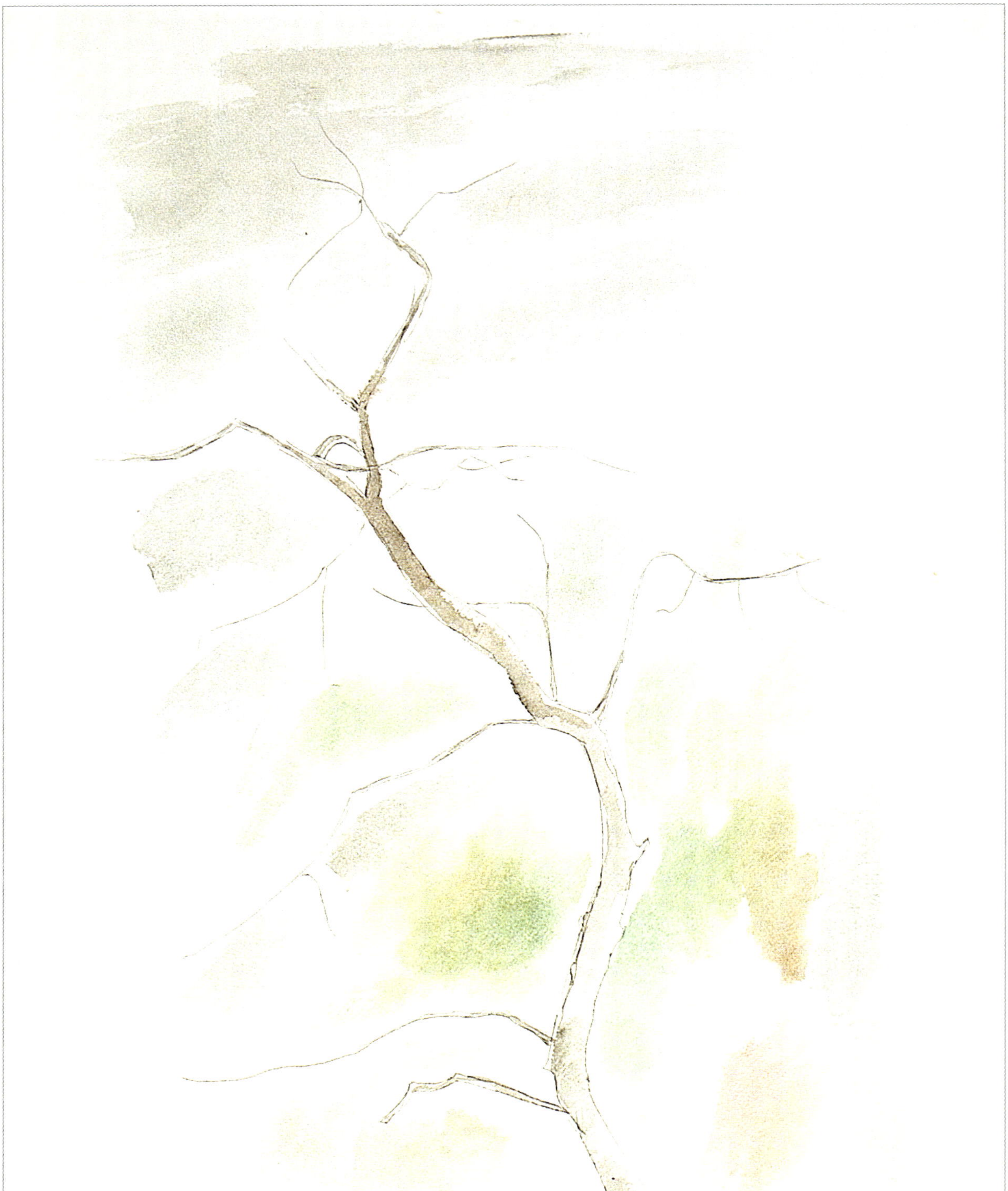

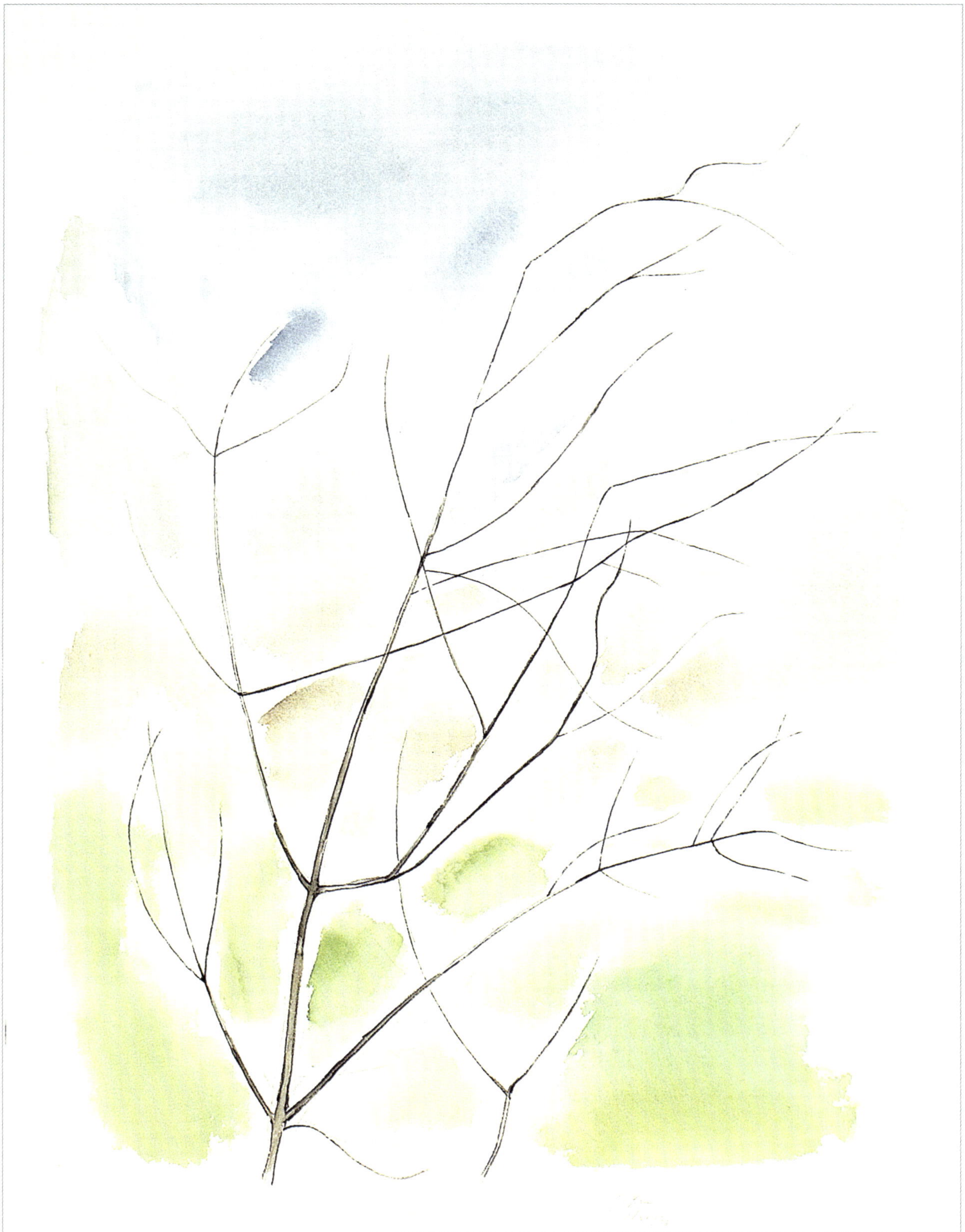

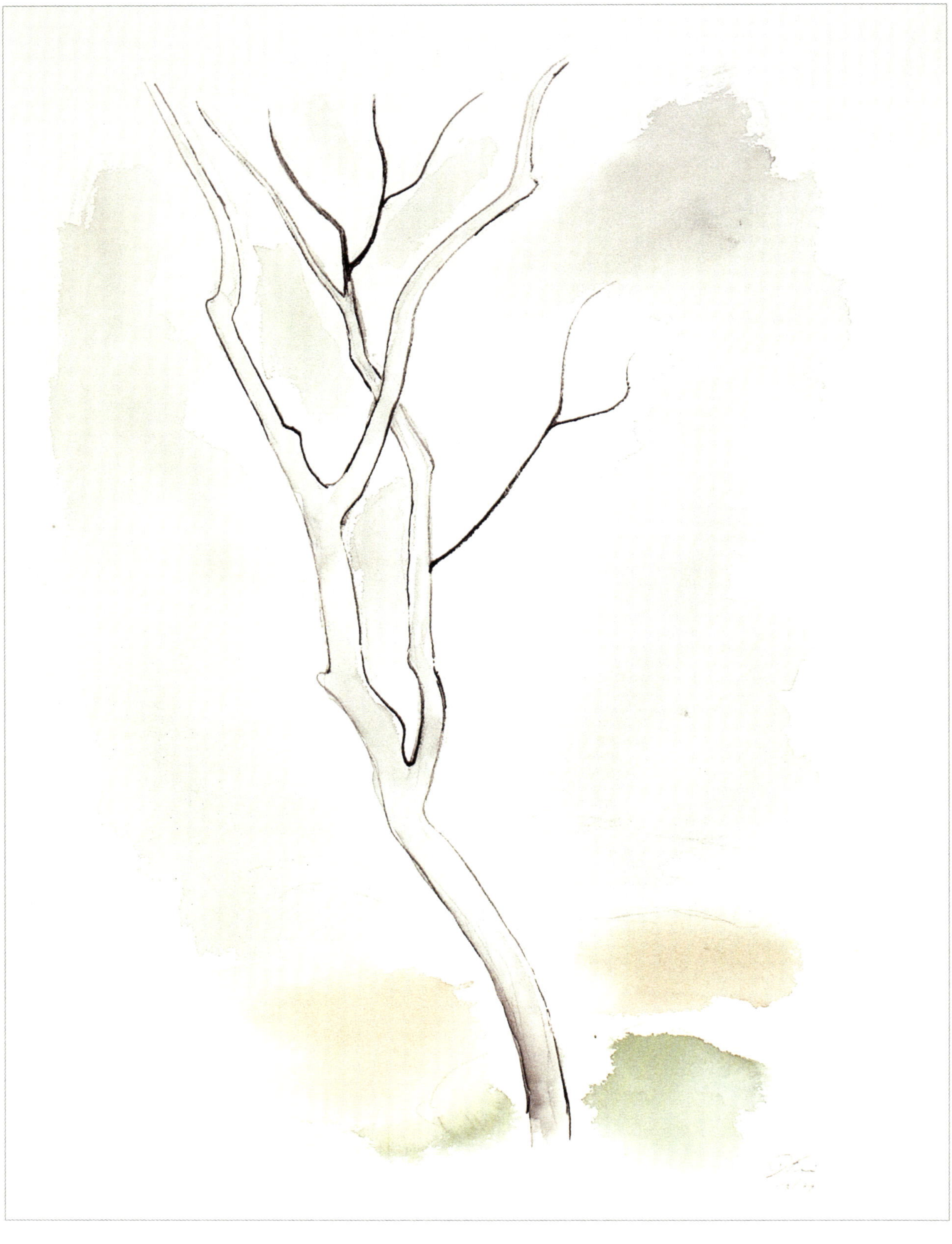

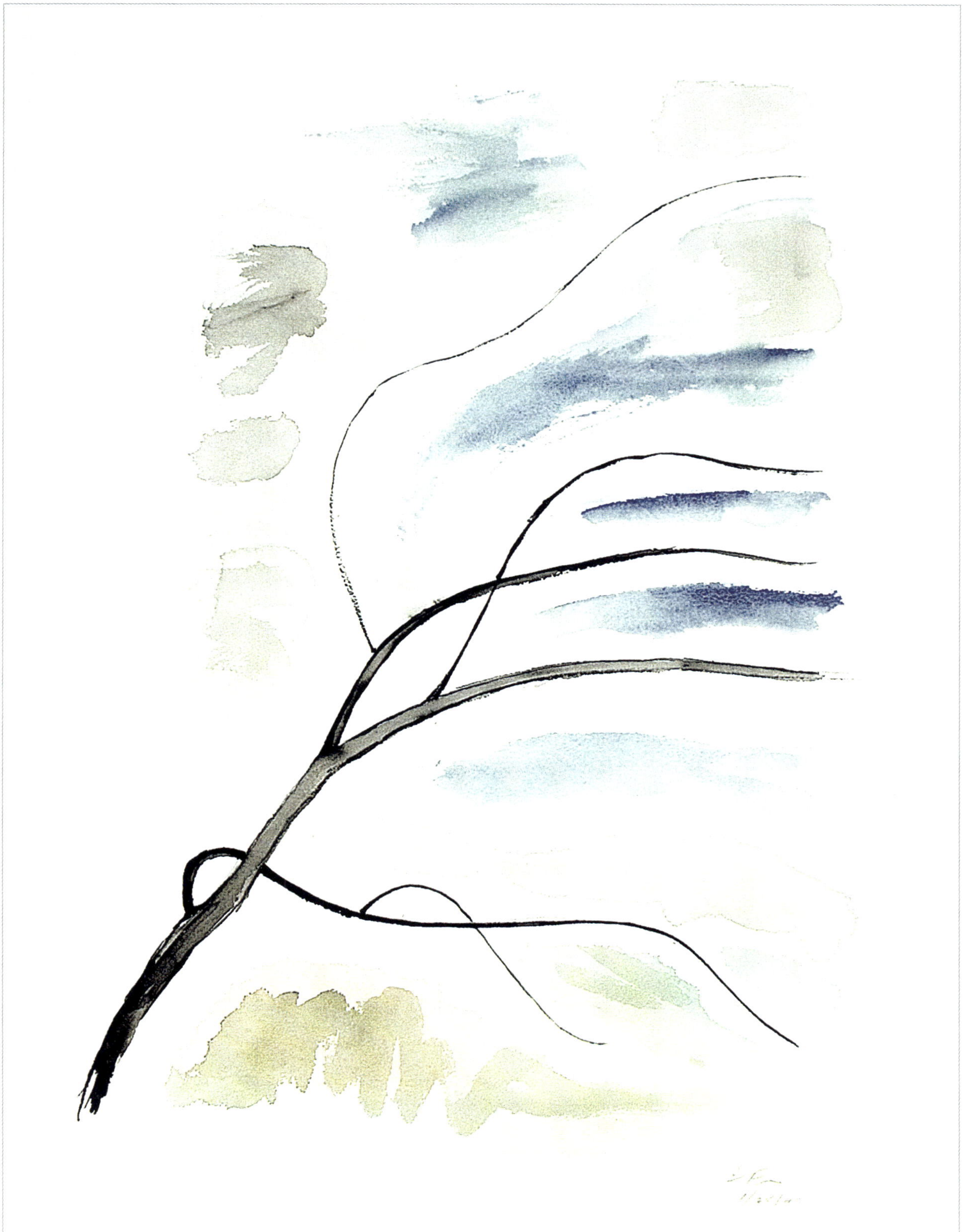

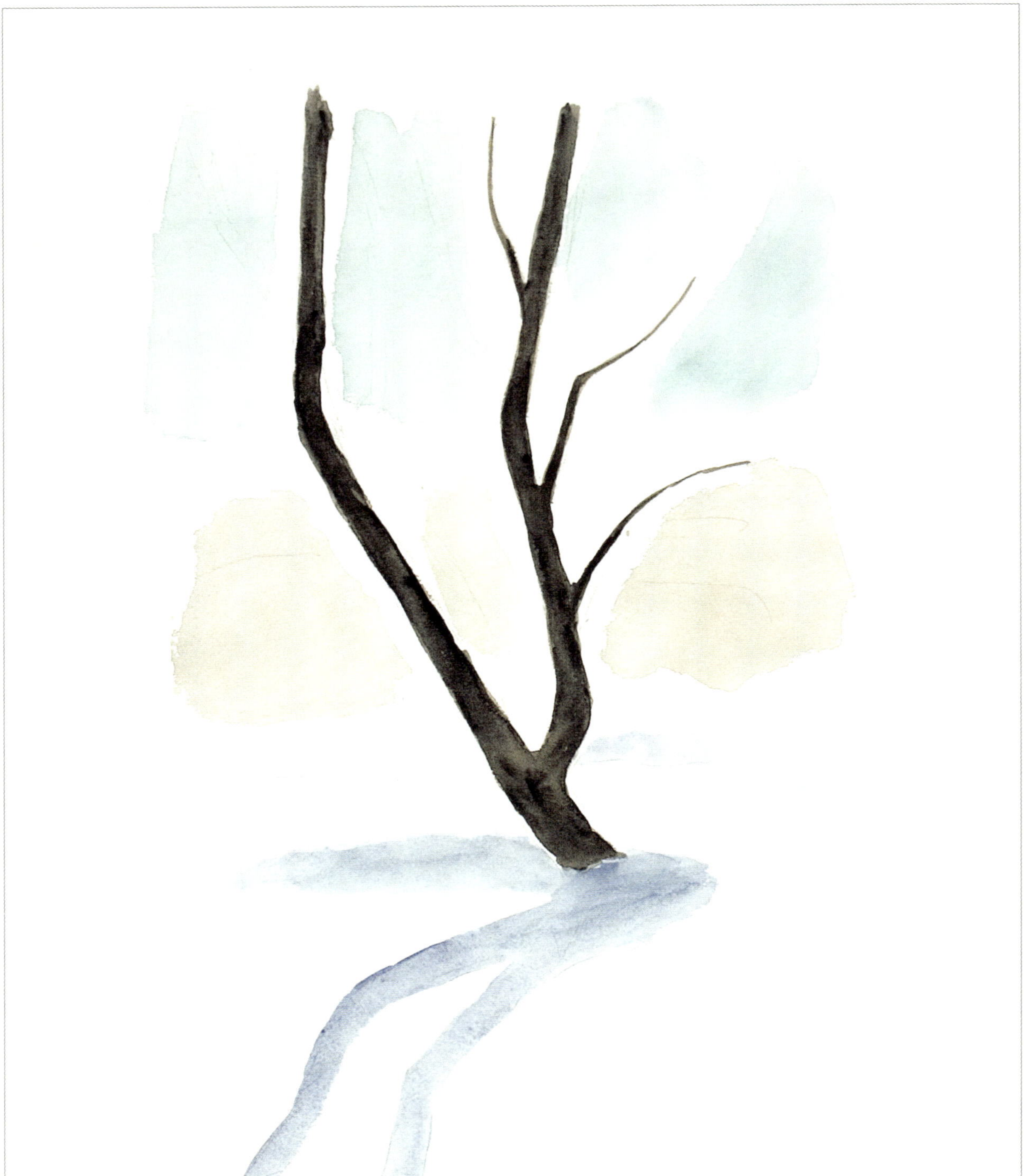

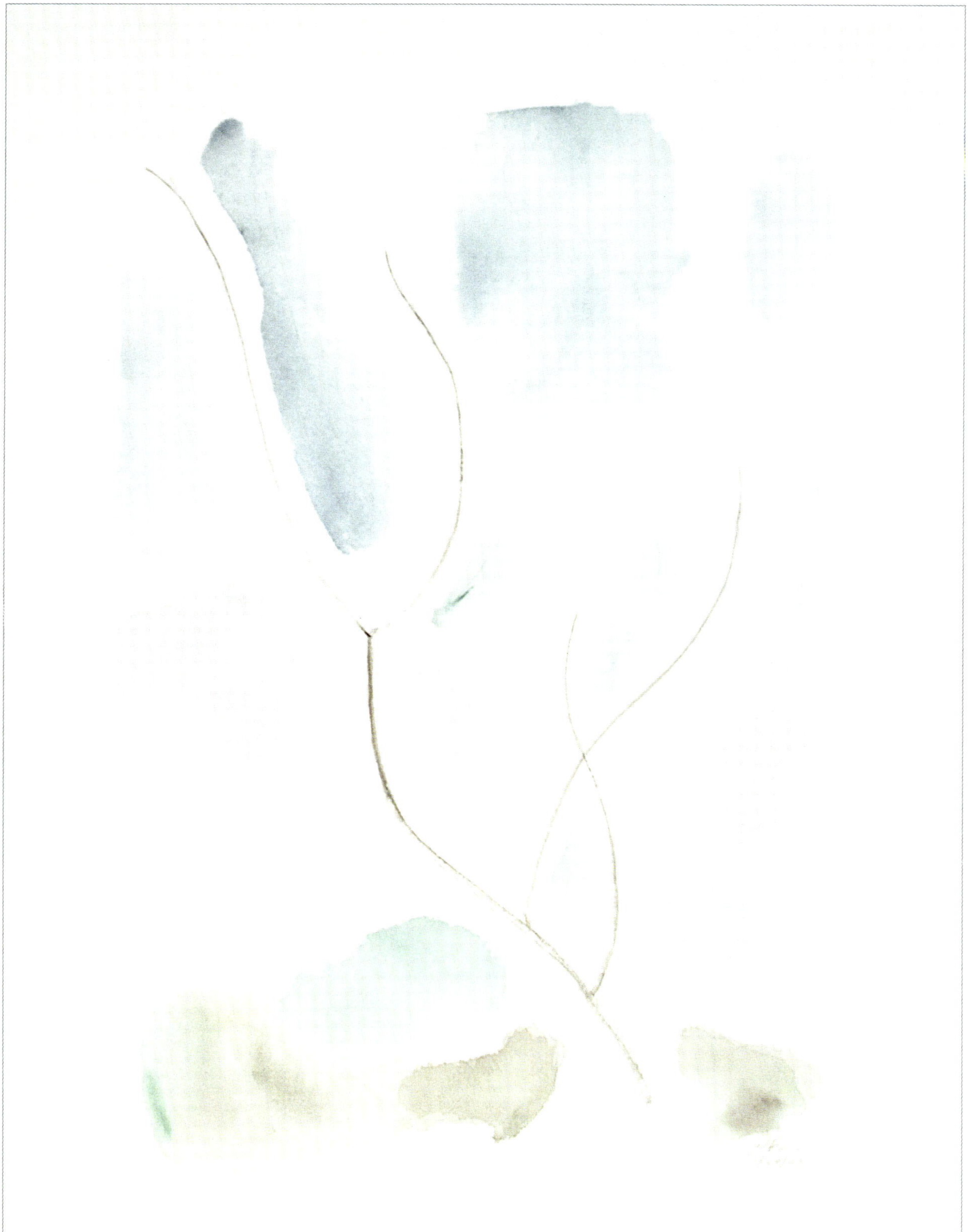

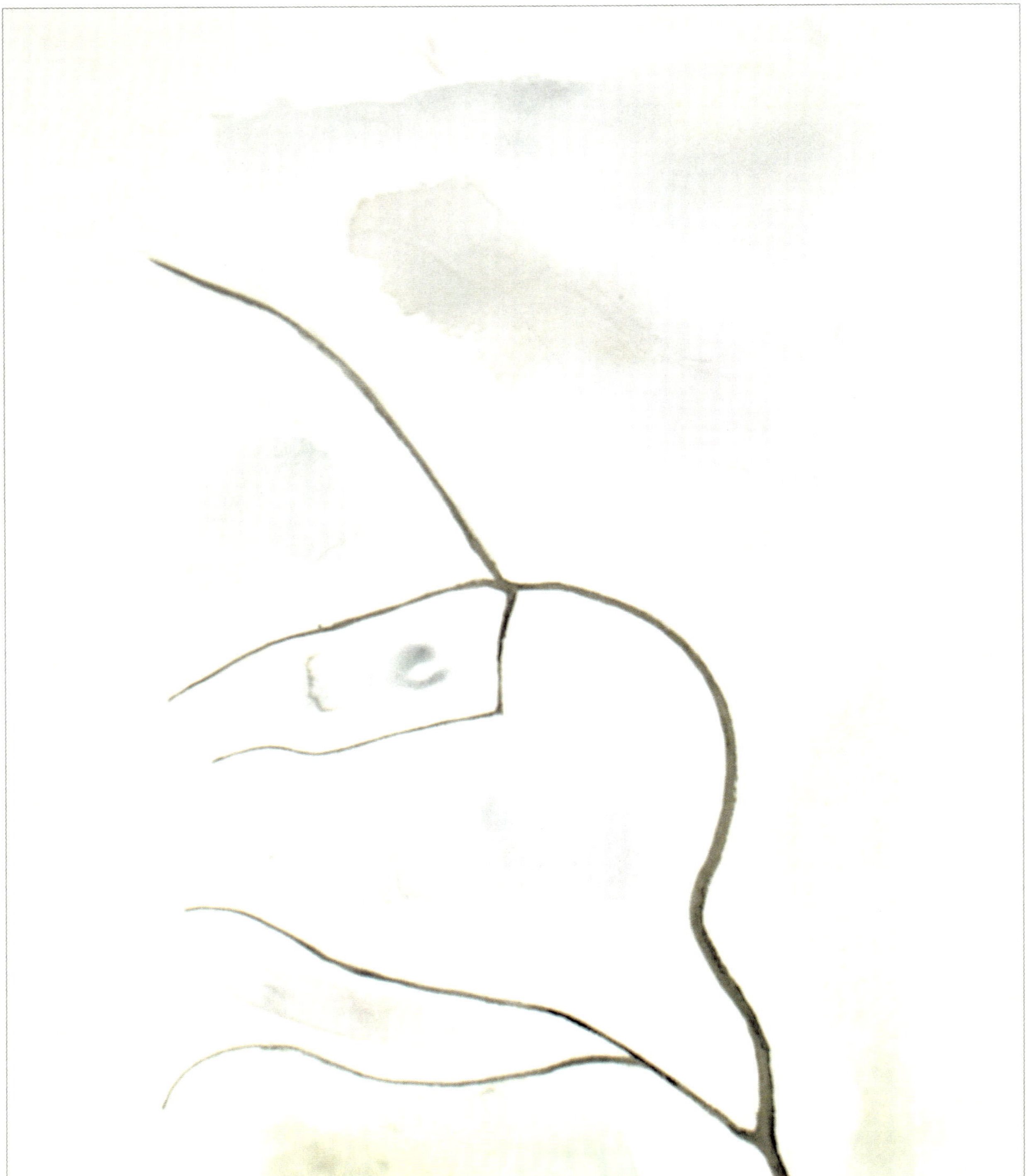

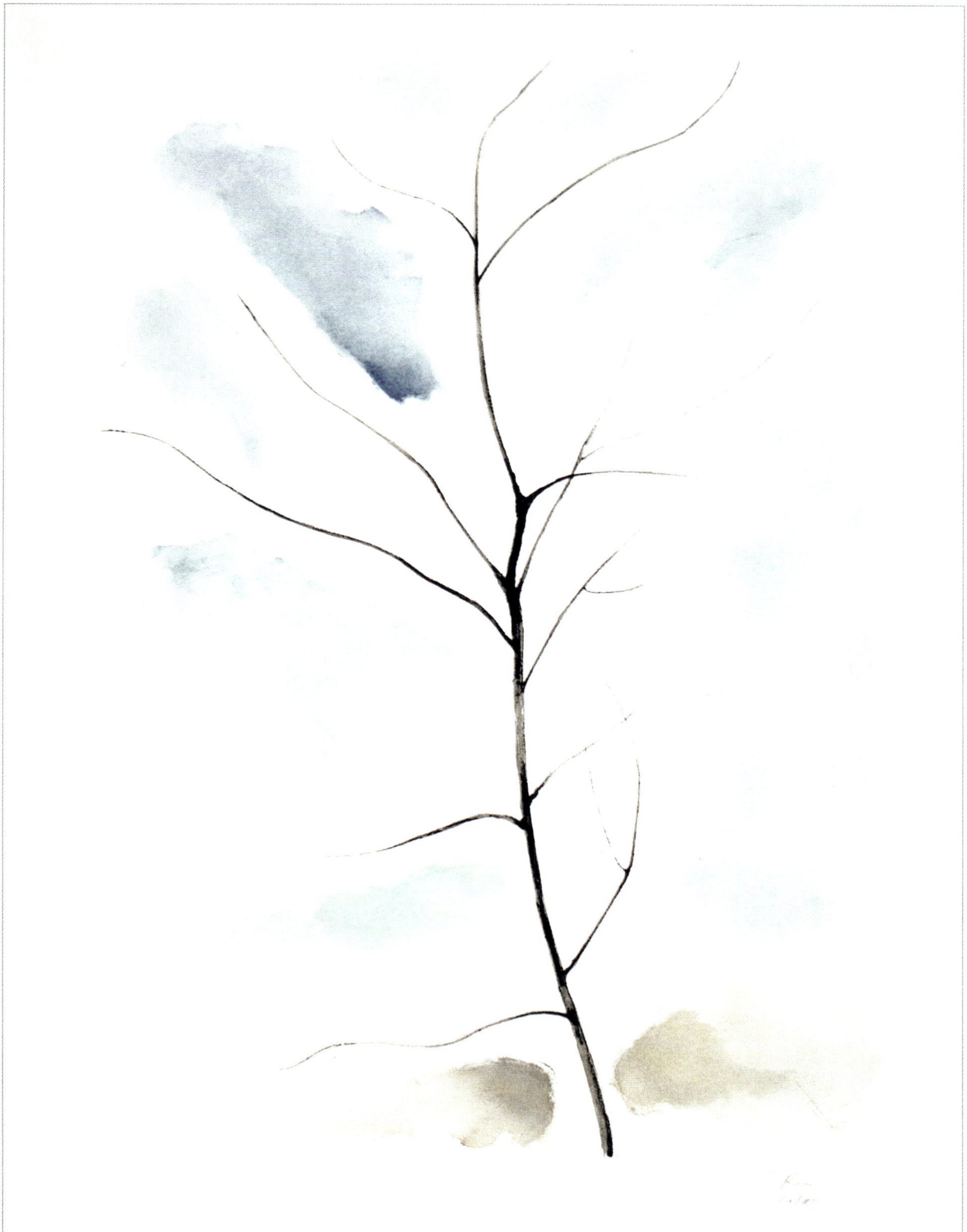

February

Cold air,

cold colors—blue,

grey, brown, yellow; lines

sweeping across the sky, trees

bending in the wind, stretching upwards,

creating geometric forms, framing

the space with curving

branches.

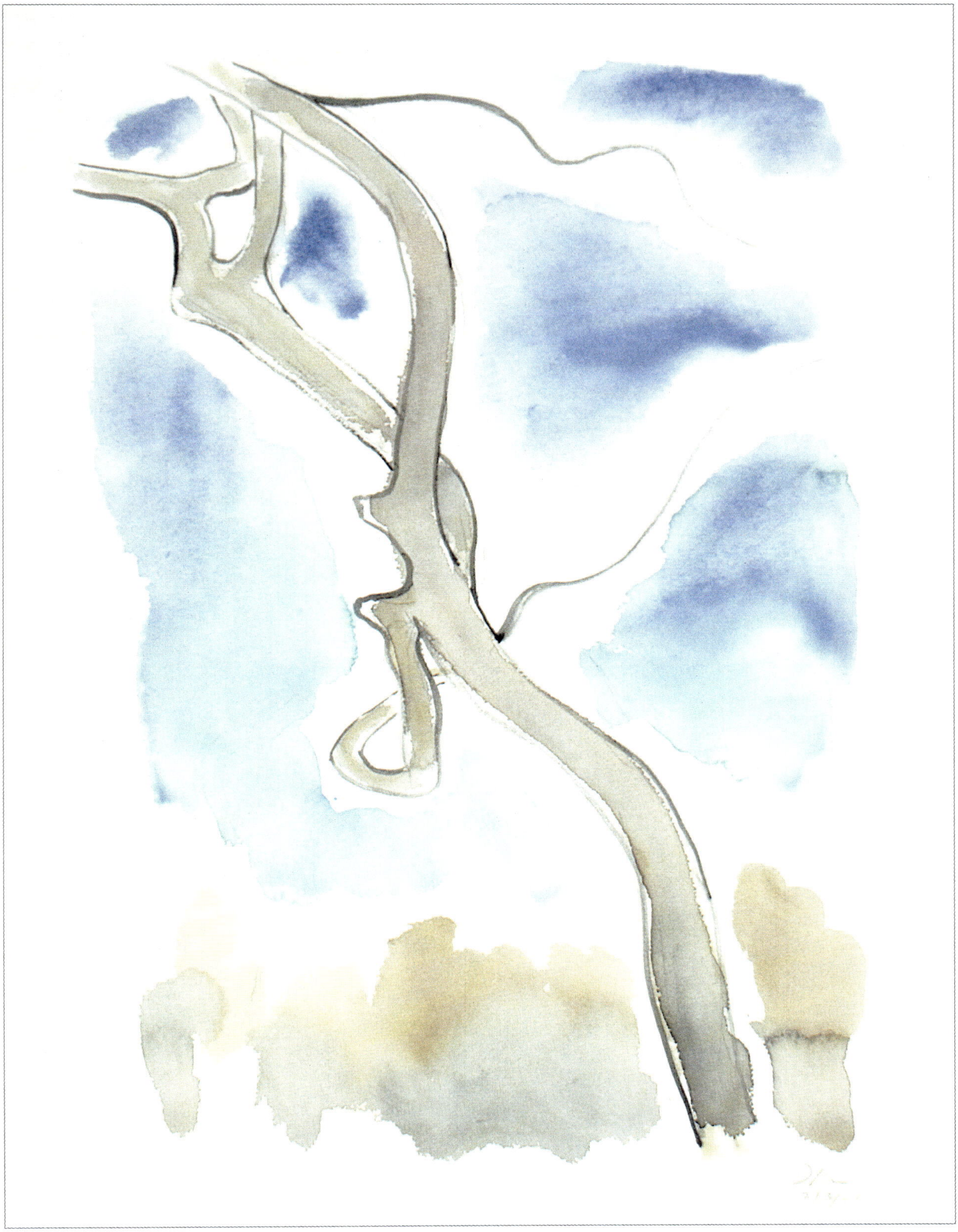

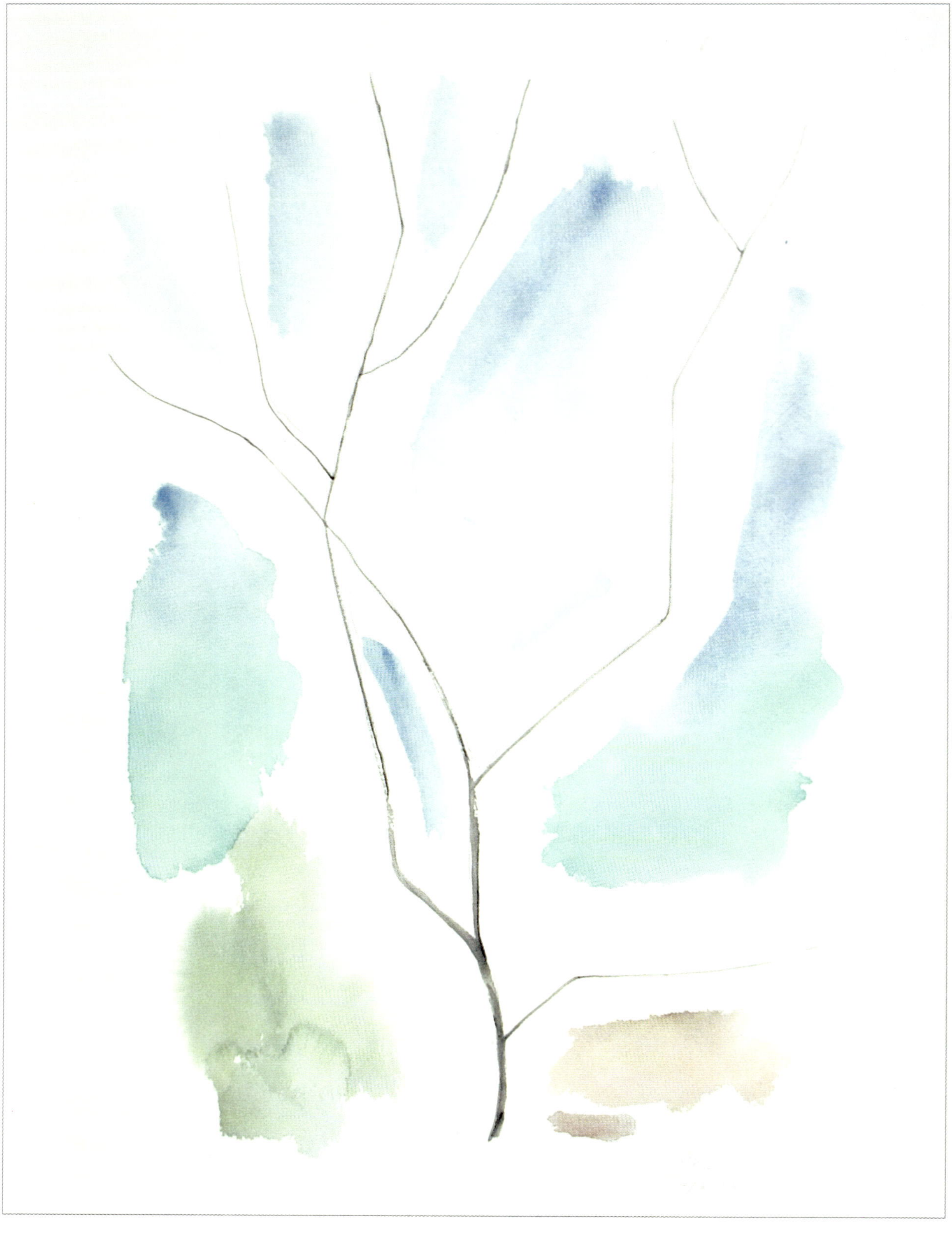

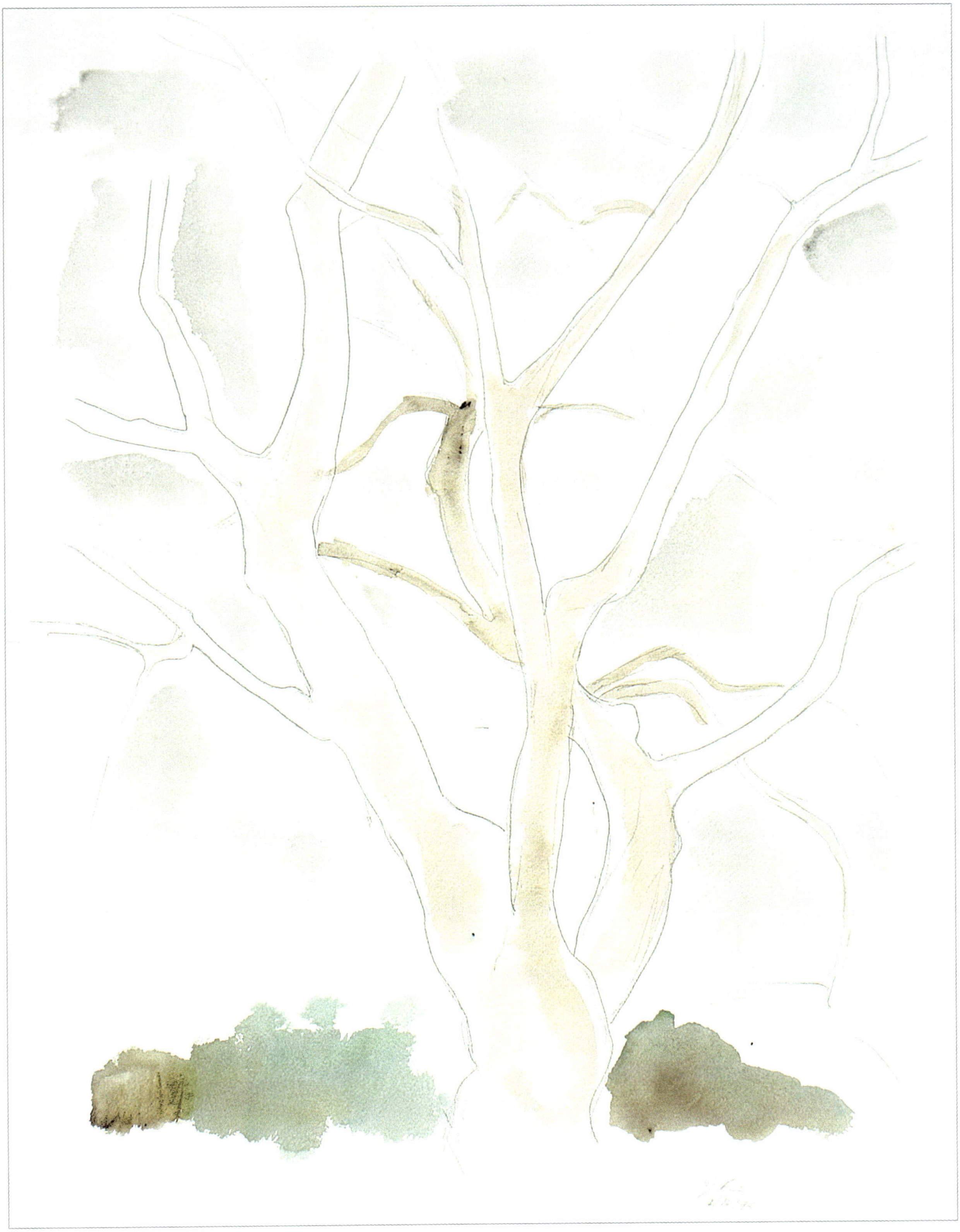

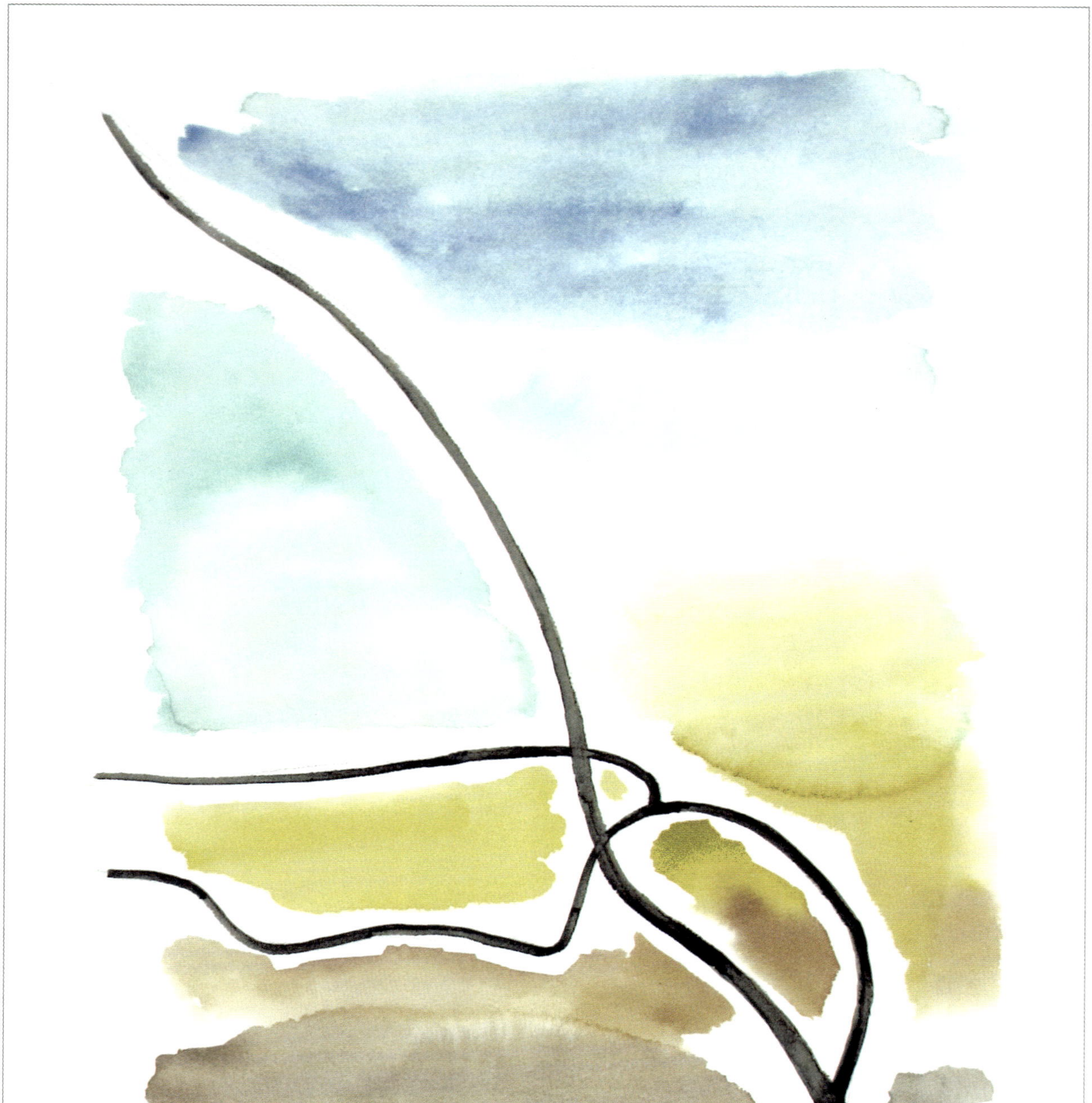

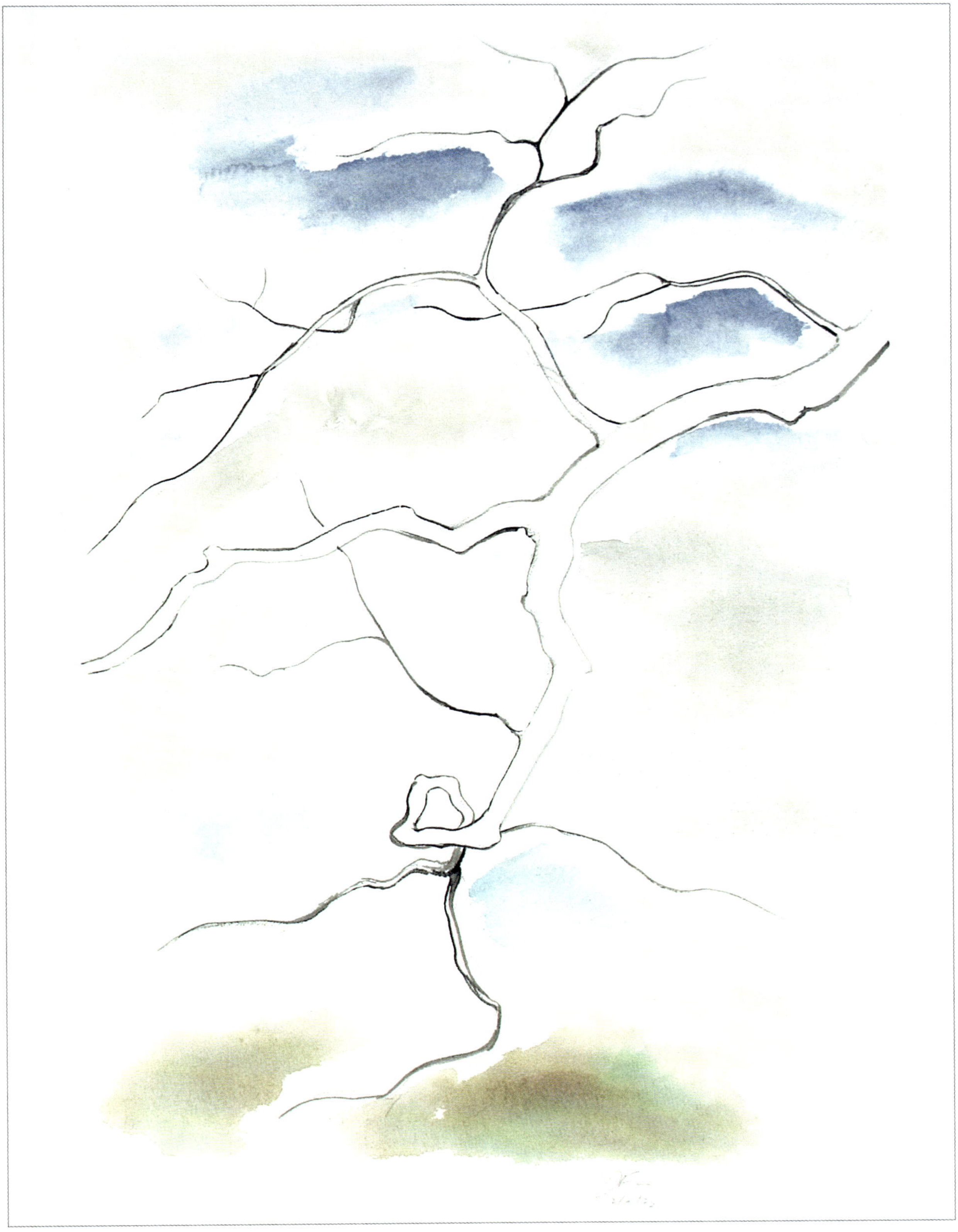

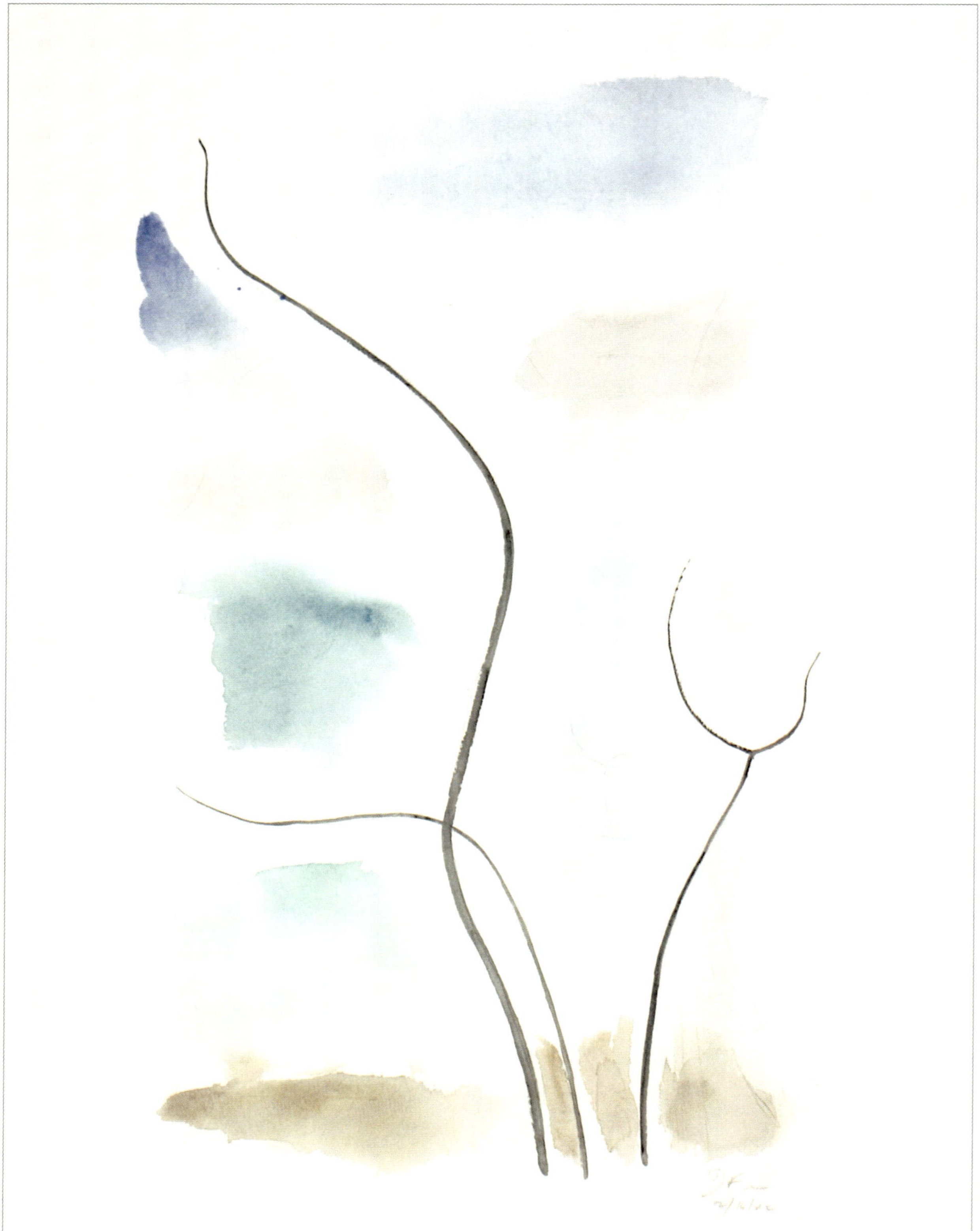

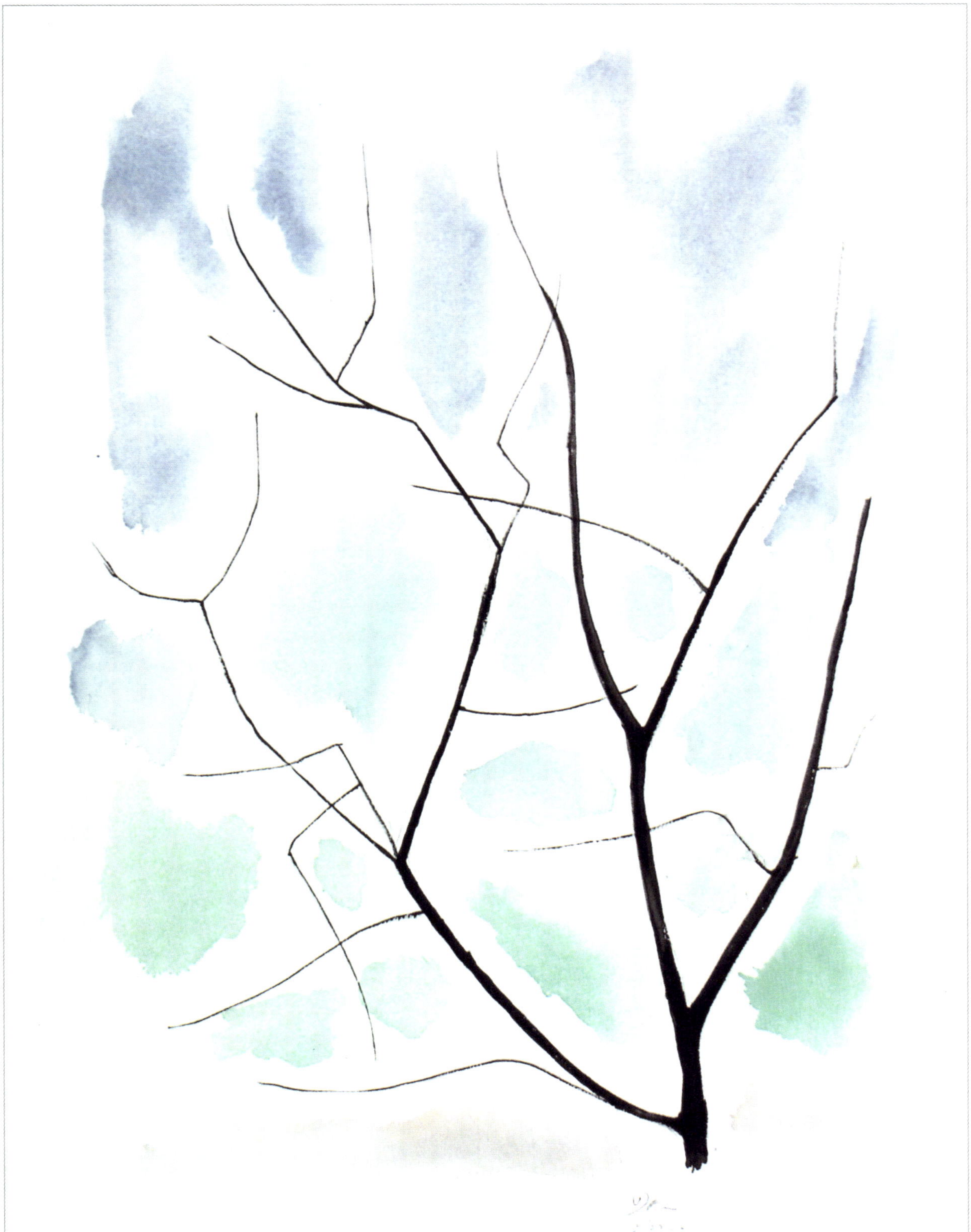

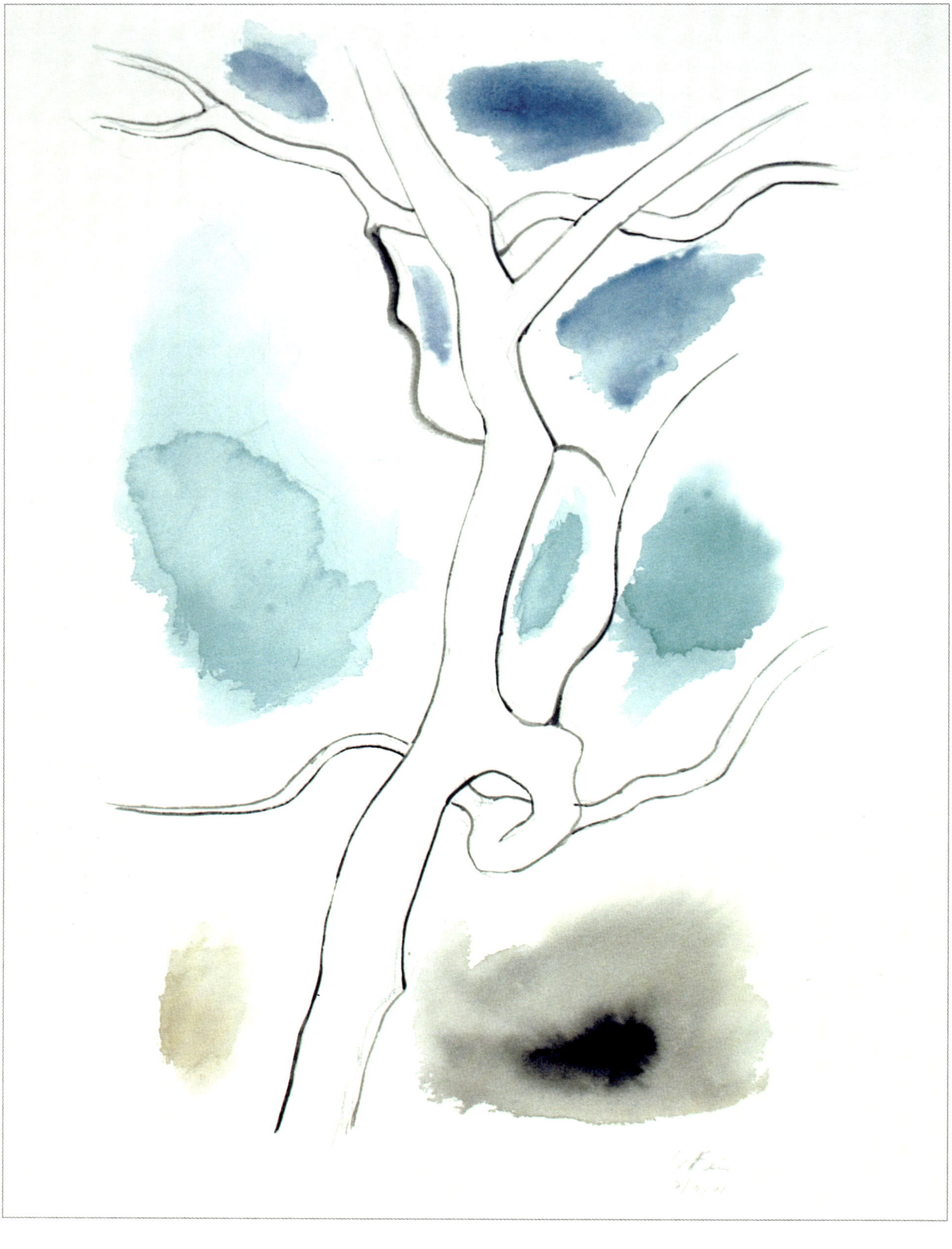

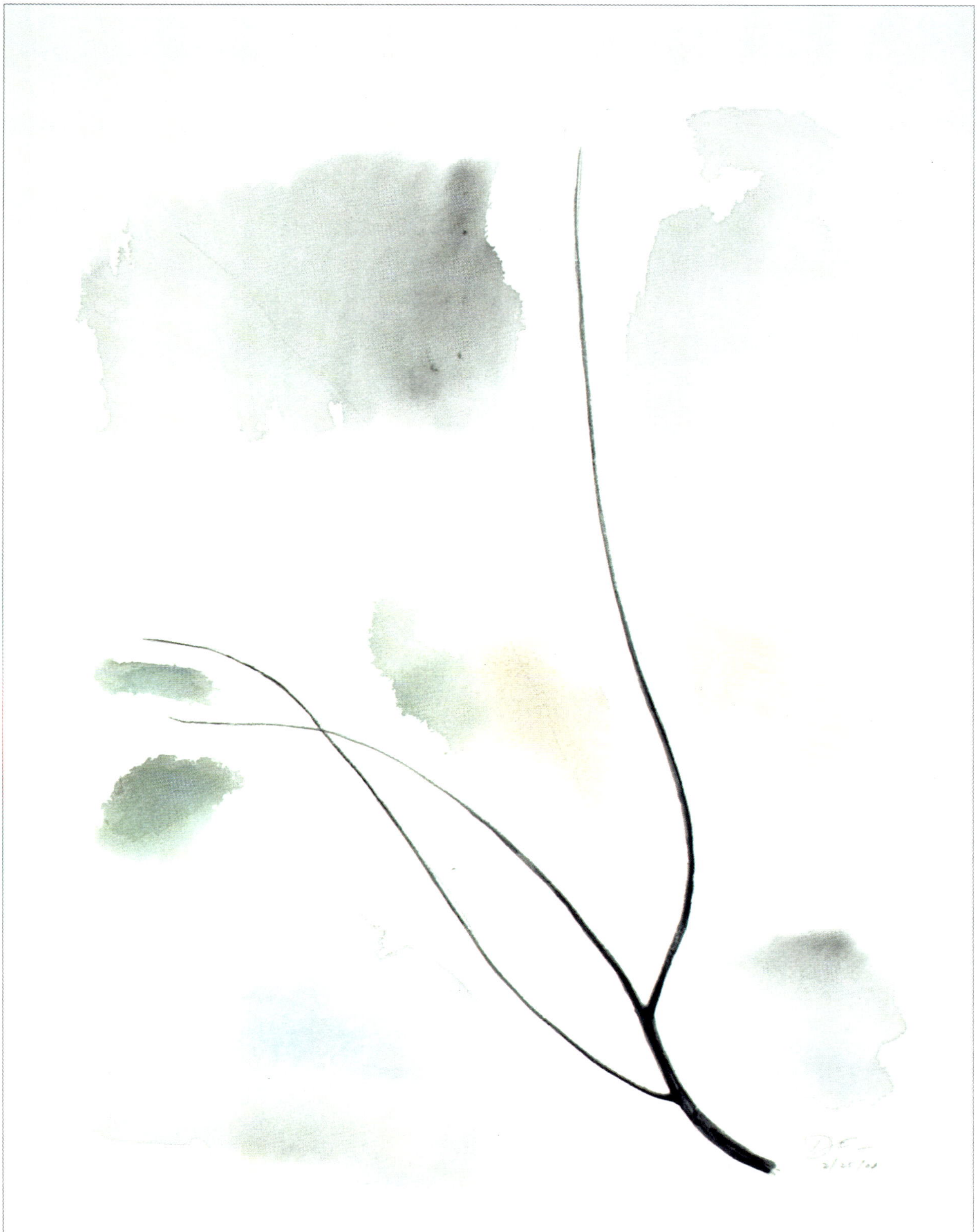

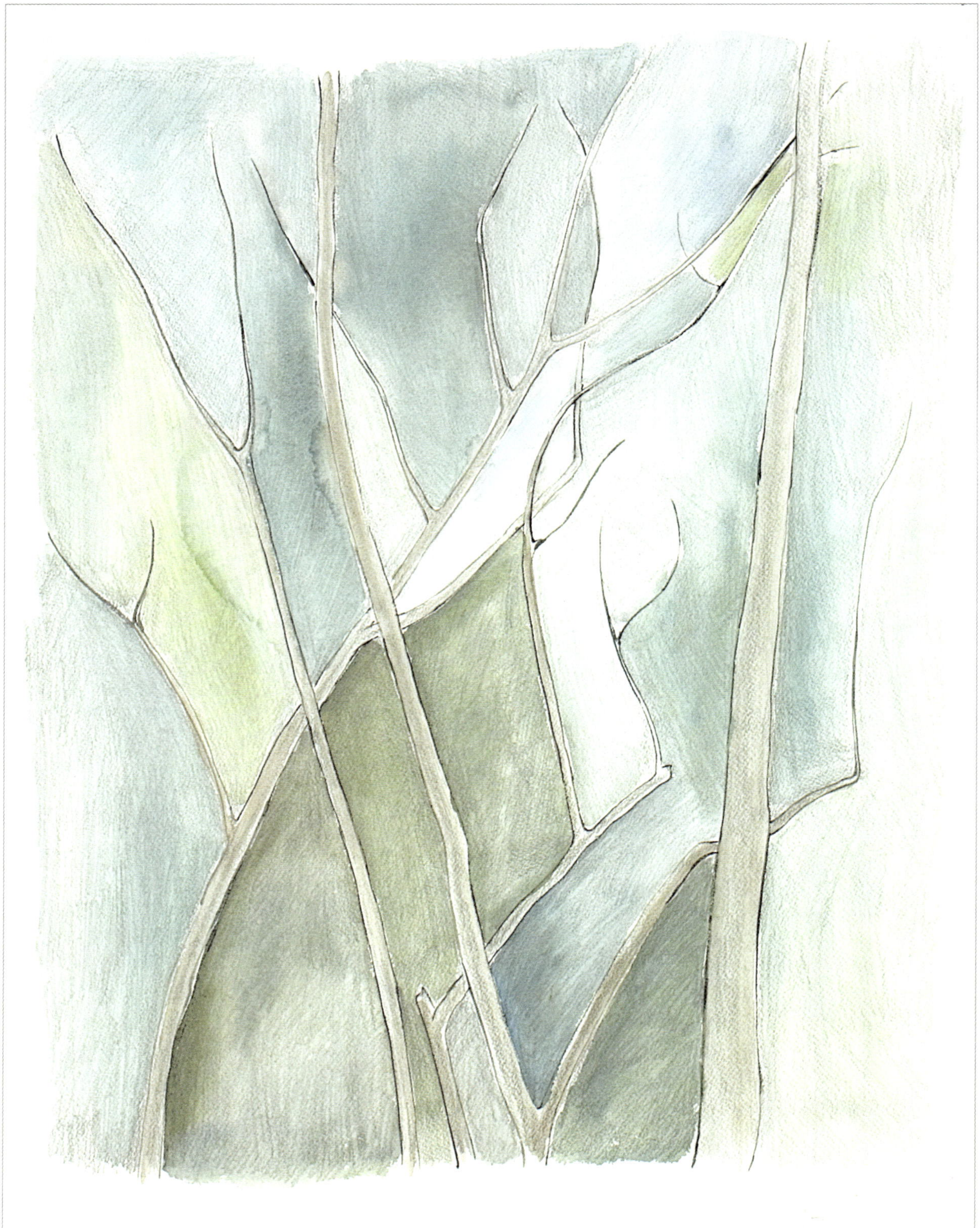

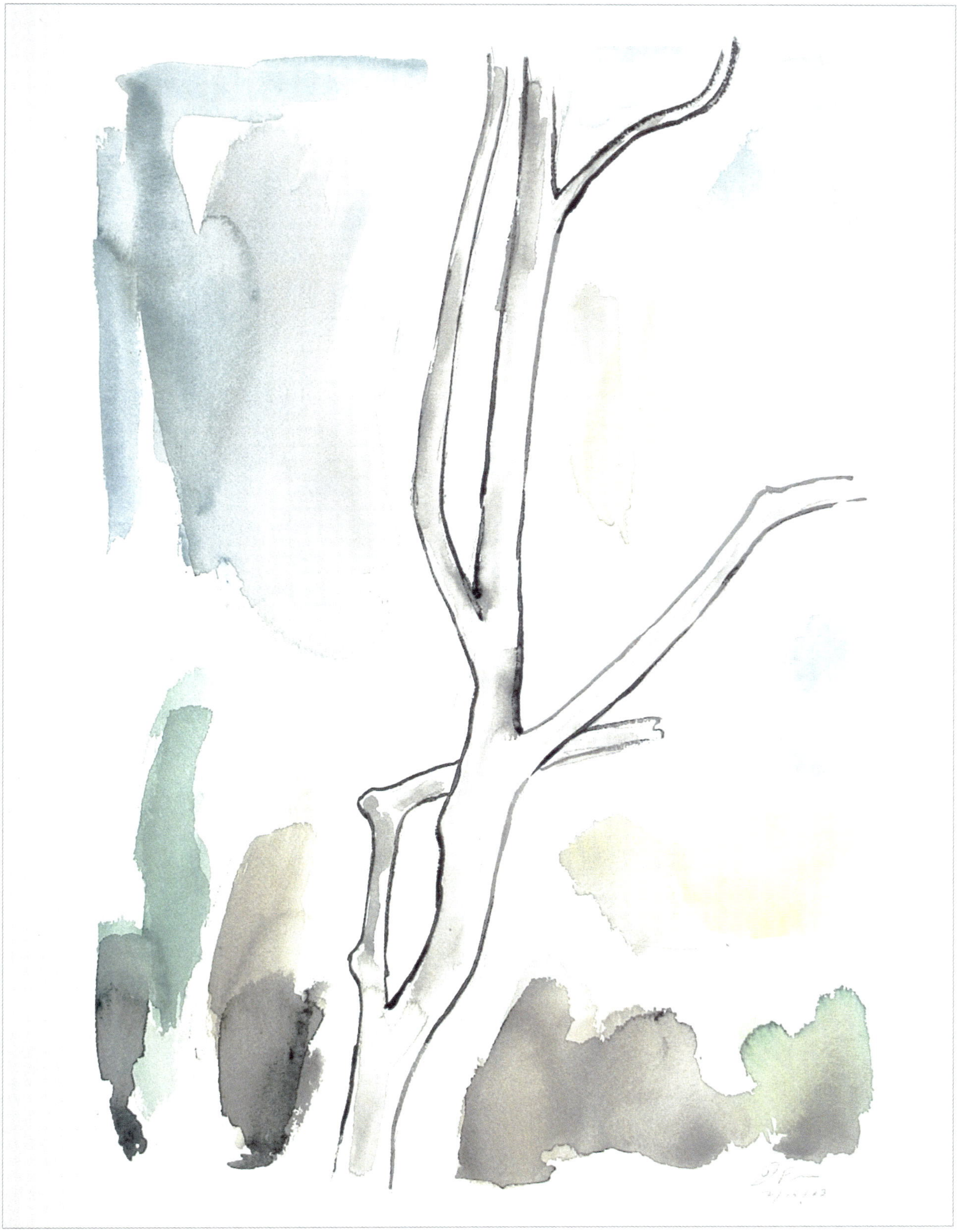

March

The colors,
like the air, become
warmer; lines swing with
new life; hints of Spring arise—
the branches are rounder, softer, more
promising, ready to burst
forth with new life
when Spring
arrives.

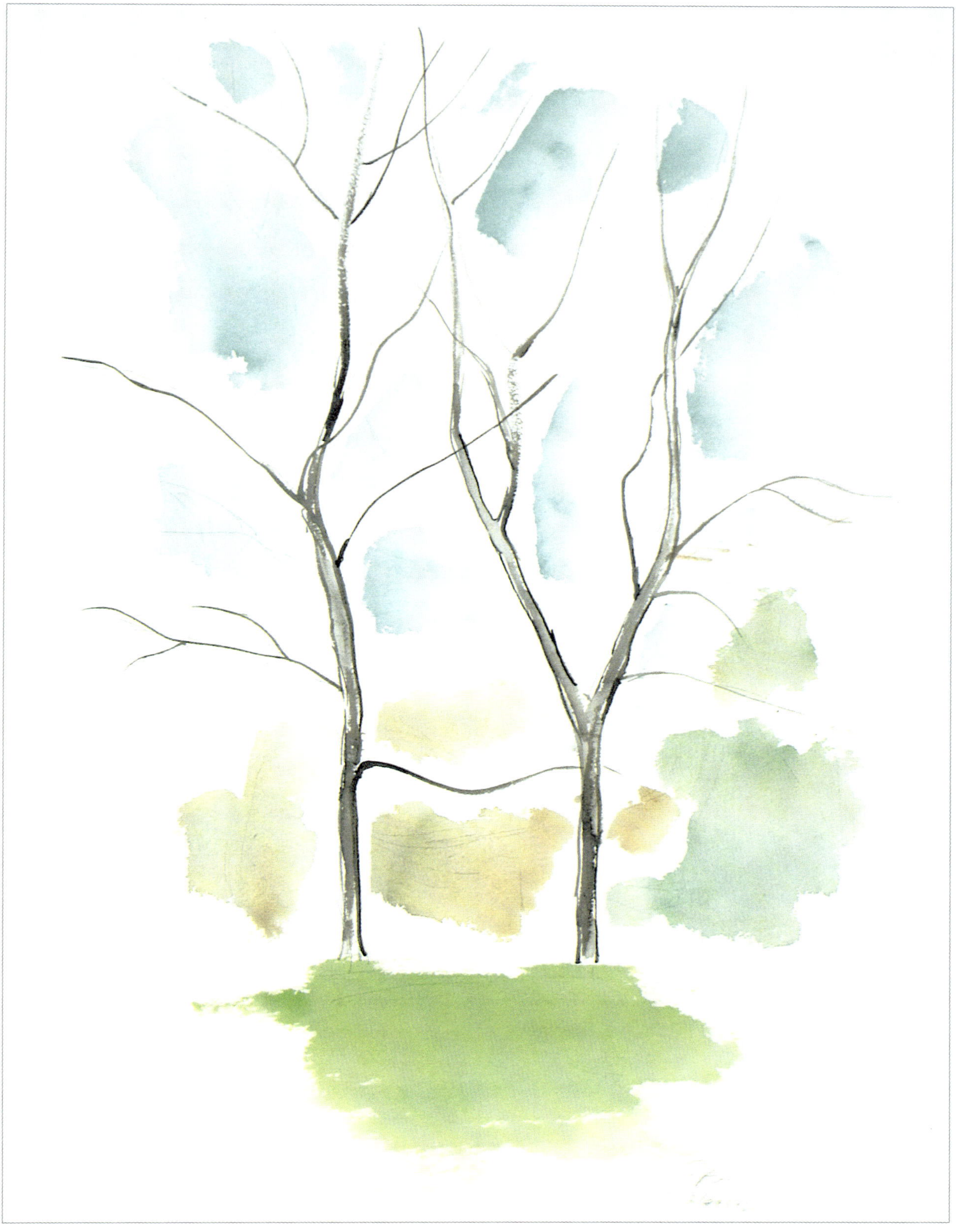

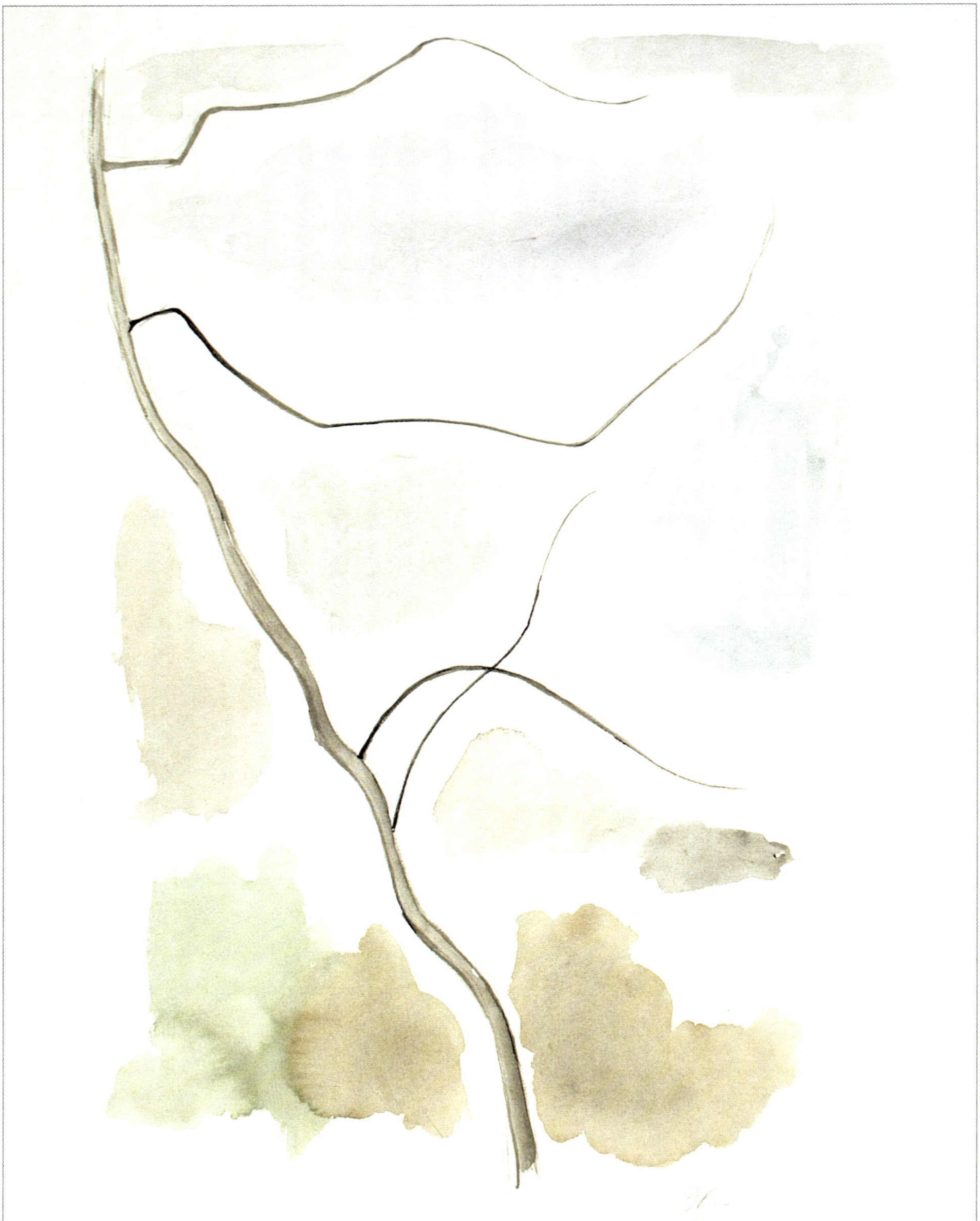

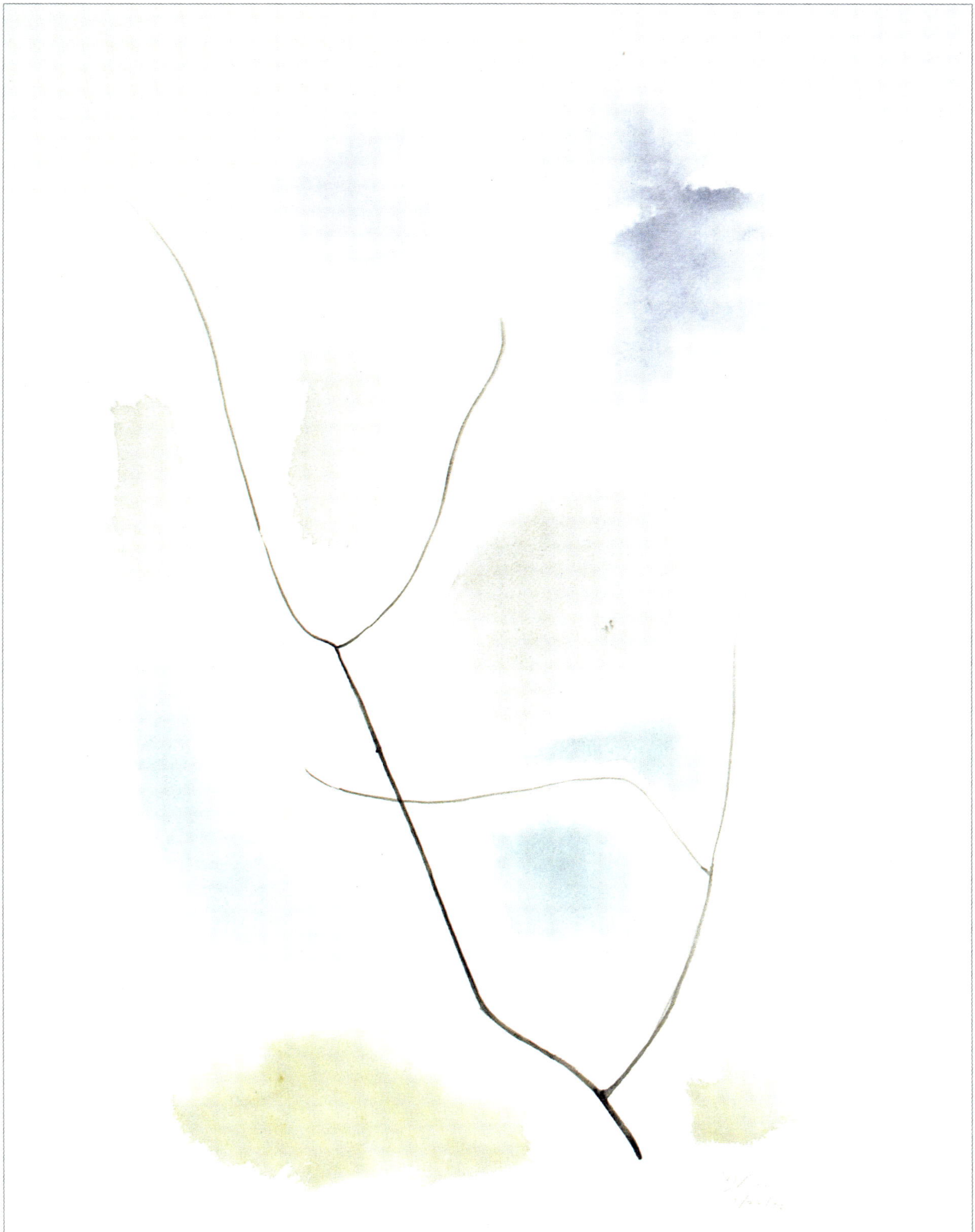

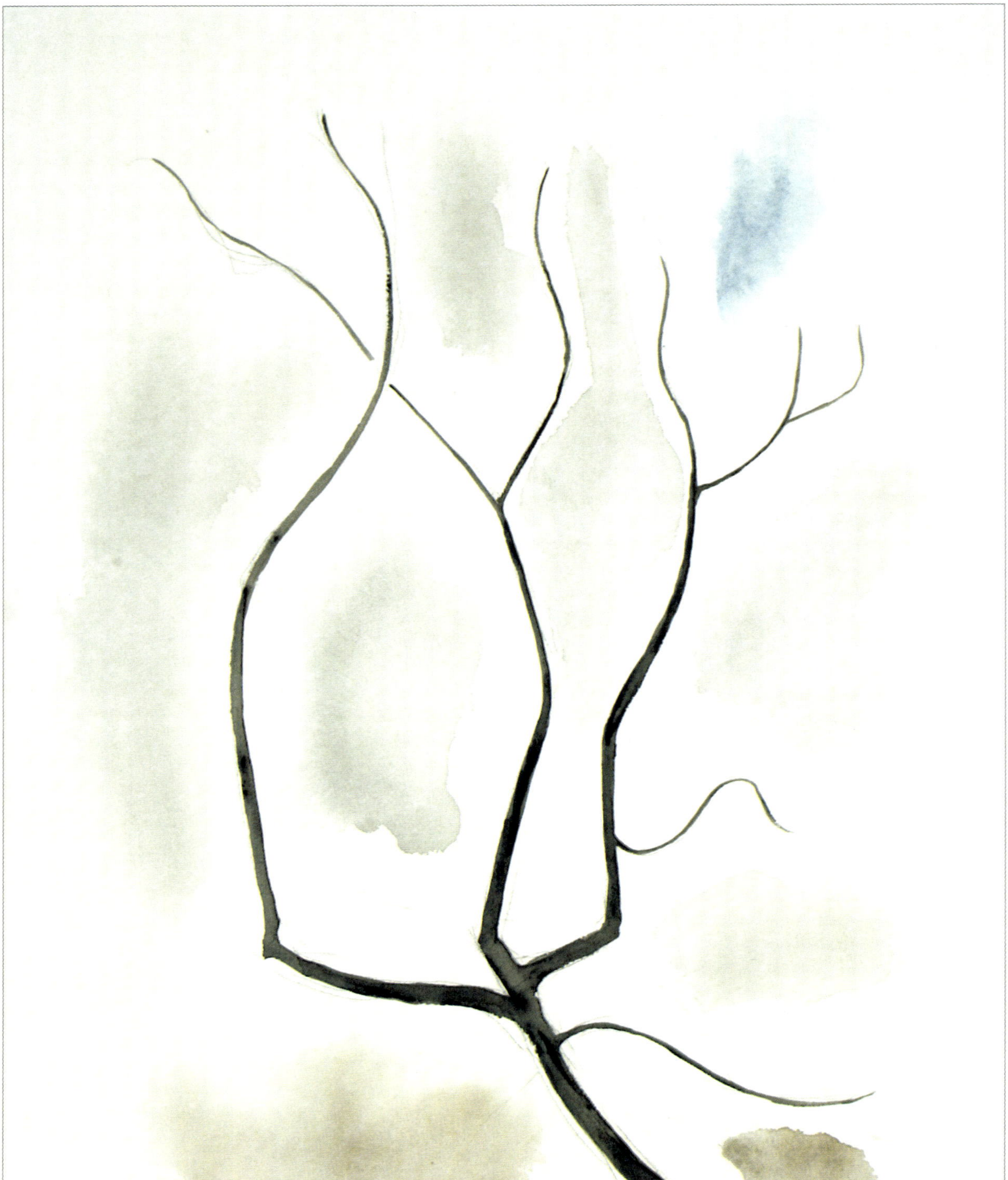

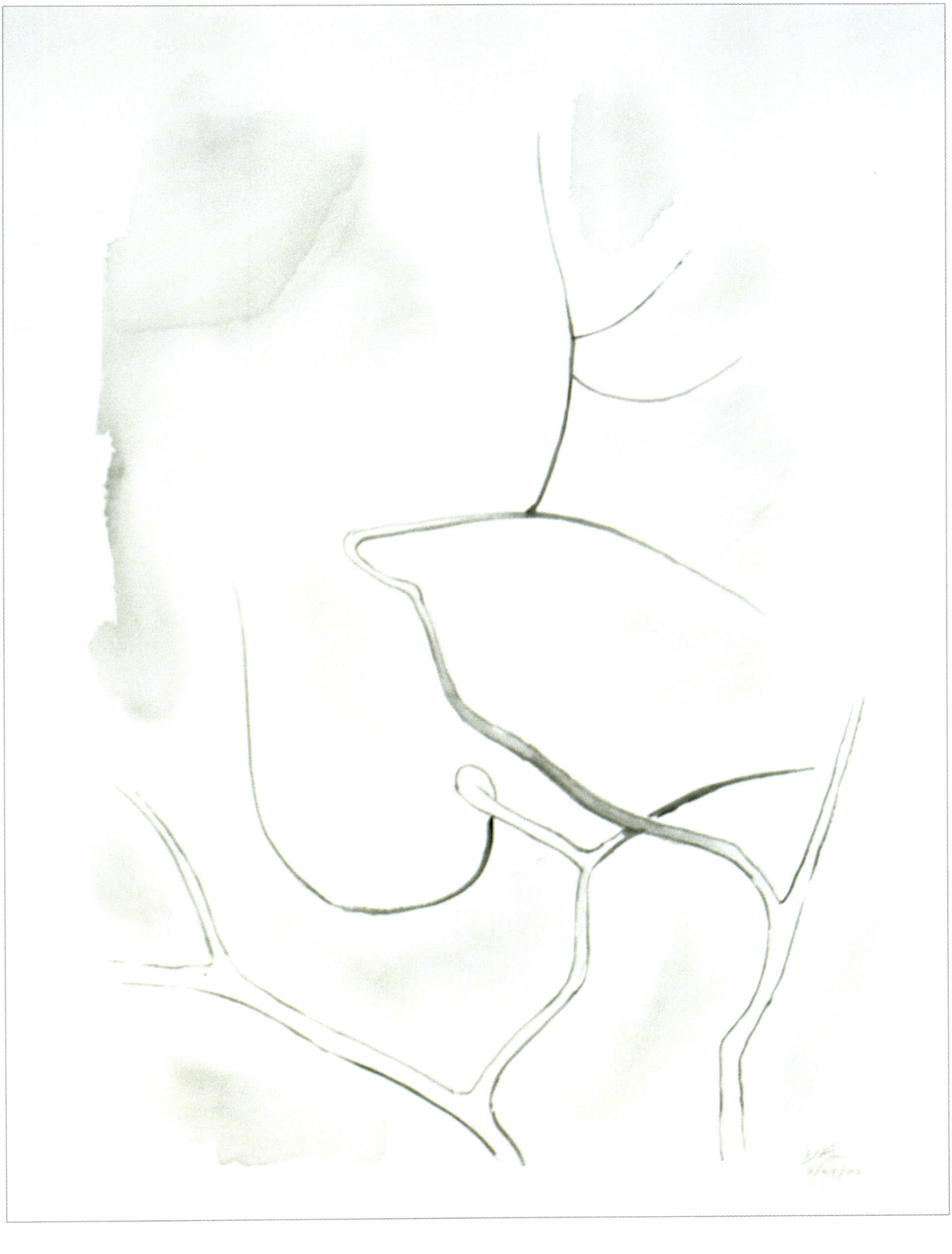

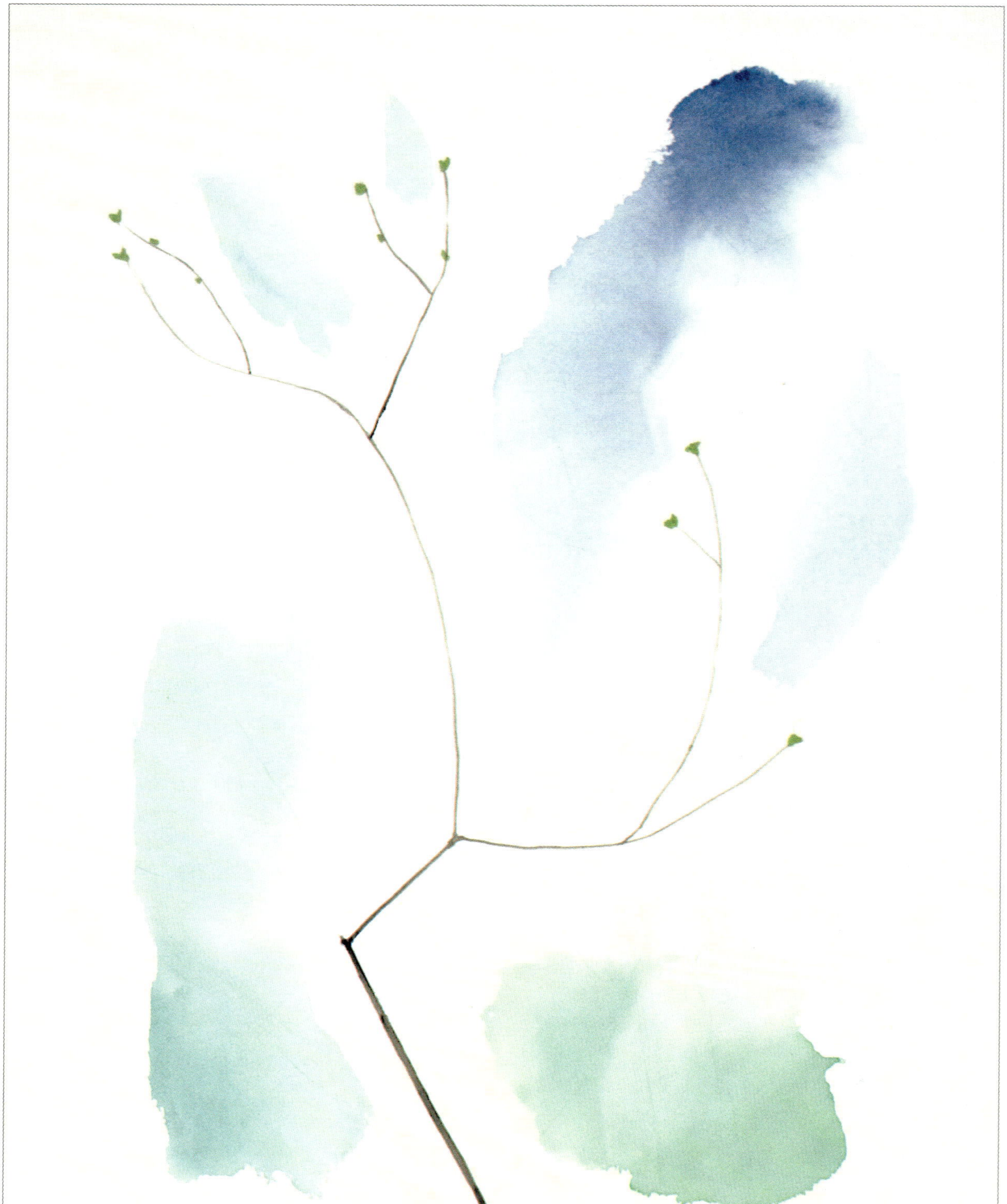

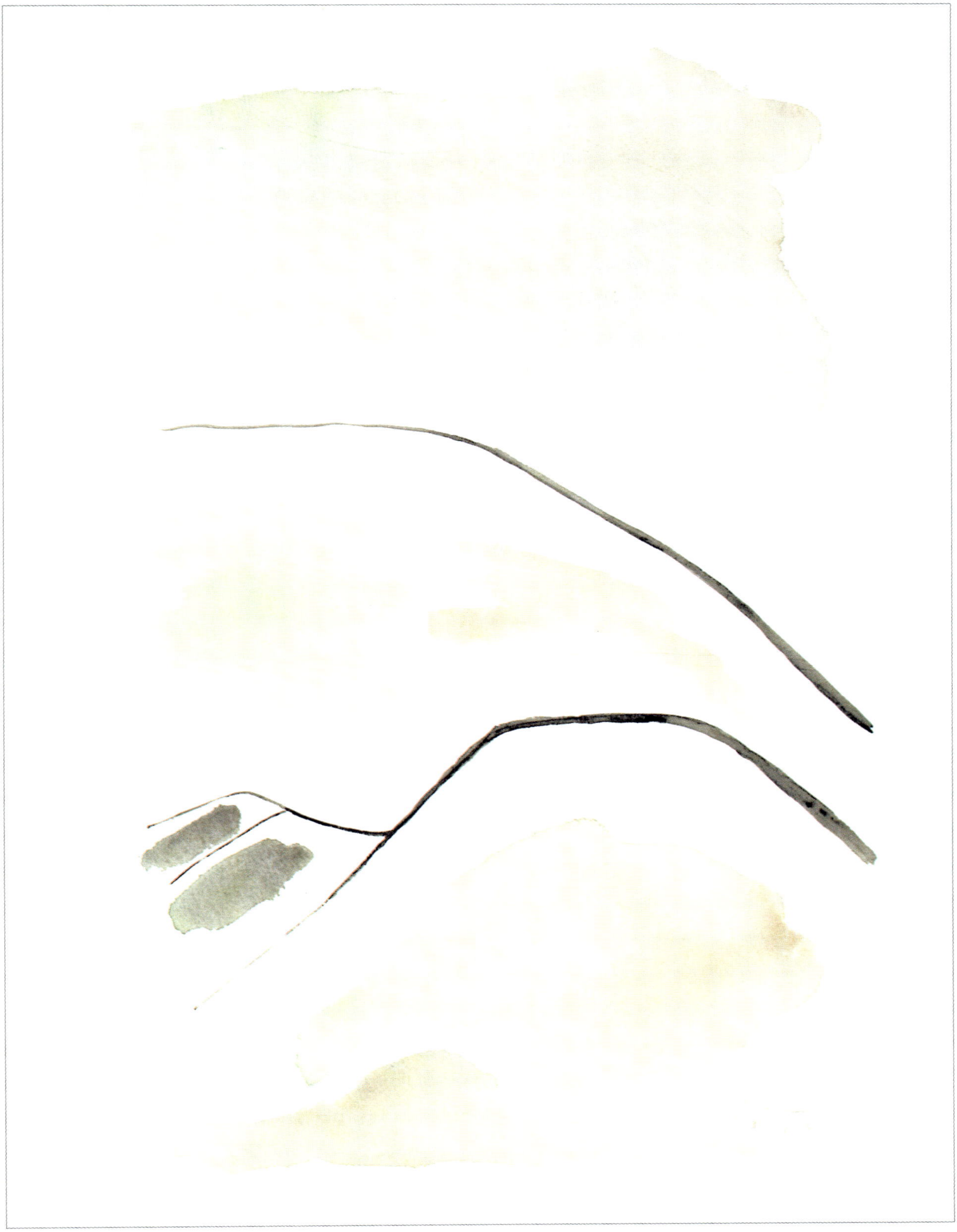

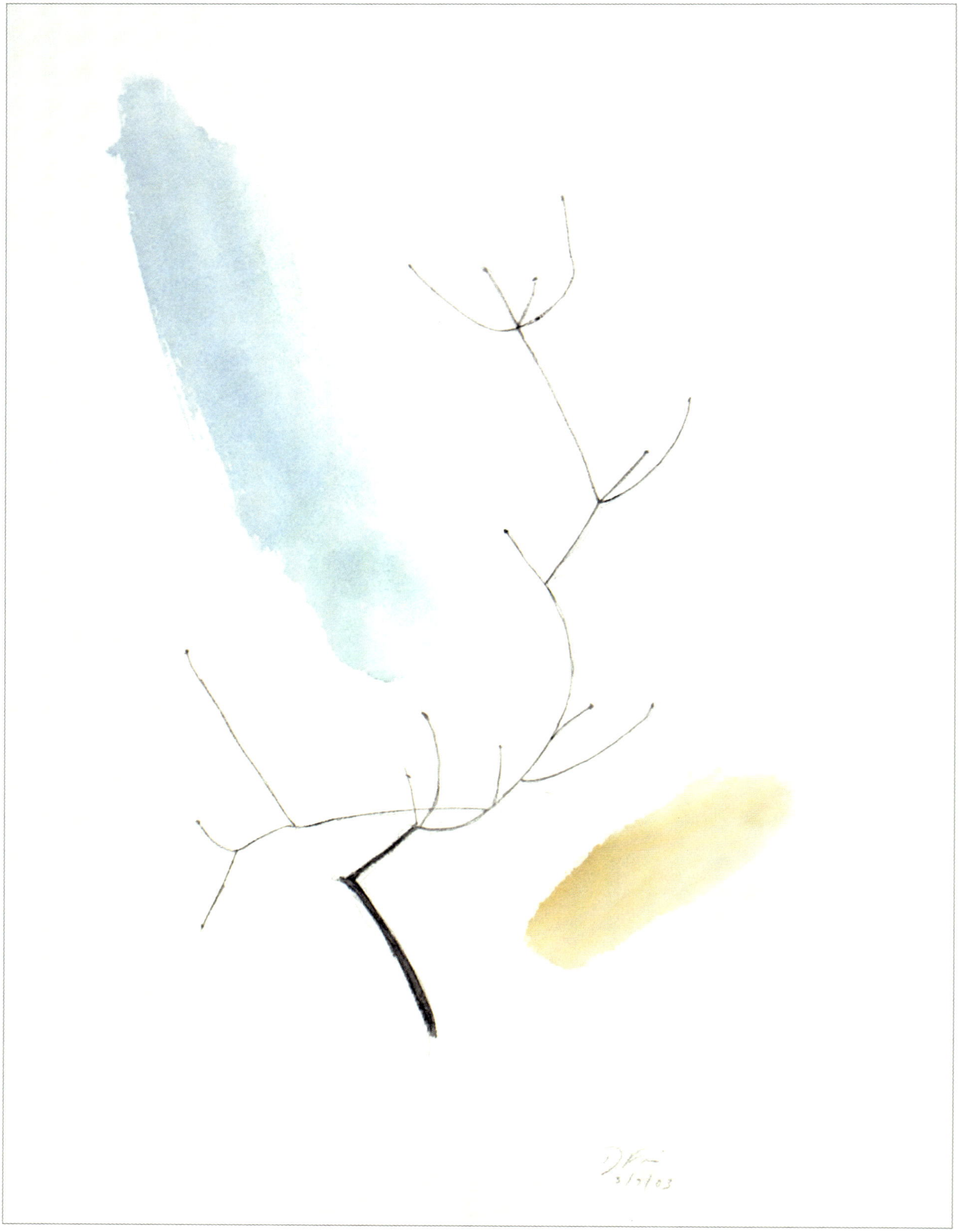

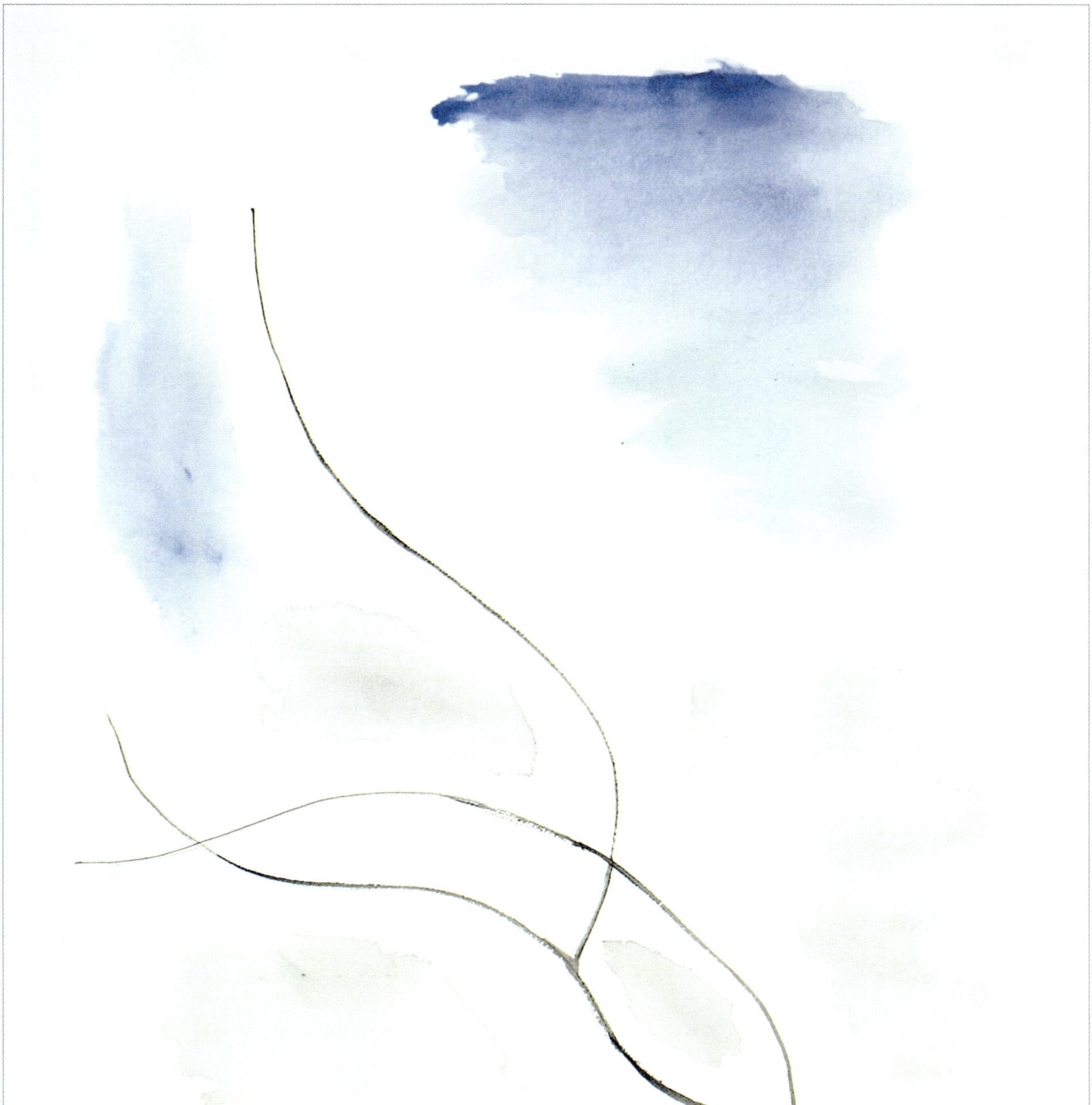

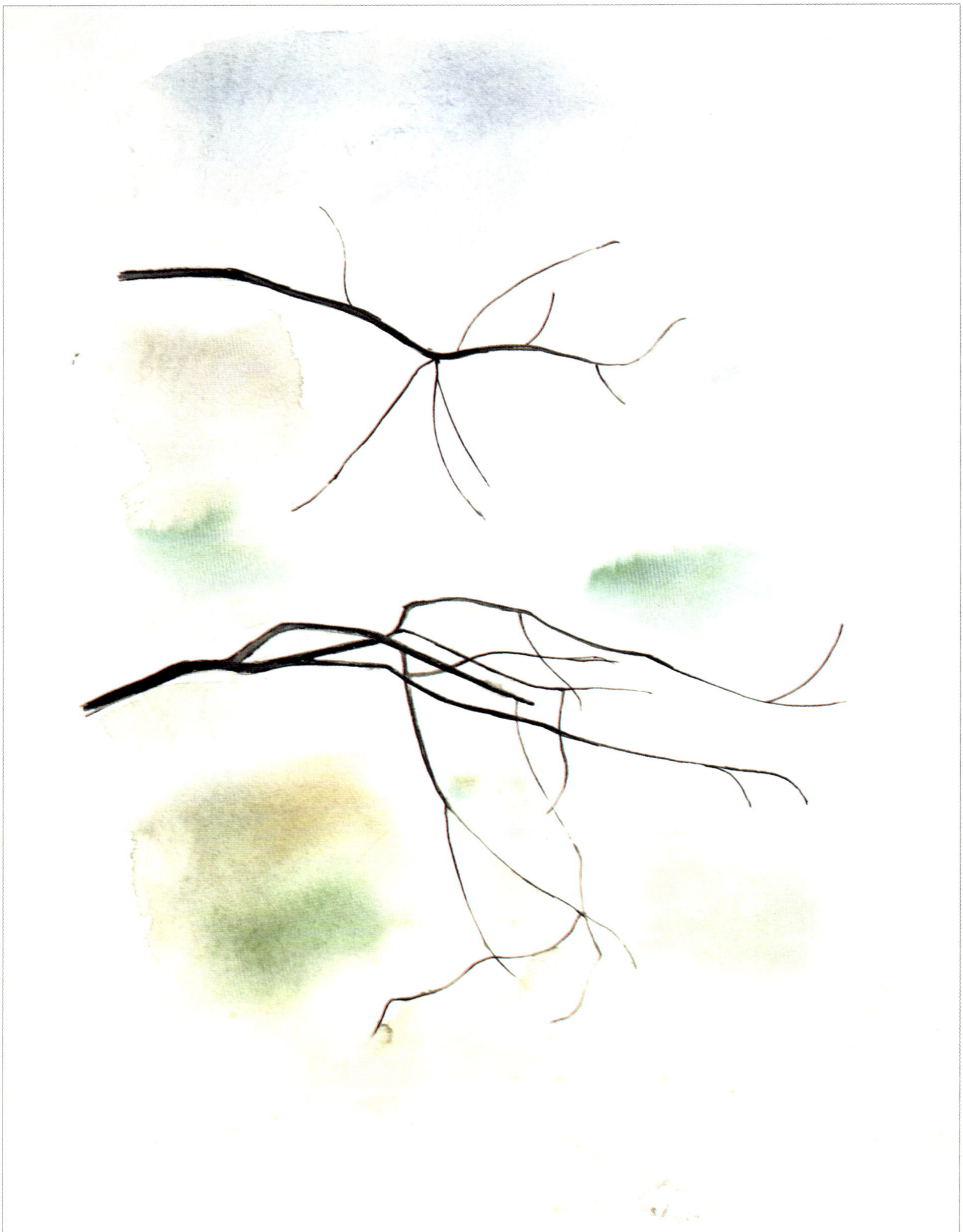

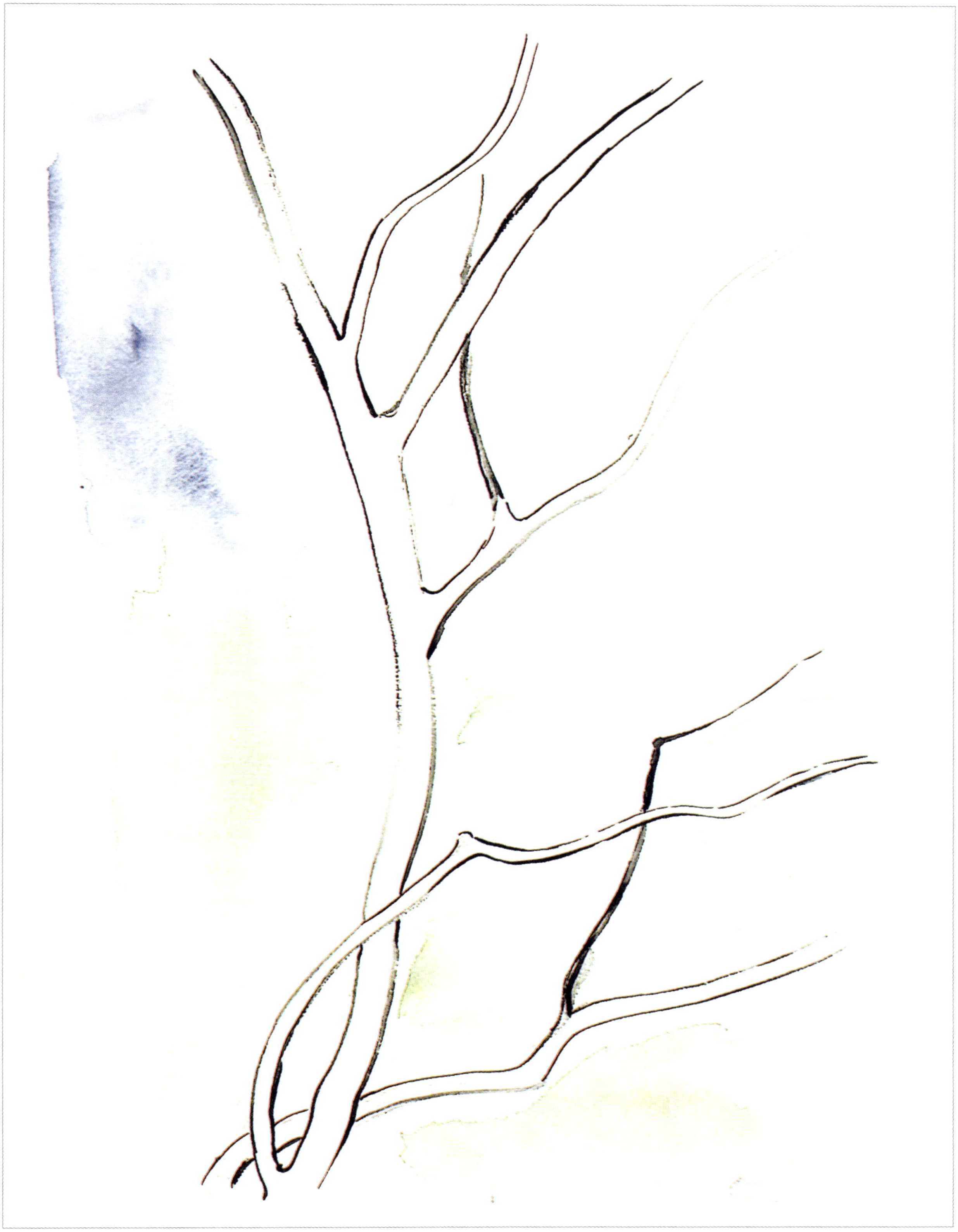

April

The mind

is dazzled looking

at the sky filled with tiny

buds; new life has been born; they

are here again: the branches are dancing

in the wind, delicate colors

are soothing the eye.

with little

specks.

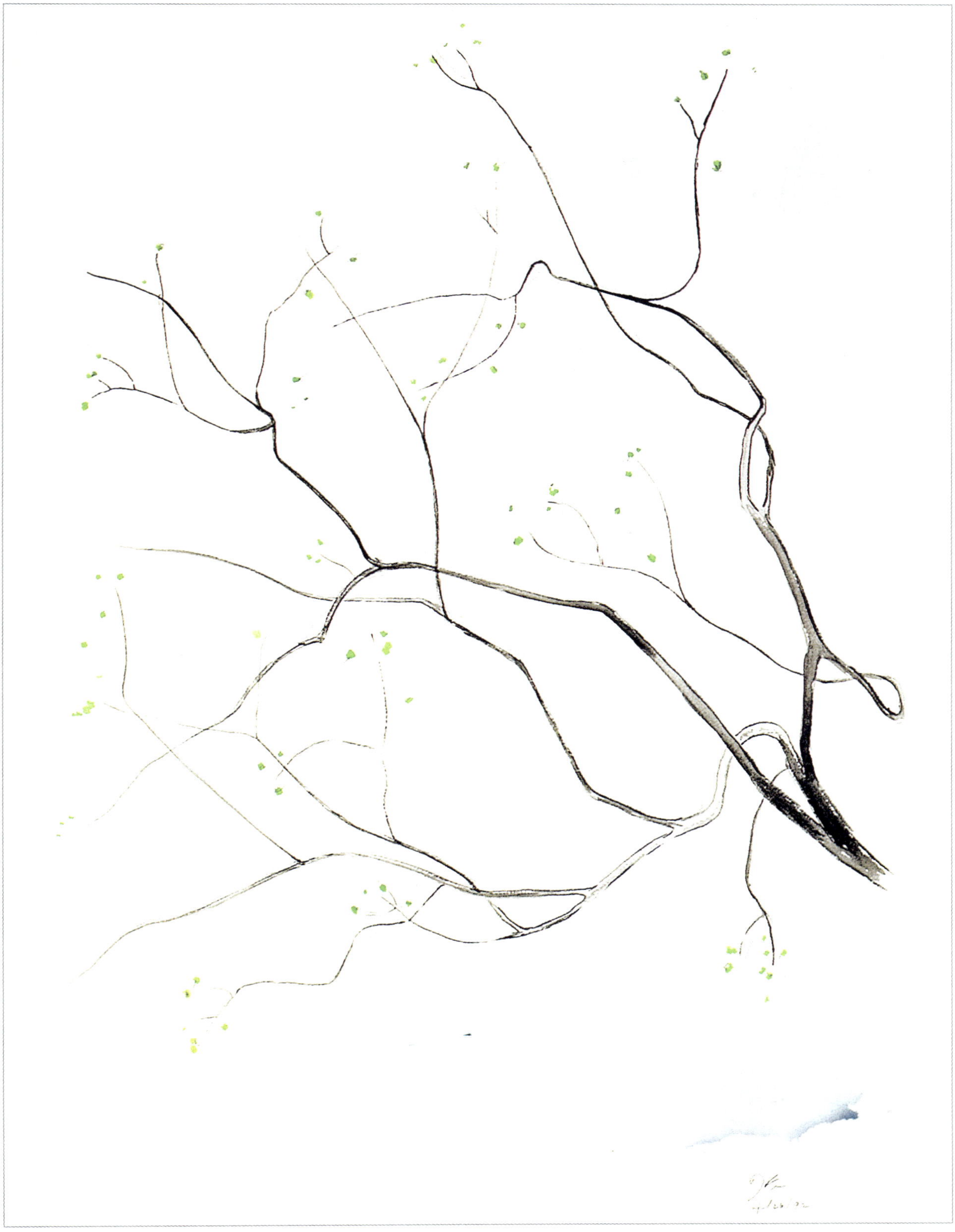

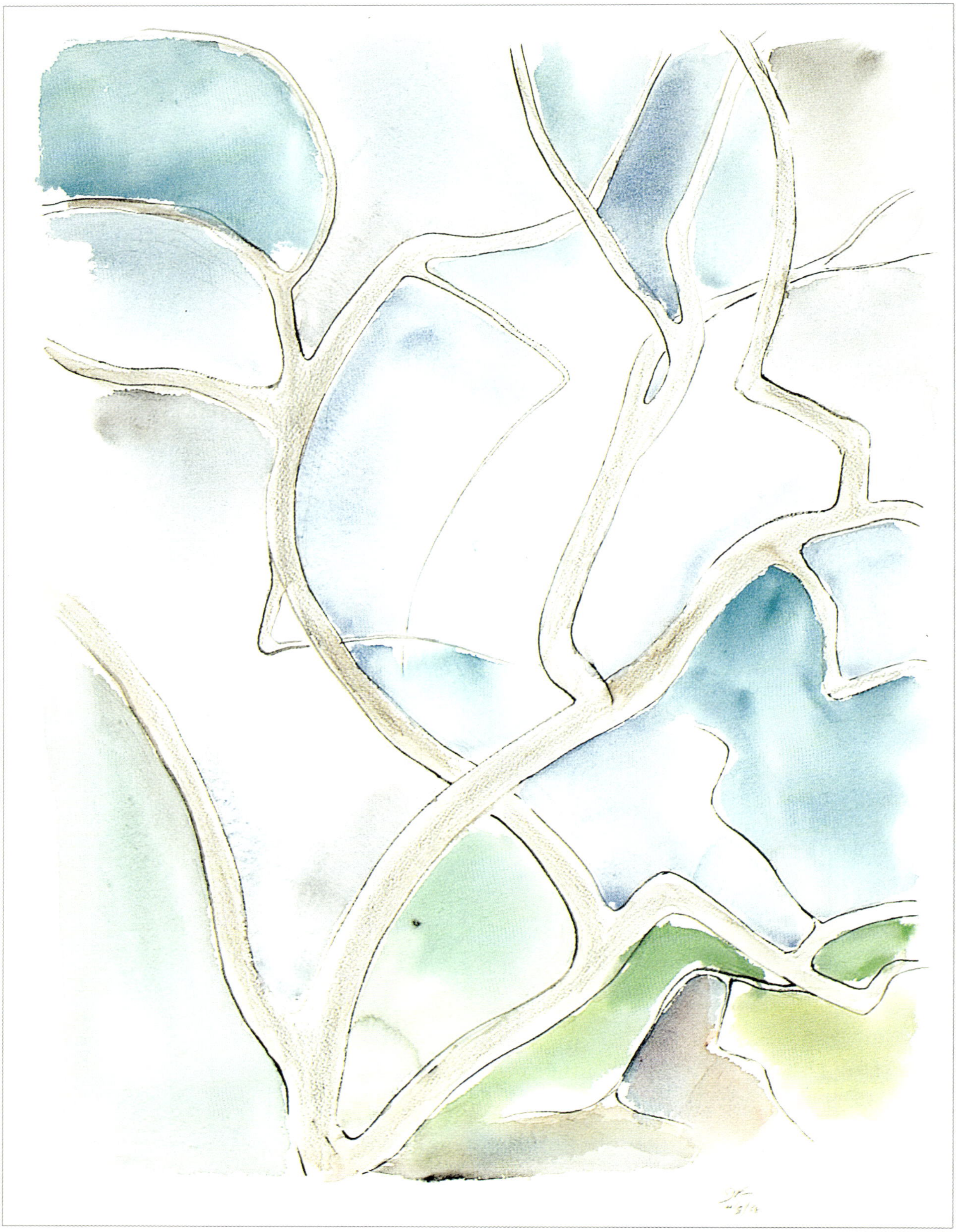

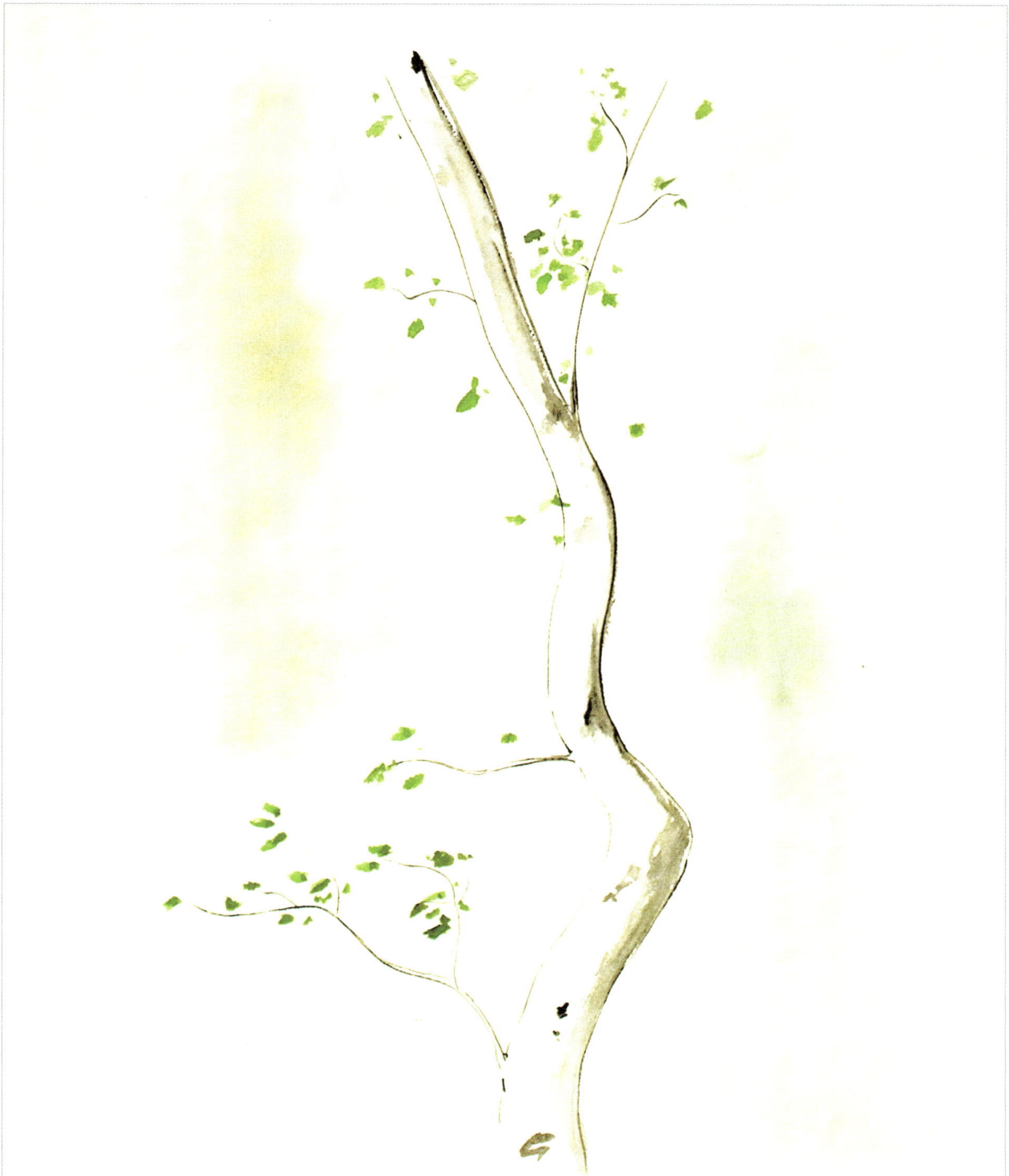

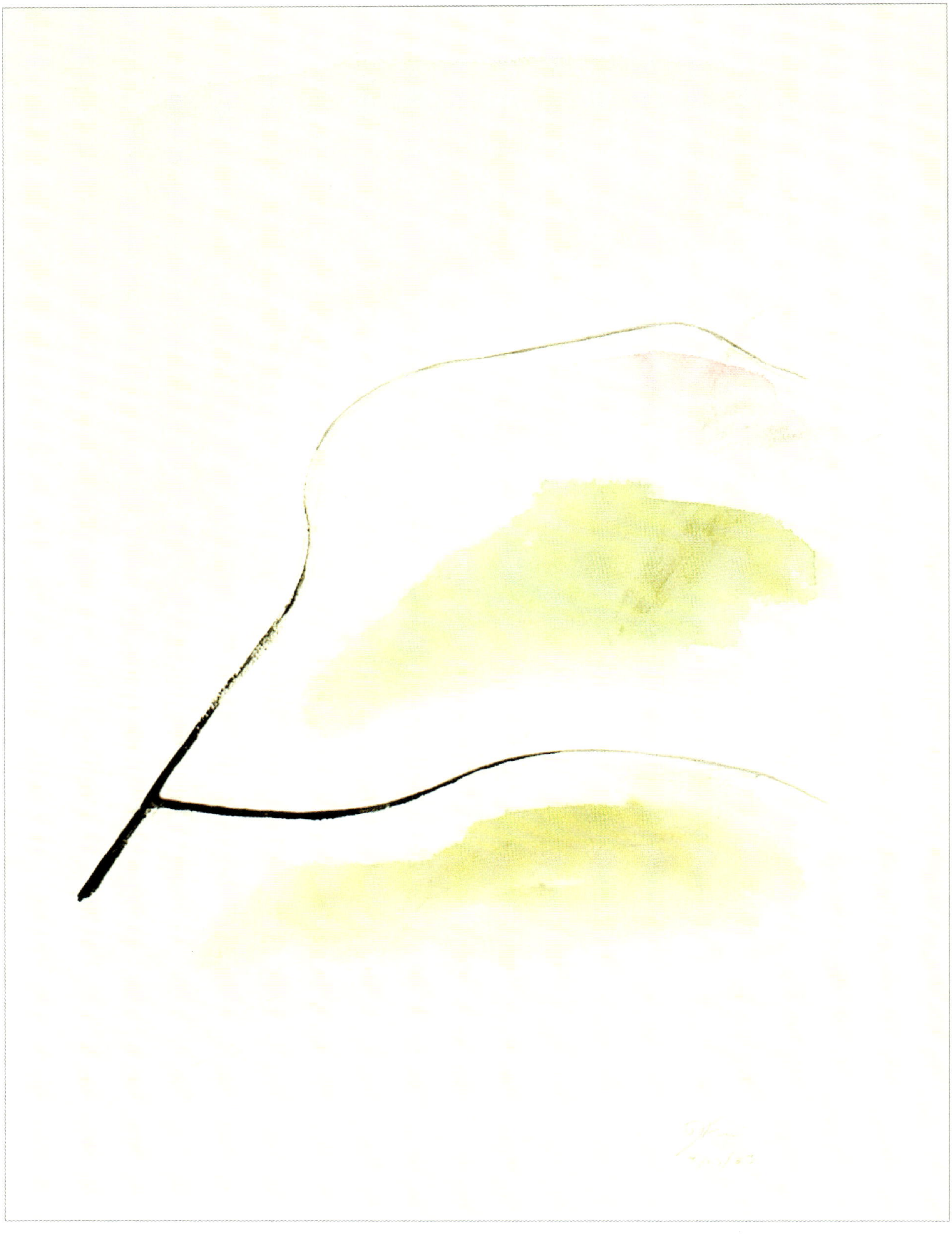

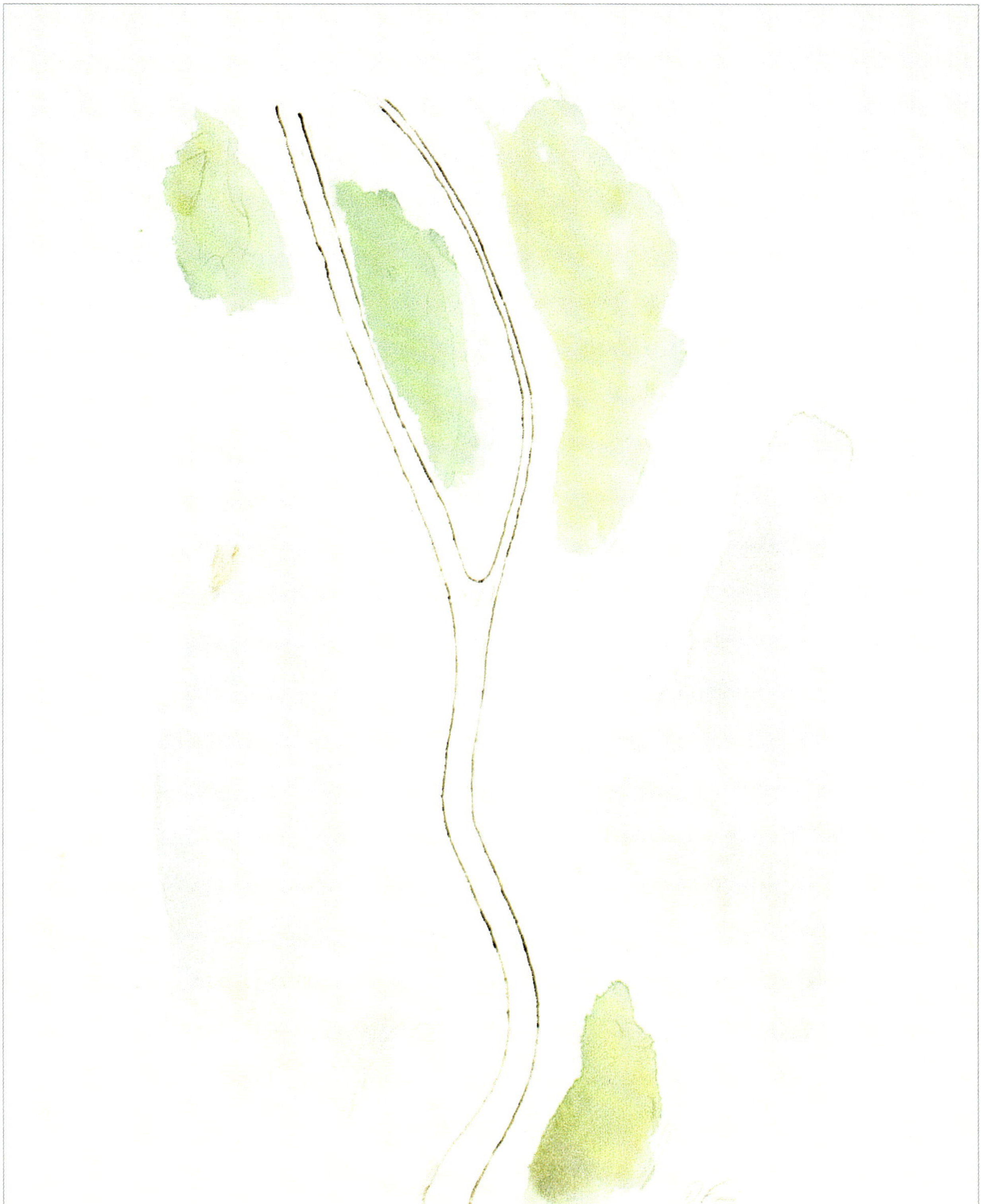

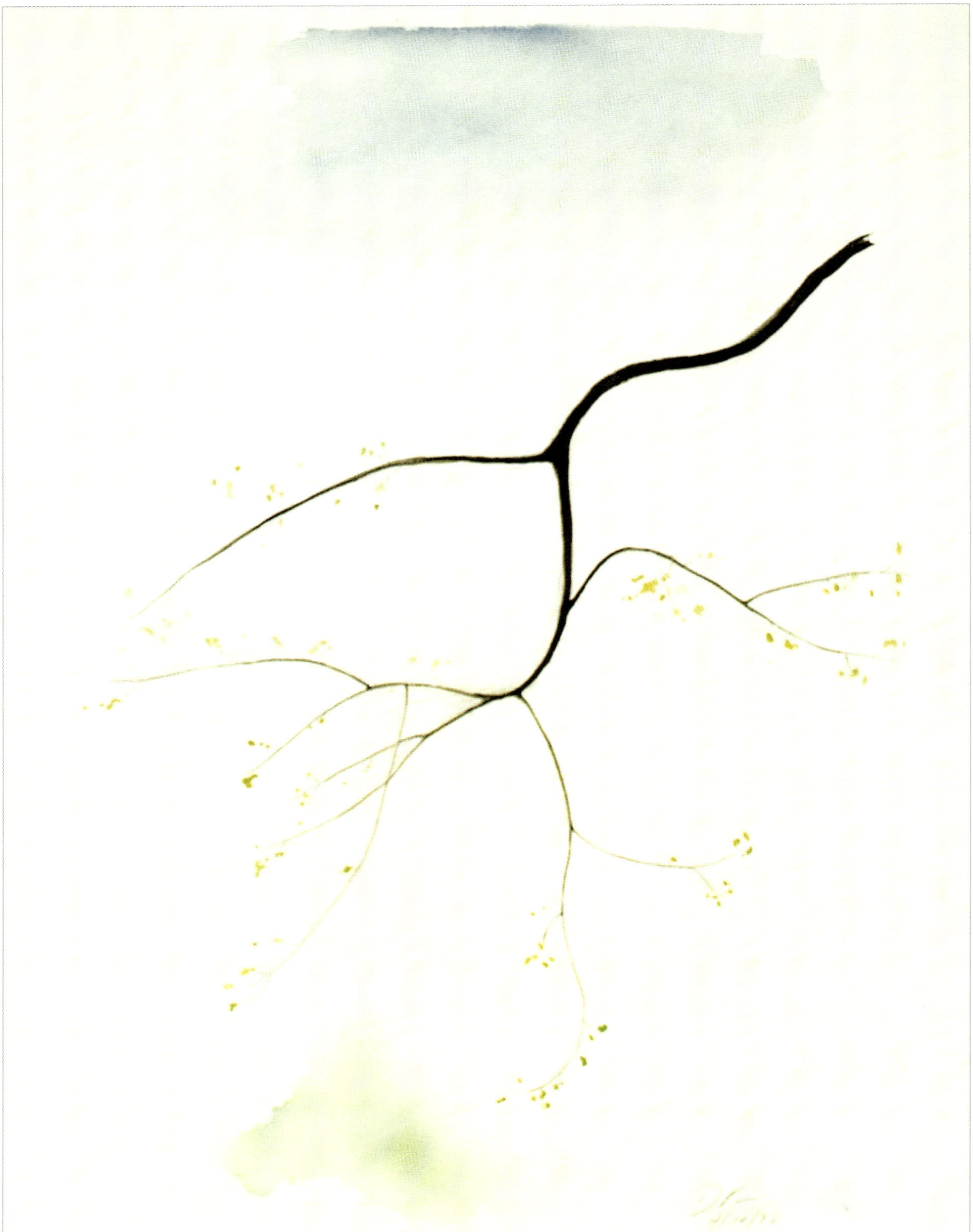

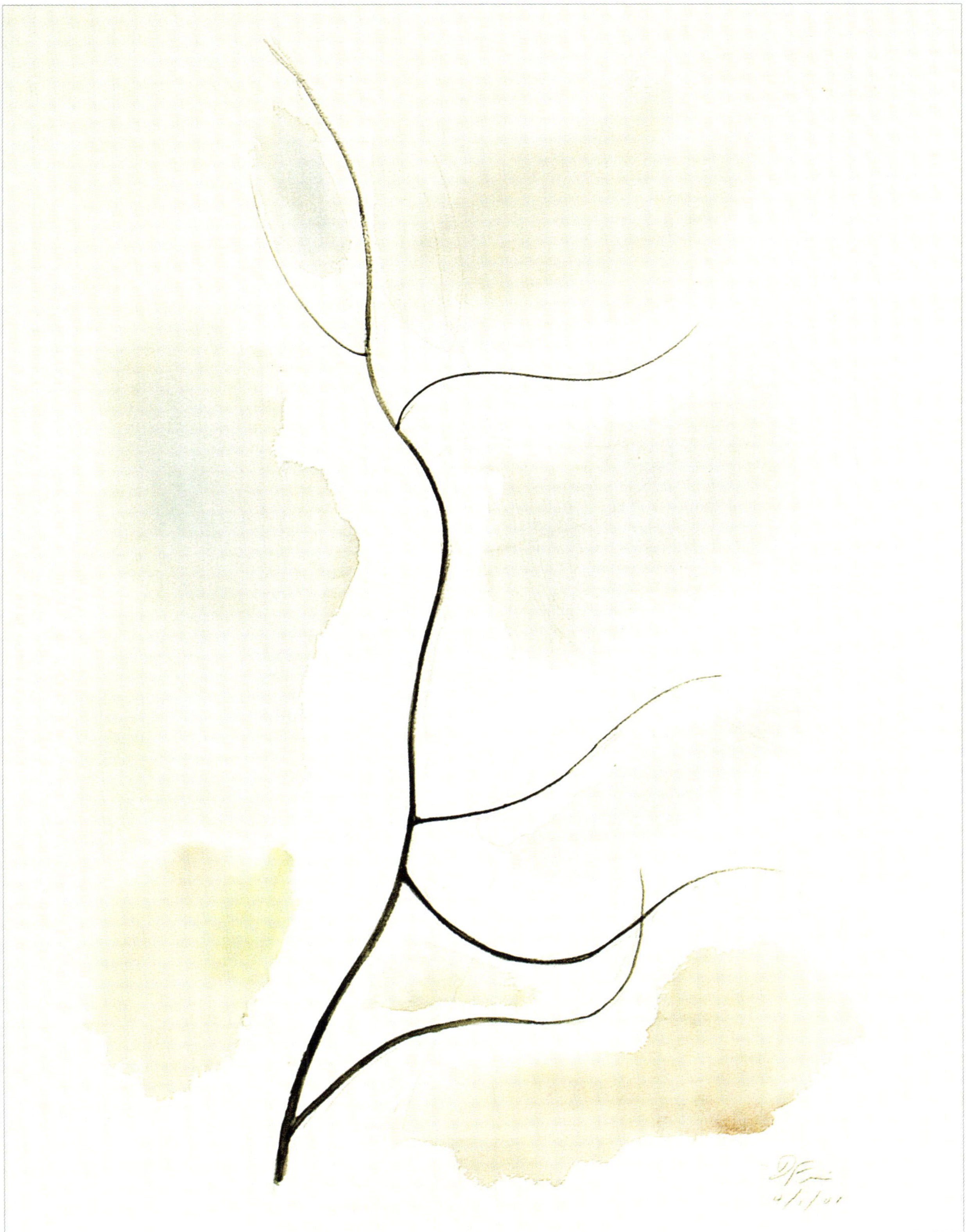

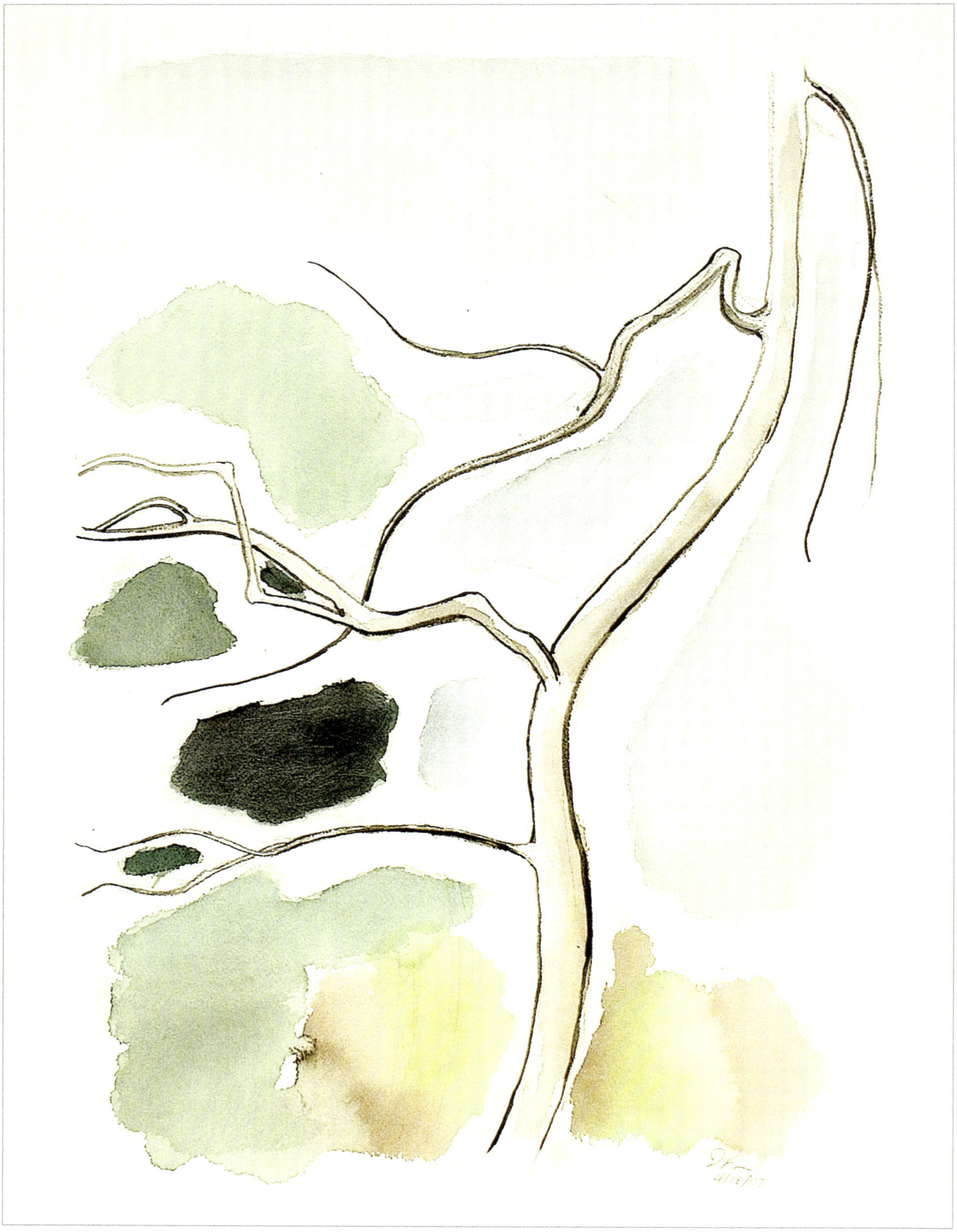

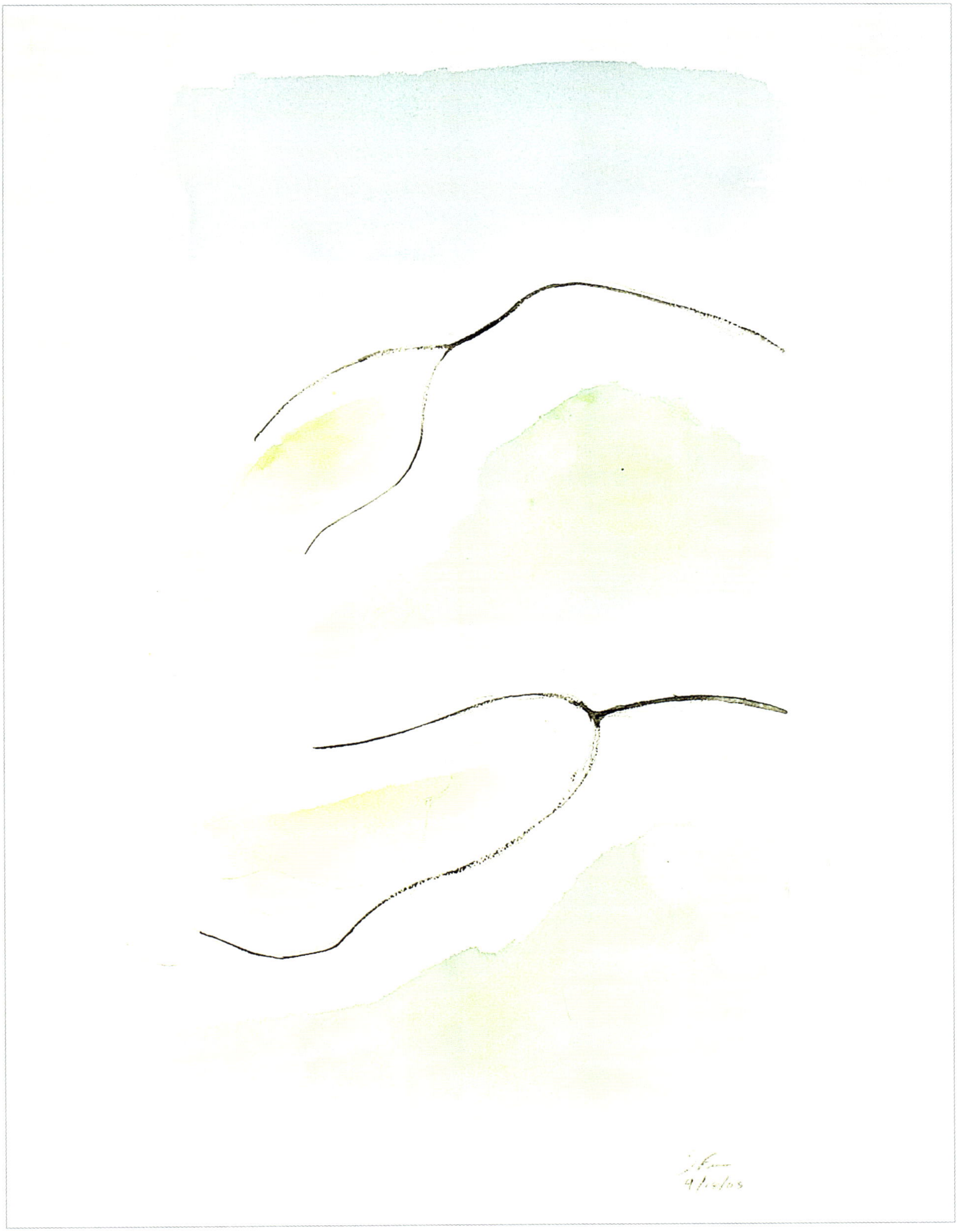

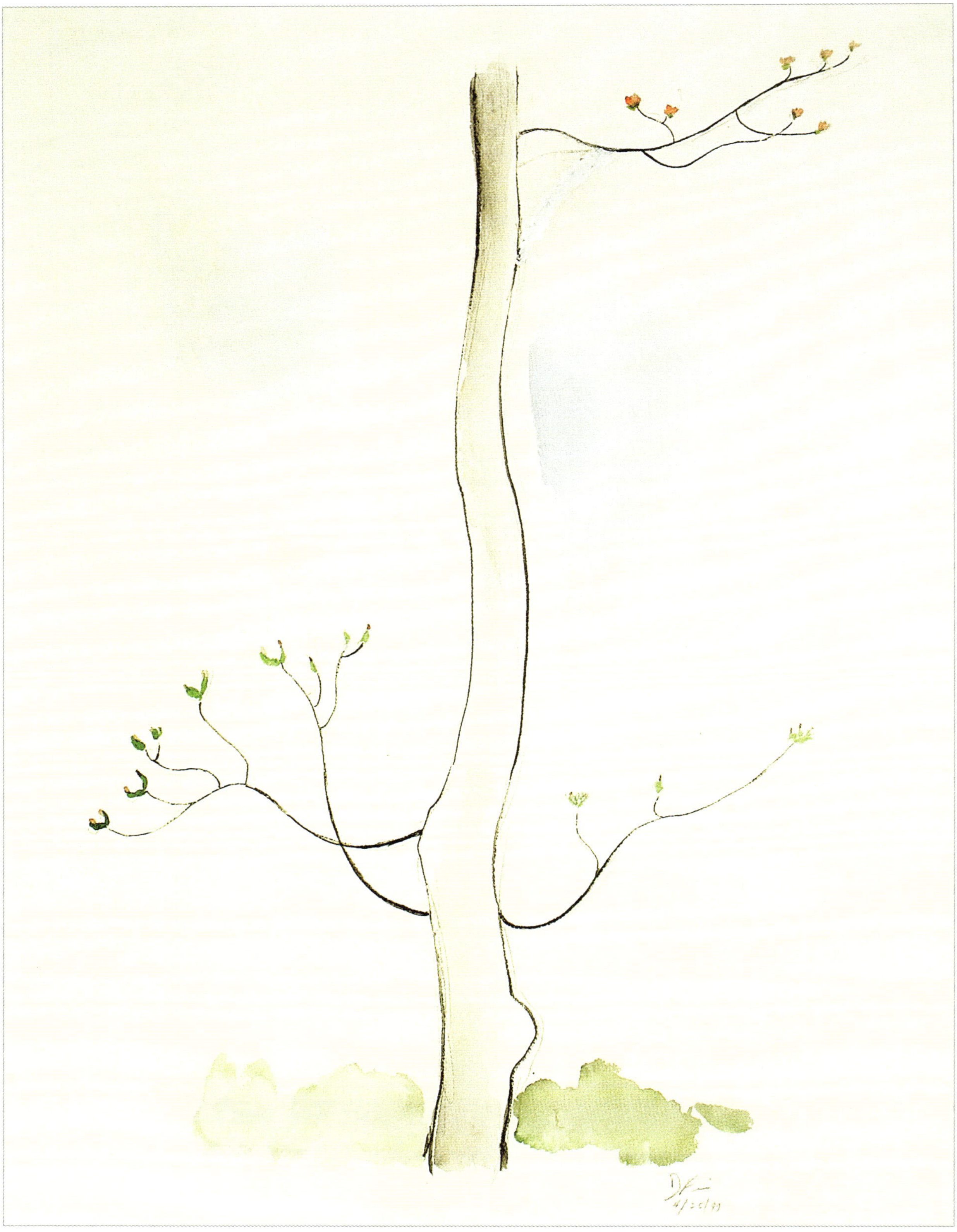

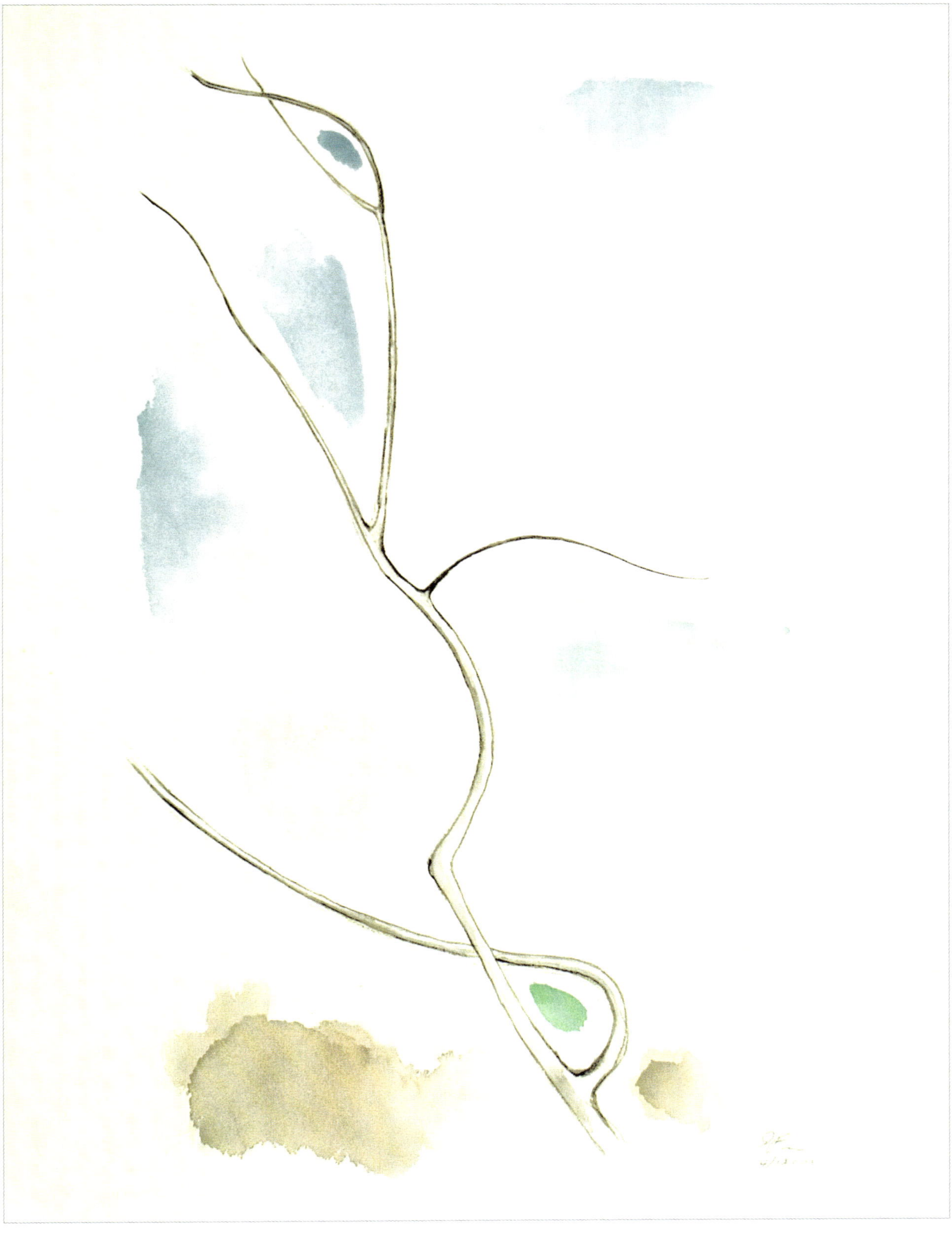

May

Green is here,
and pink blossoms
on the branches are singing,
bending with joy; leaves are floating,
filling the spaces in between
as curving branches
rise to the sky.

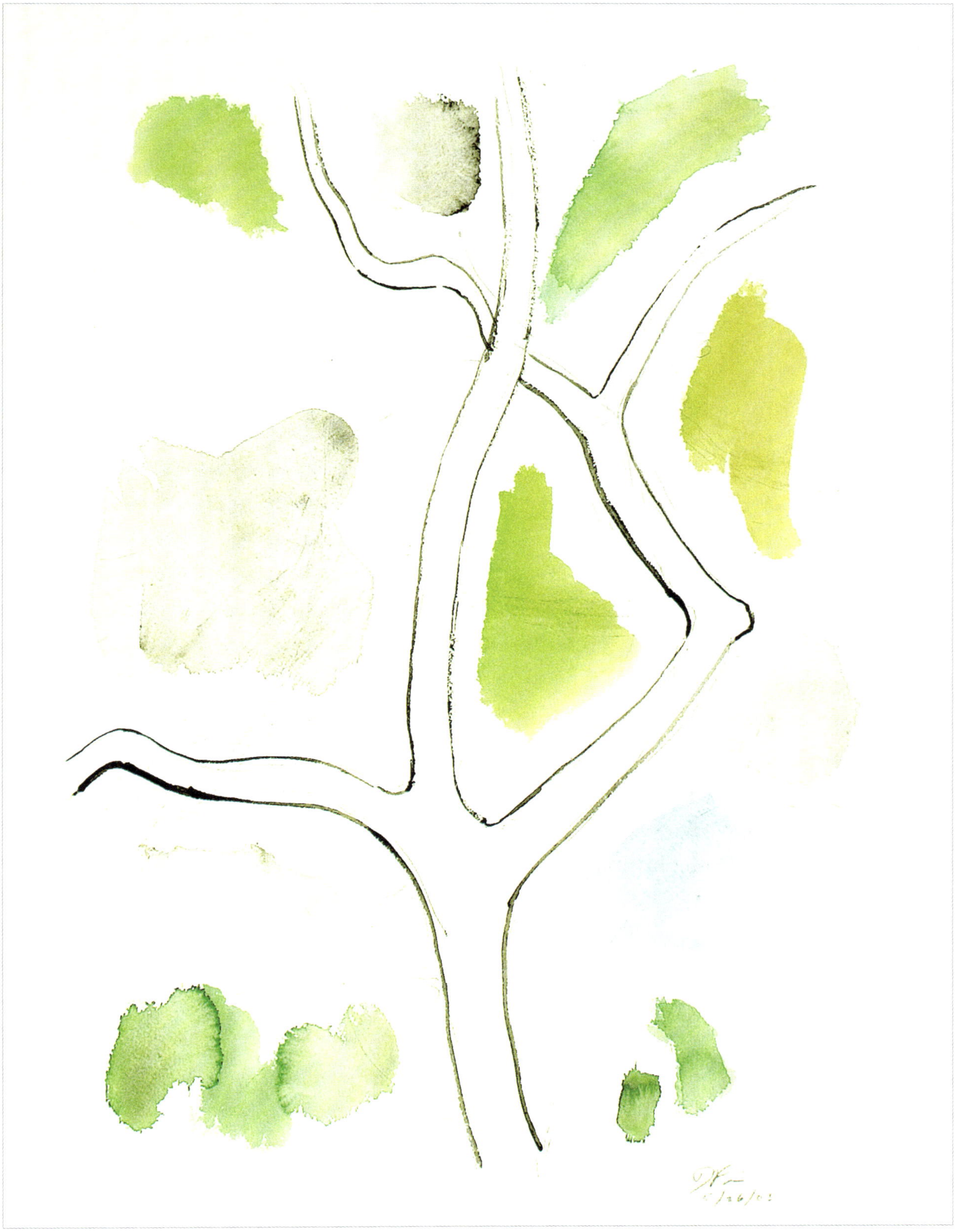

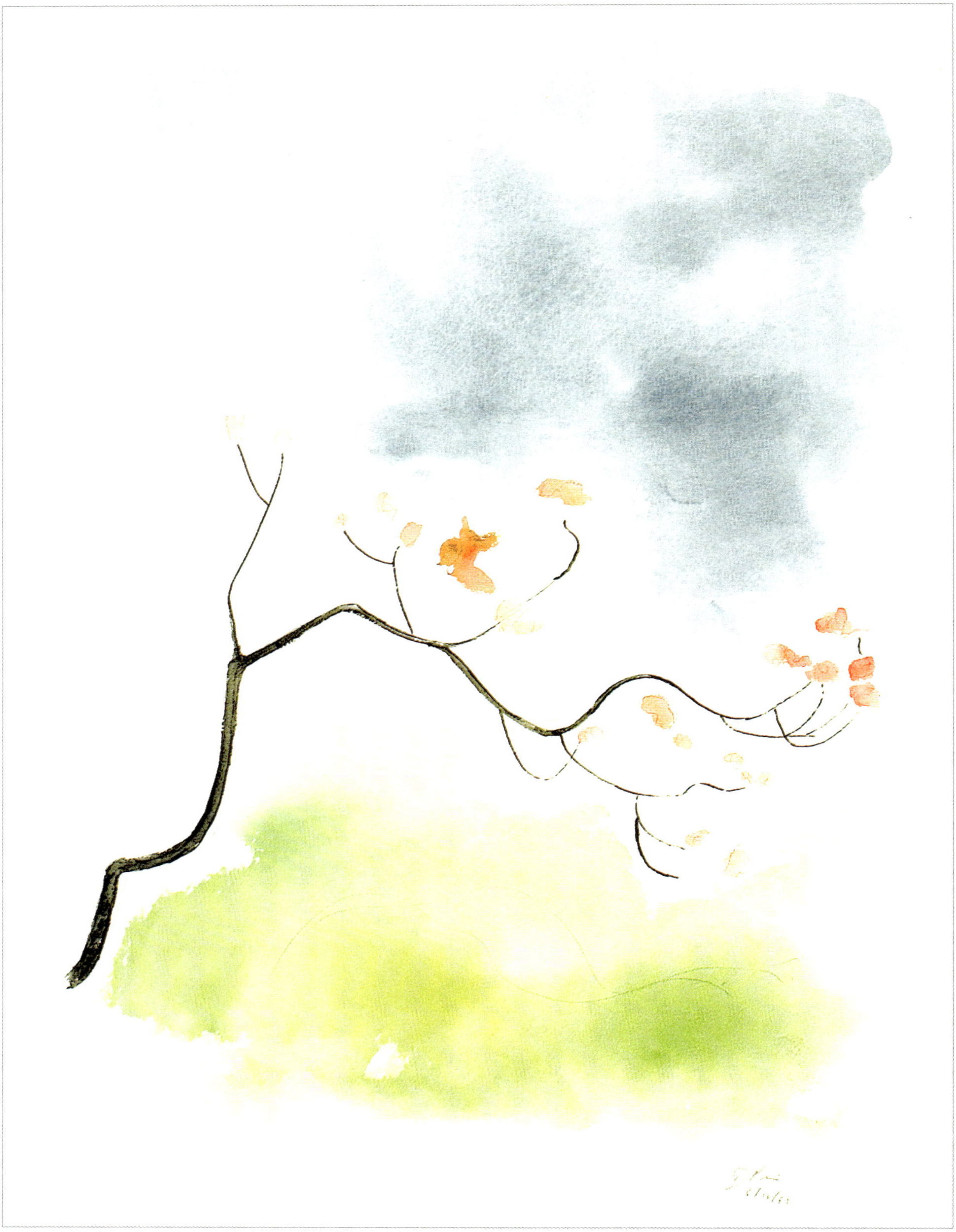

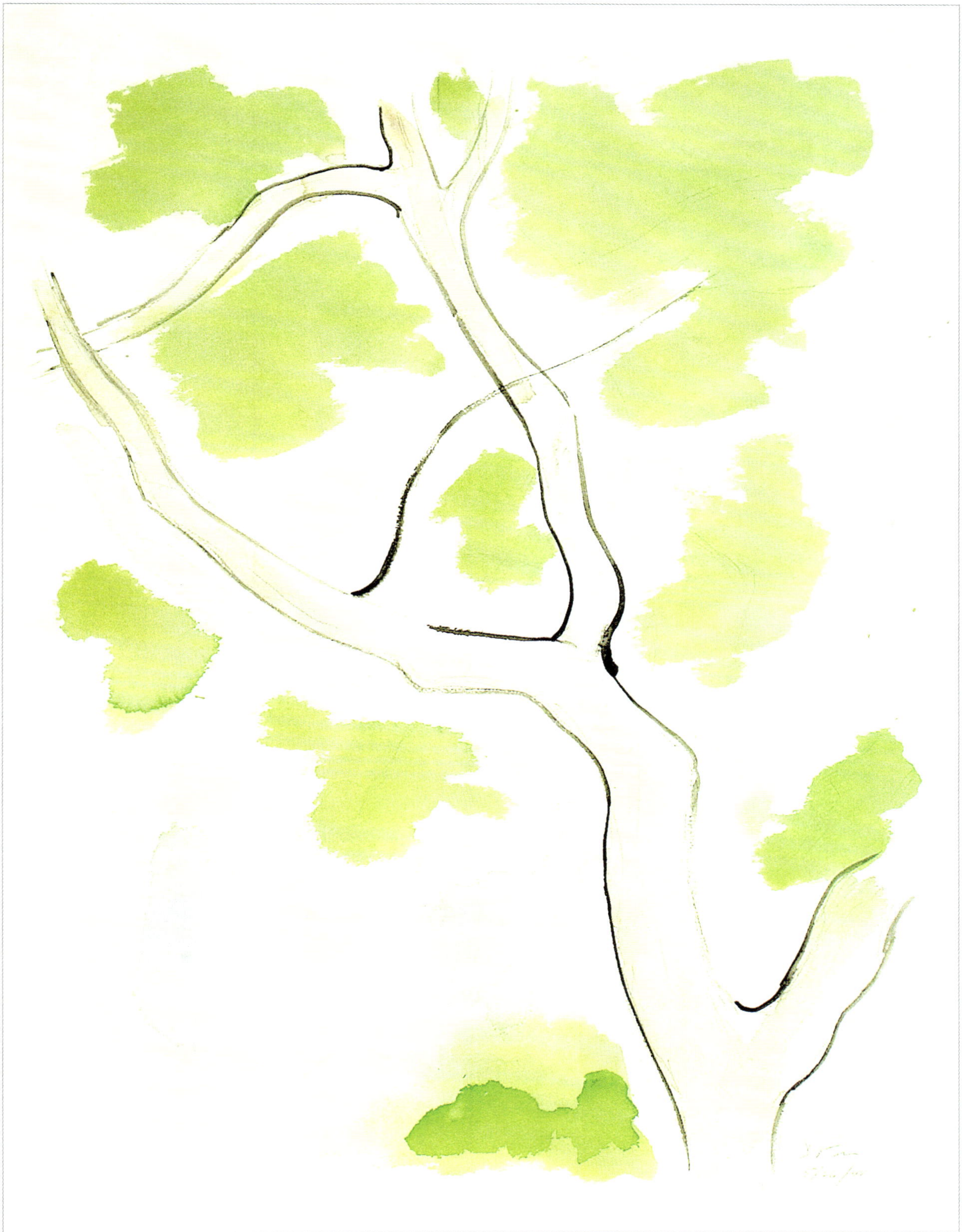

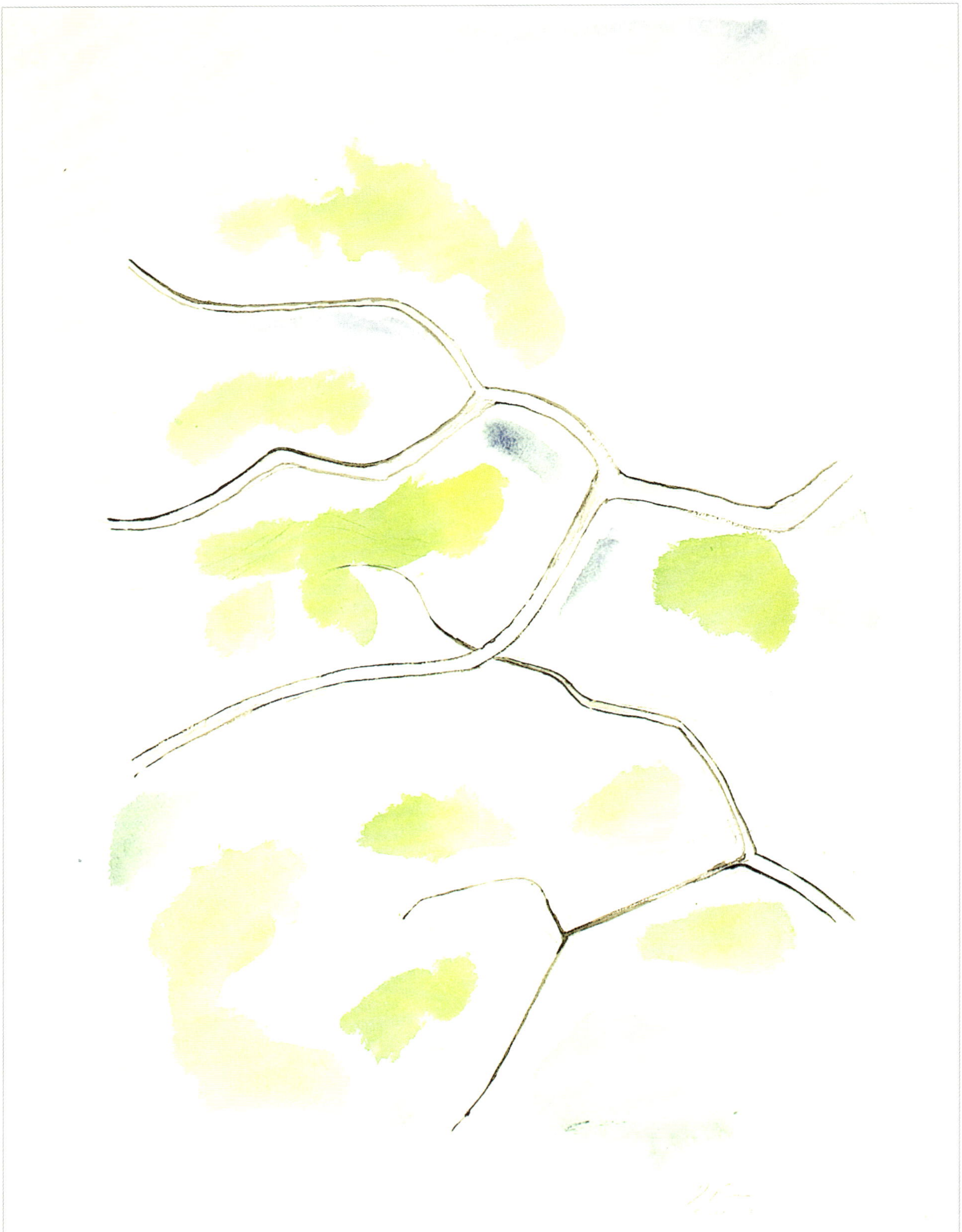

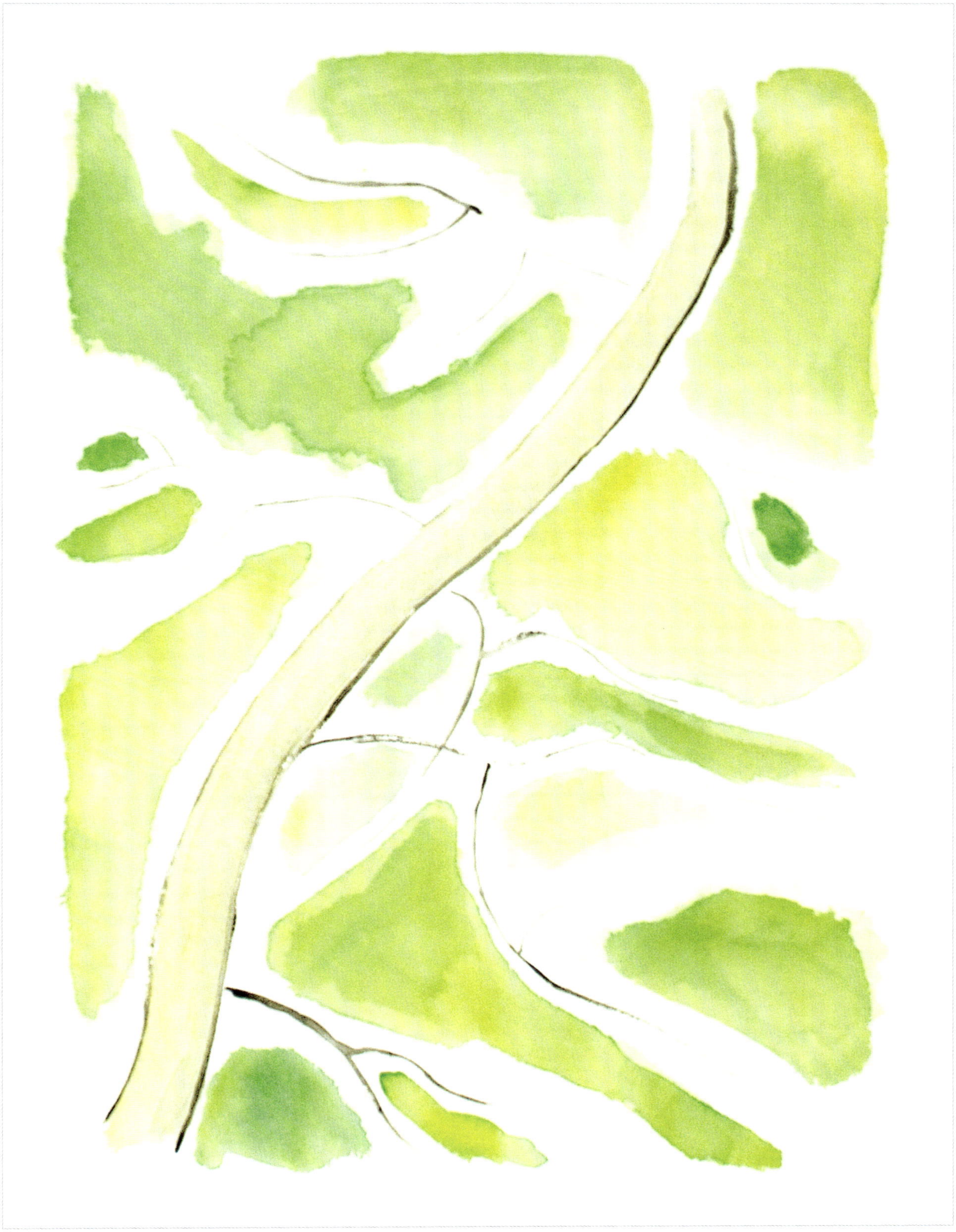

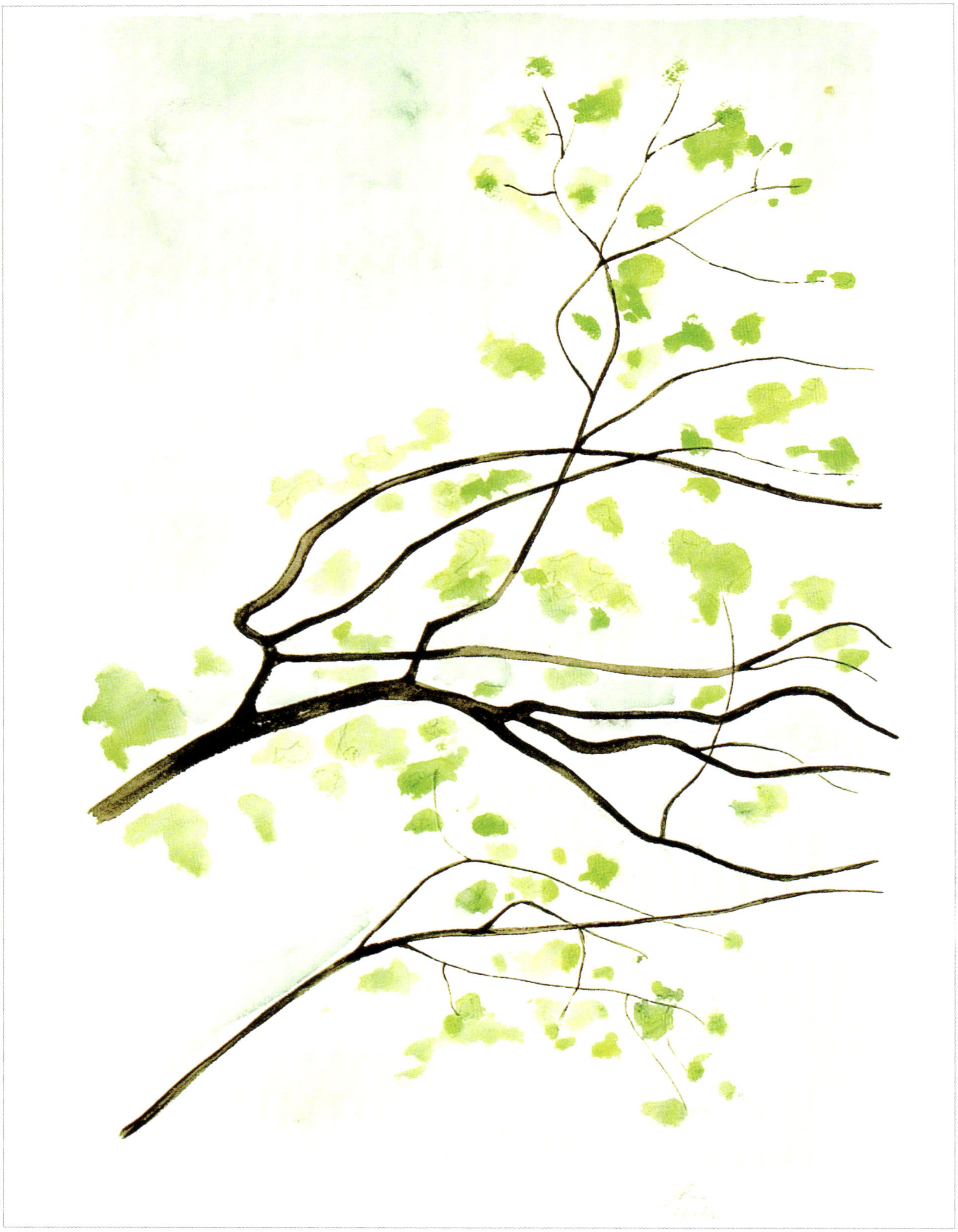

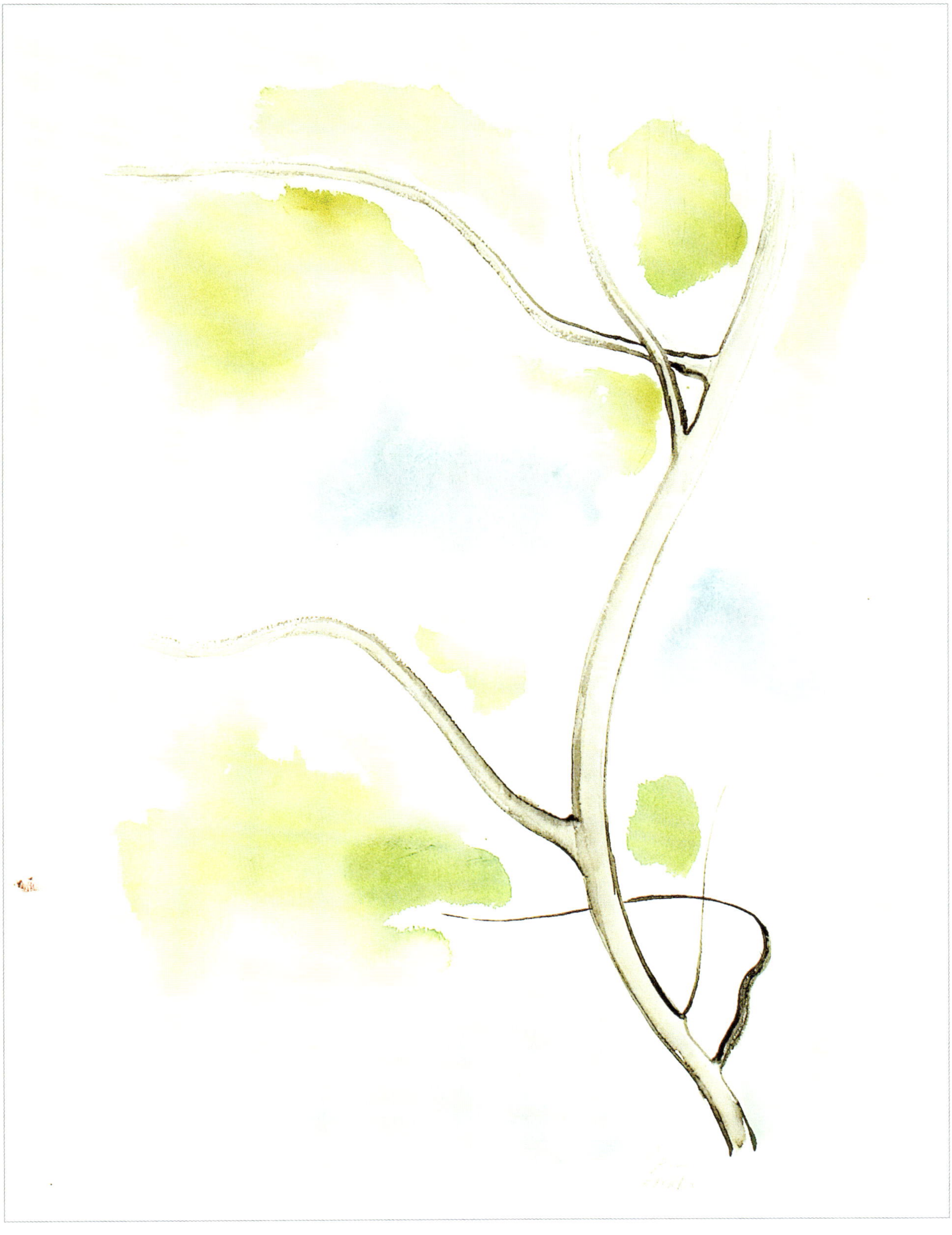

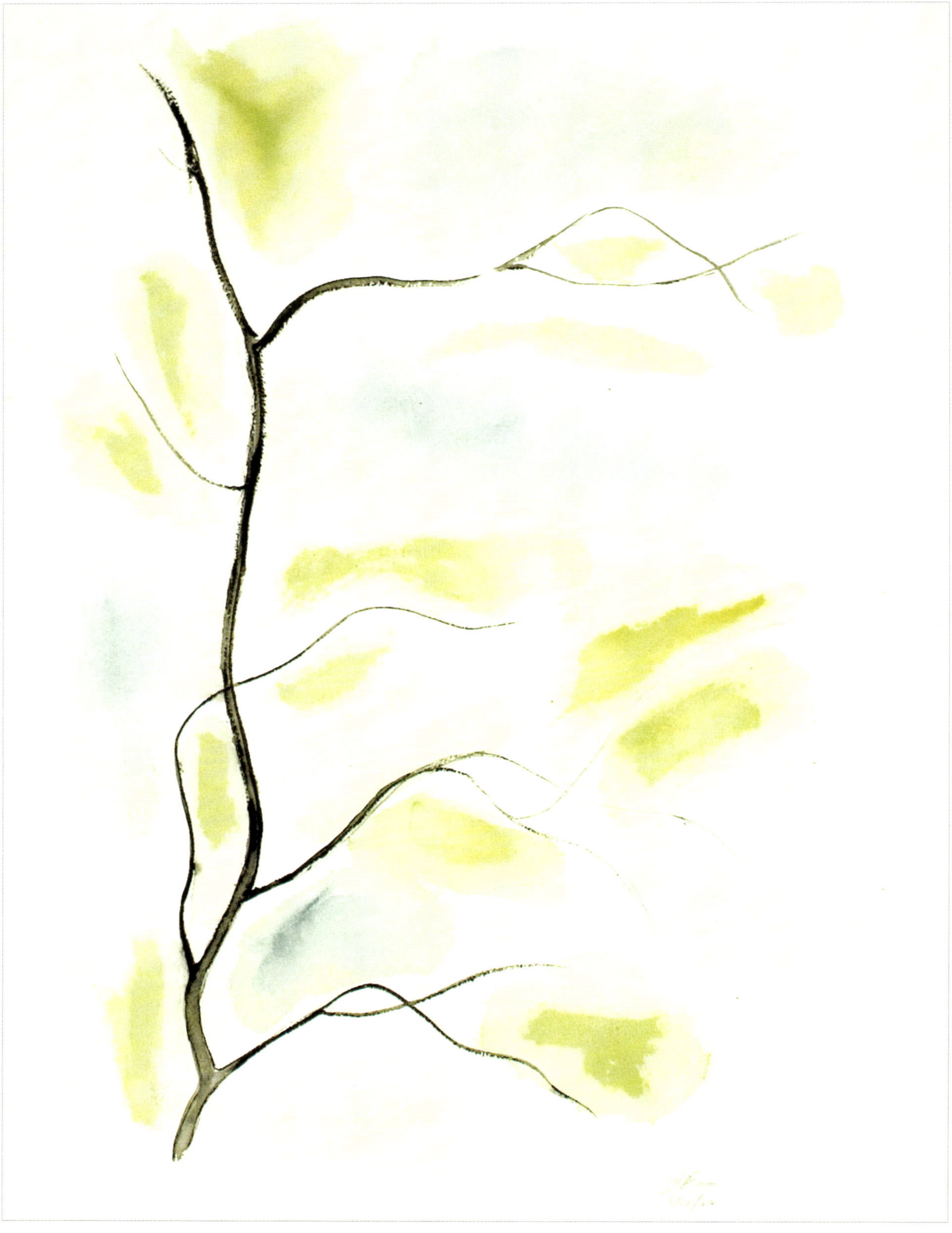

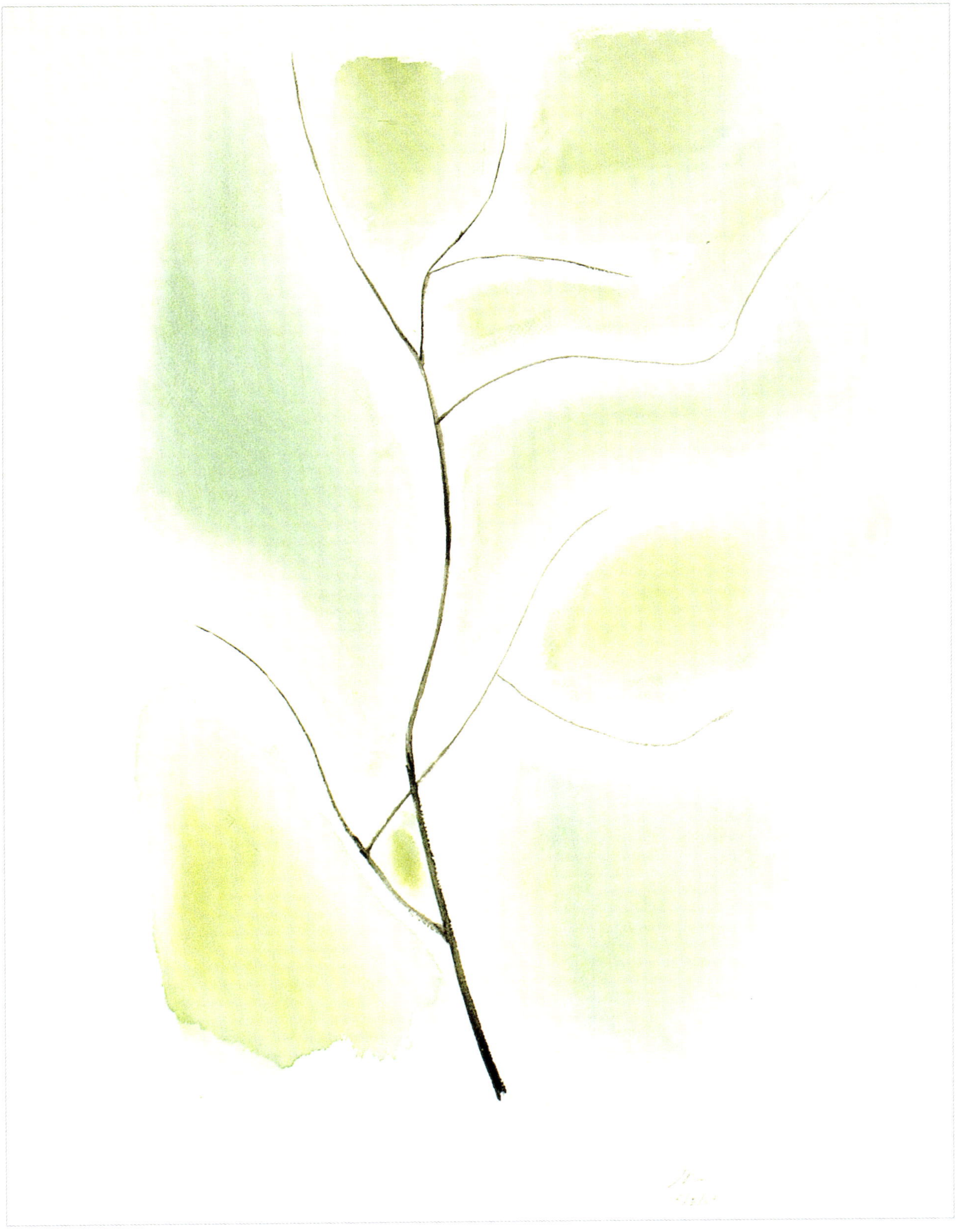

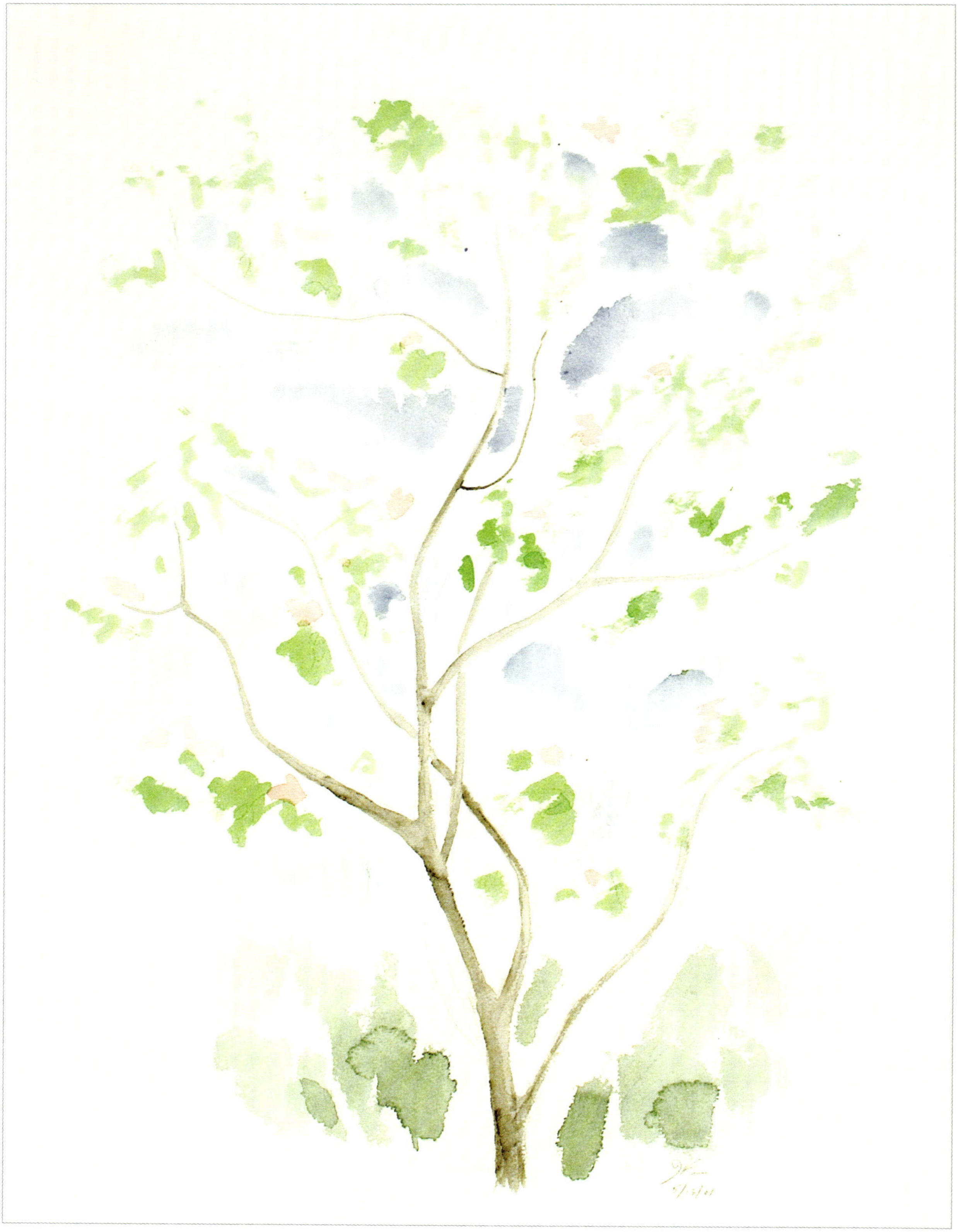

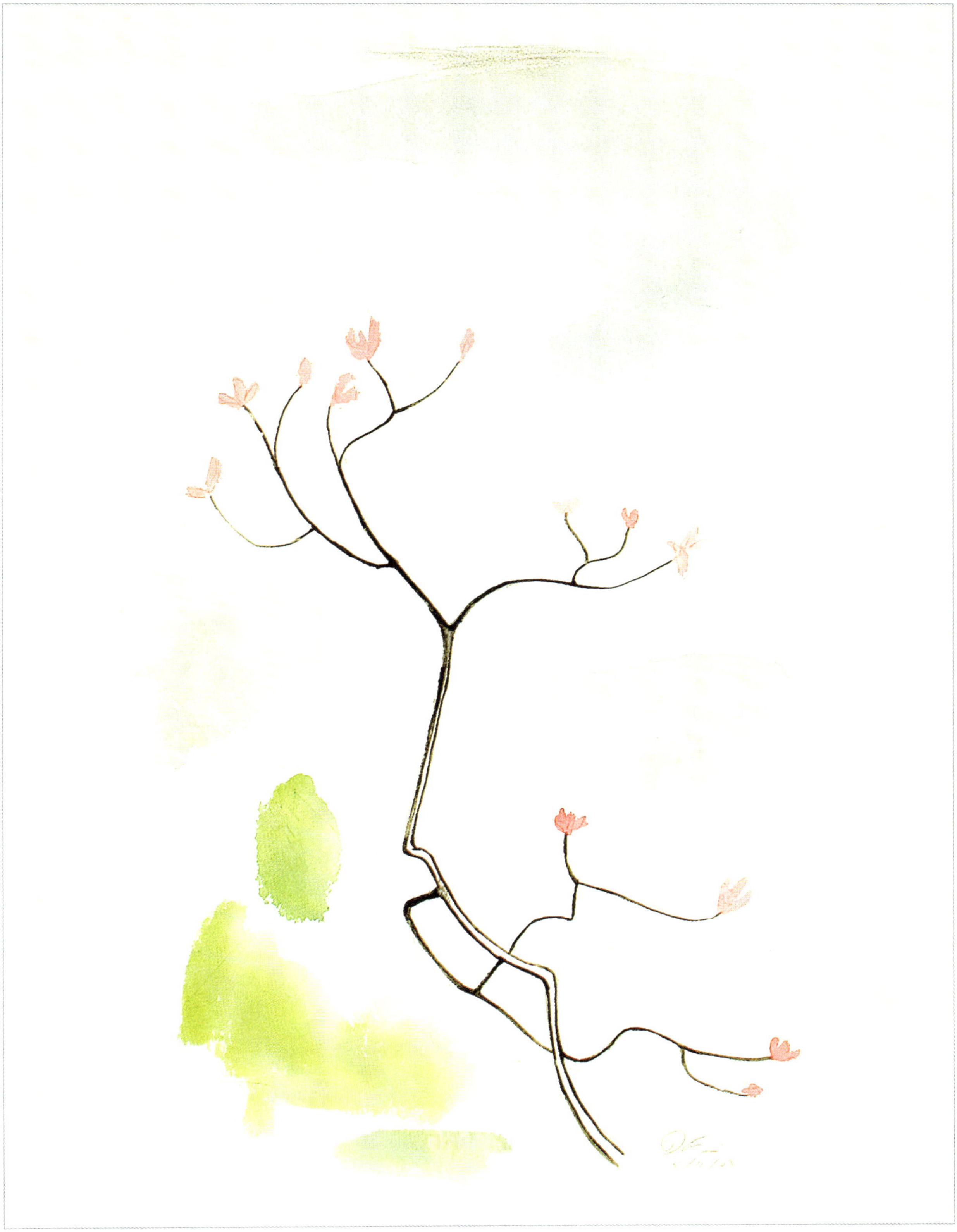

June

Now colors are full of the season's joy,
they spread through open spaces
framed by curving branches,
as new compositions arise
with washes of forms
bright, rich, warm,
full of energy,
intense,
strong.

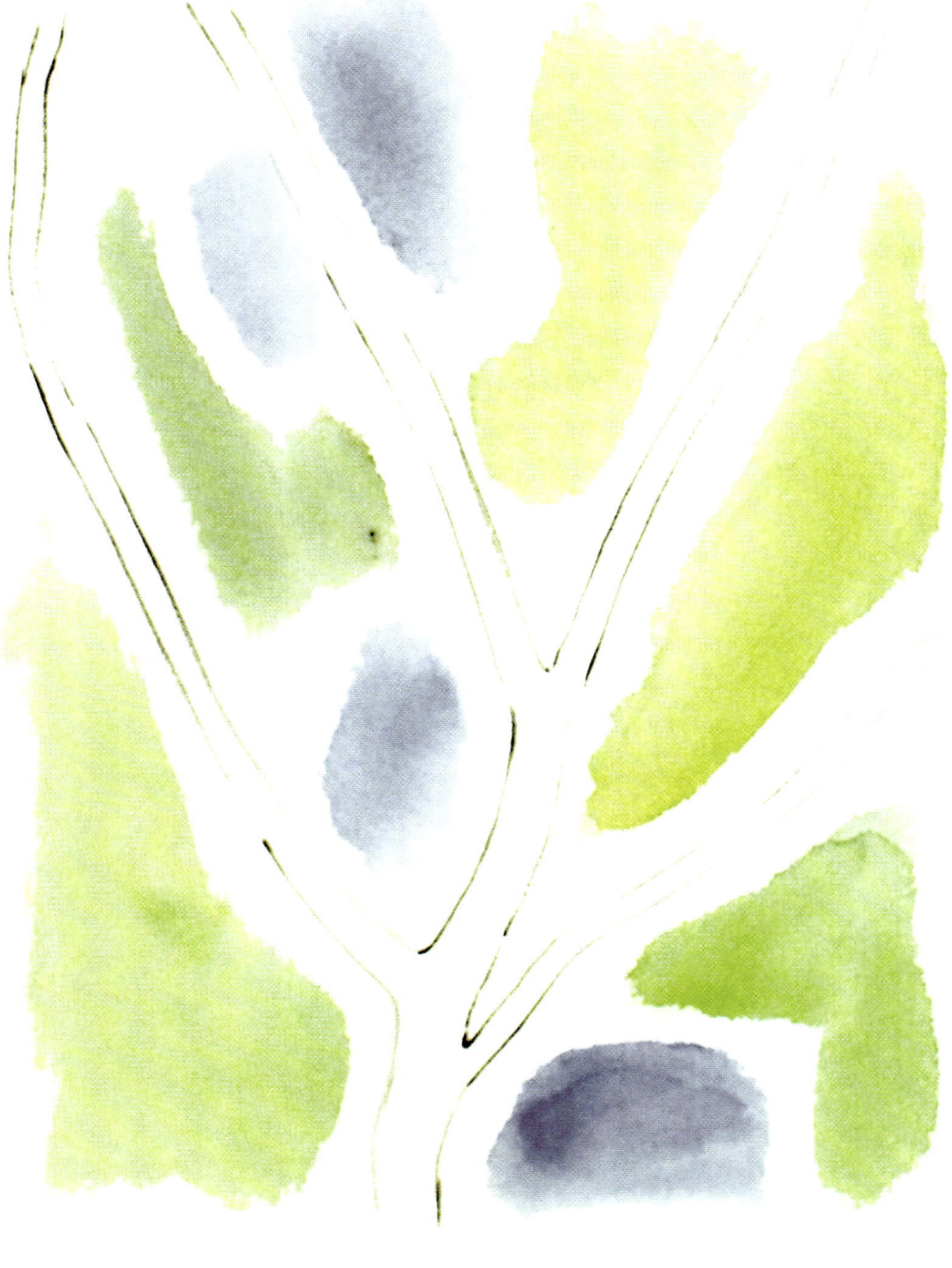

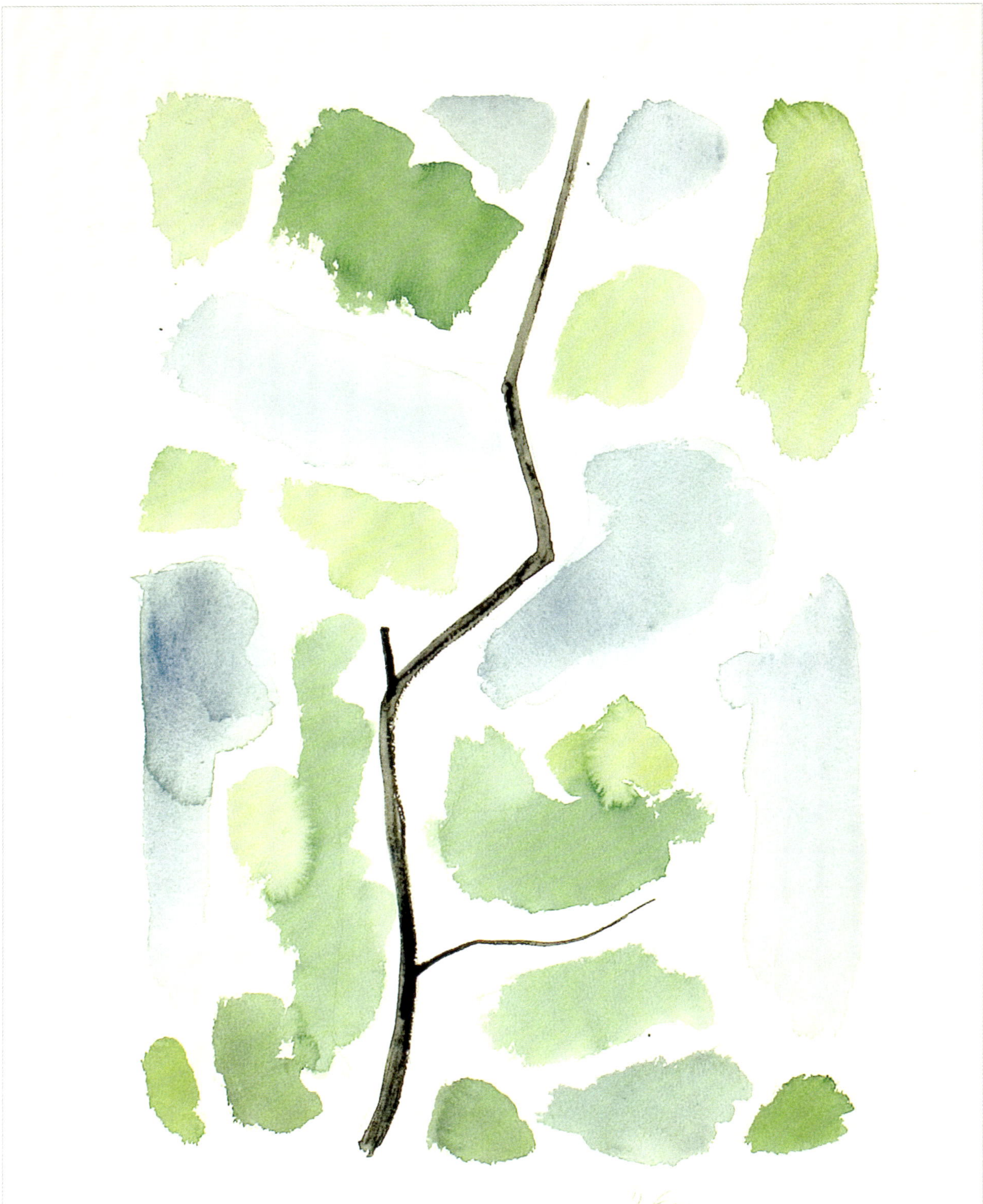

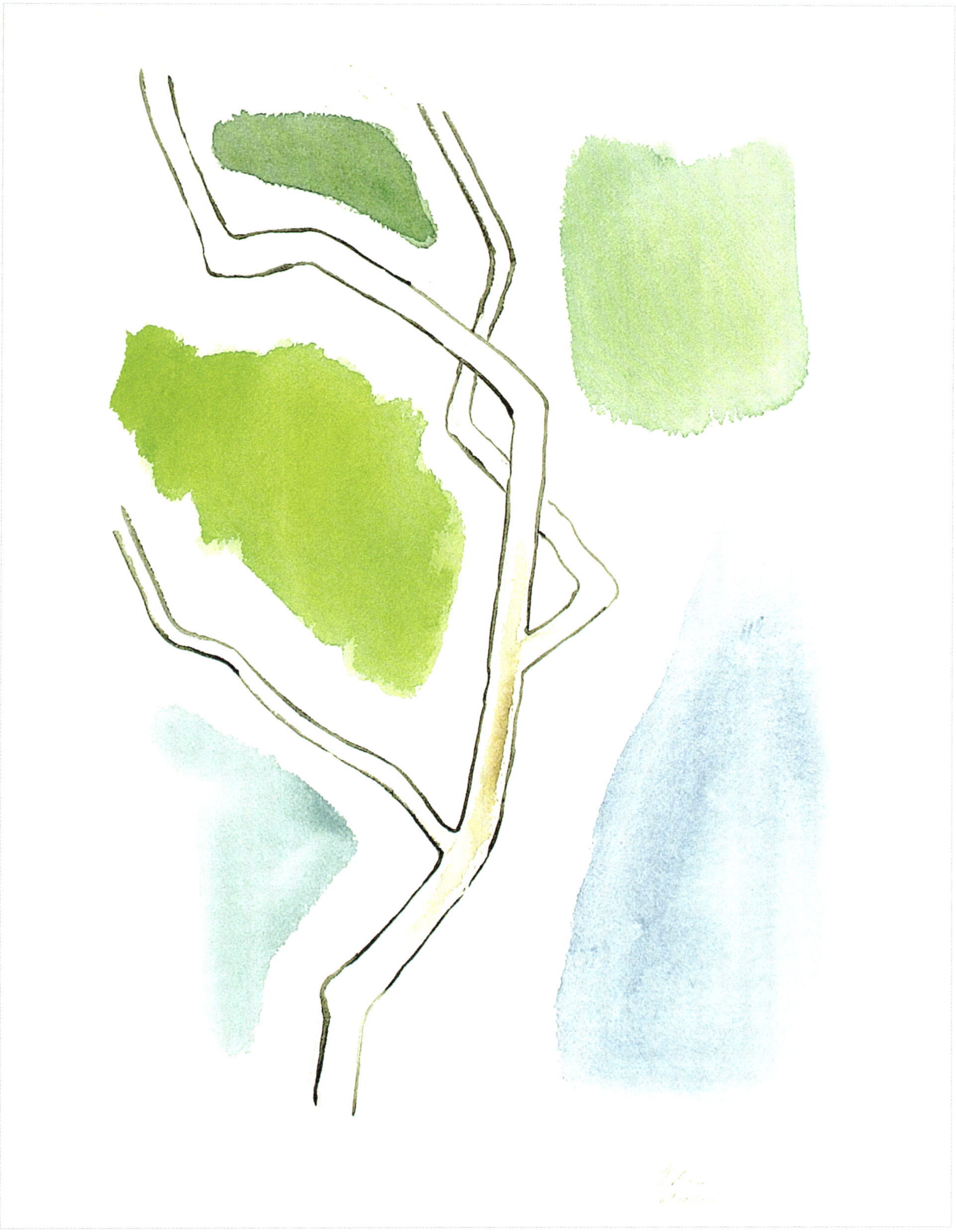

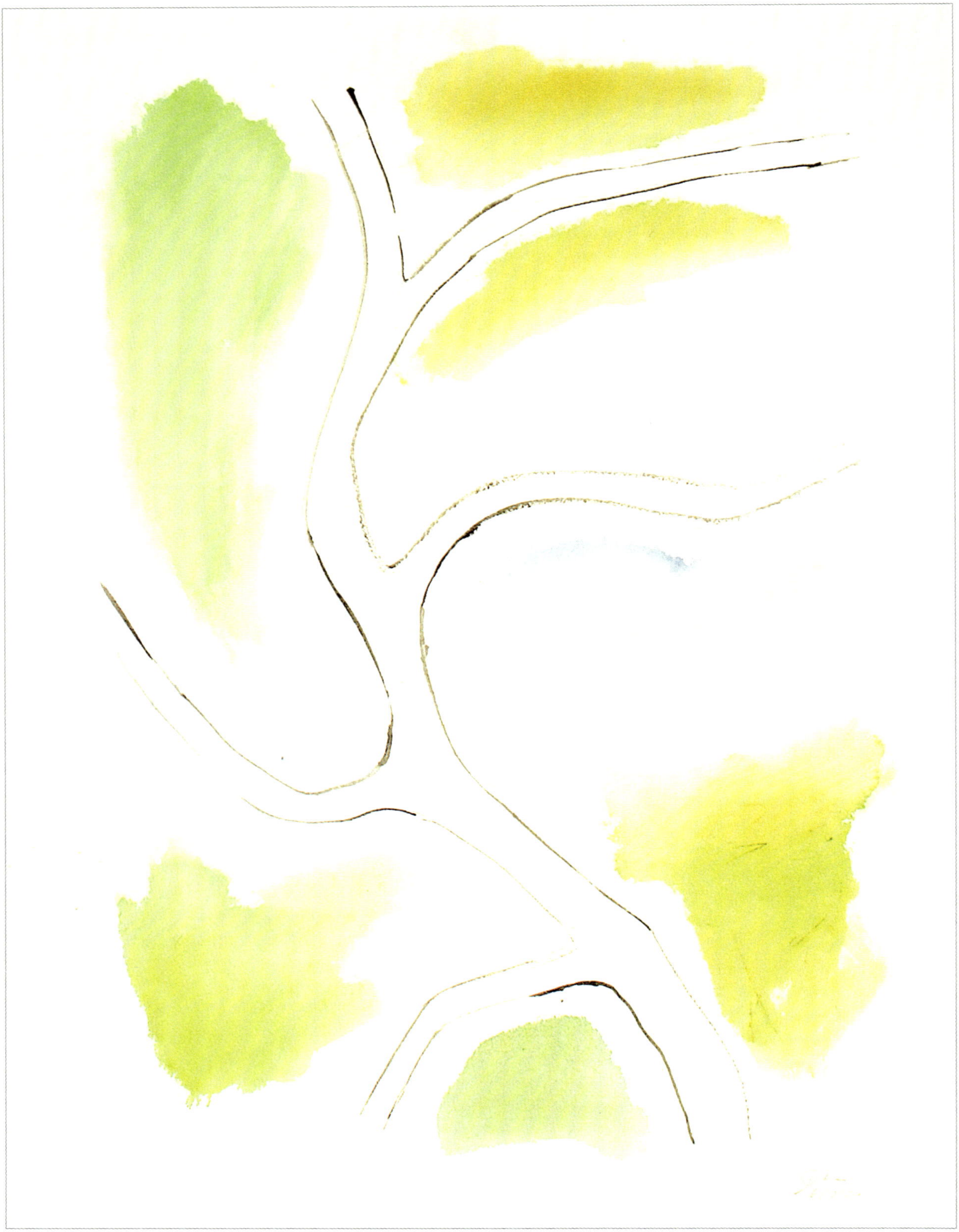

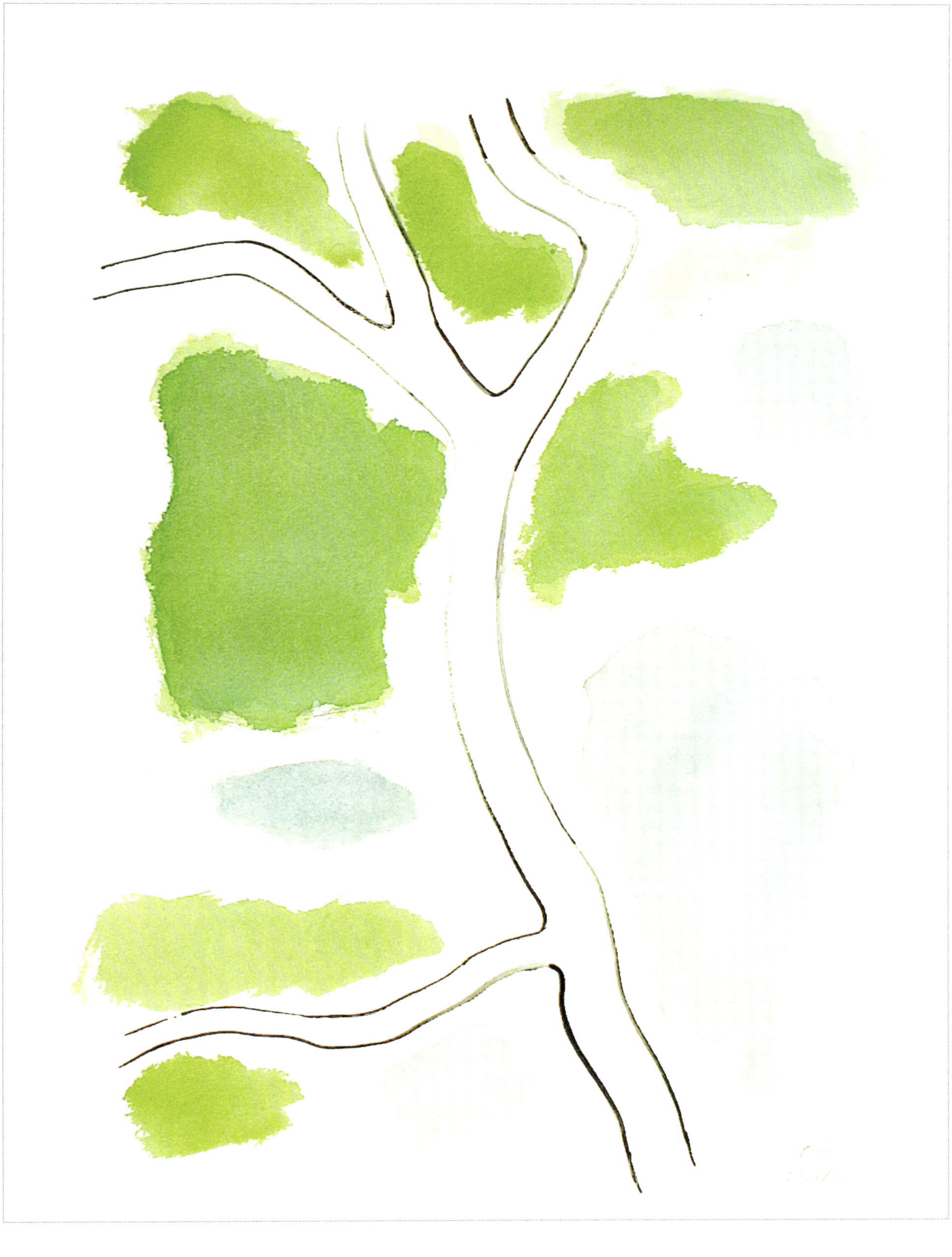

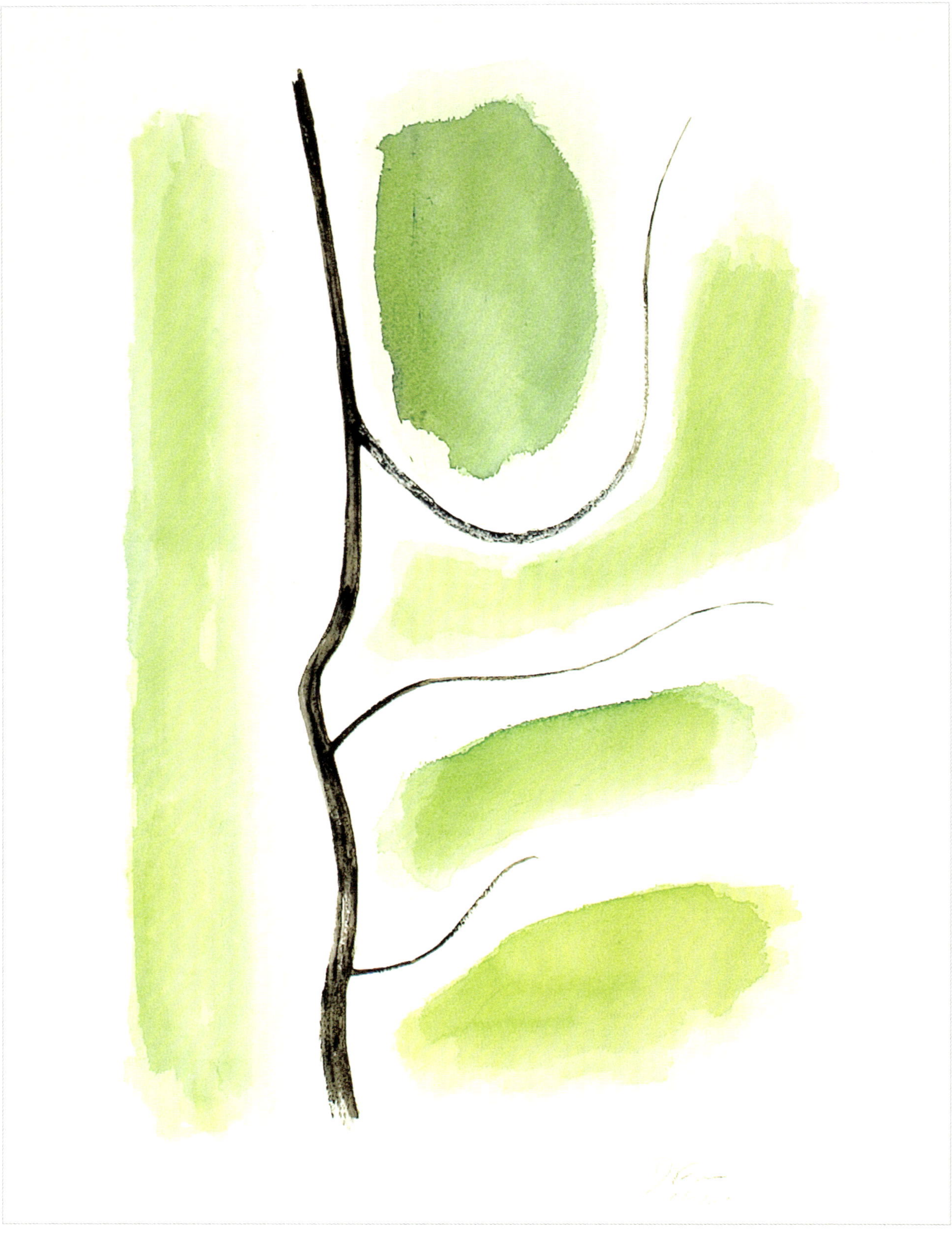

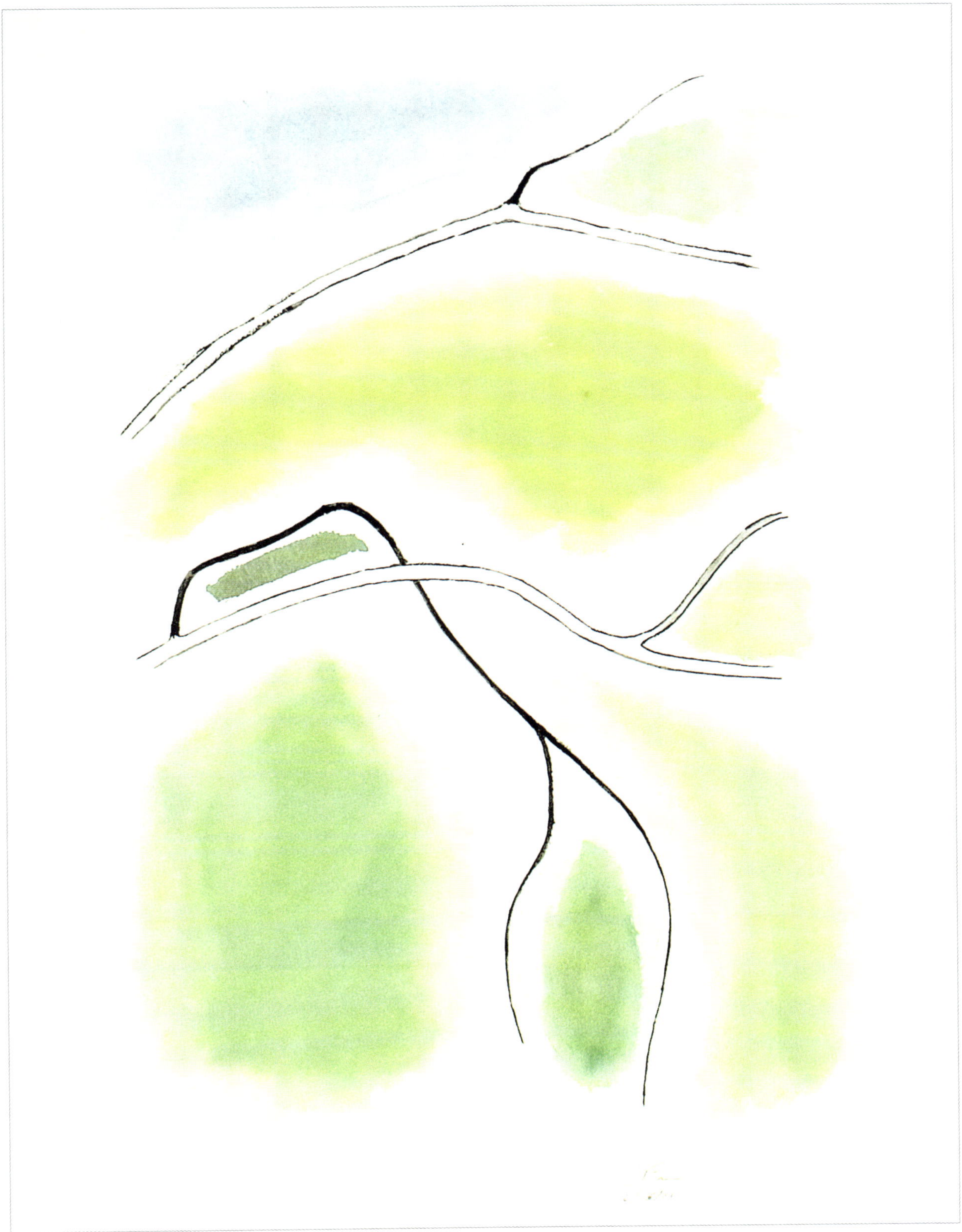

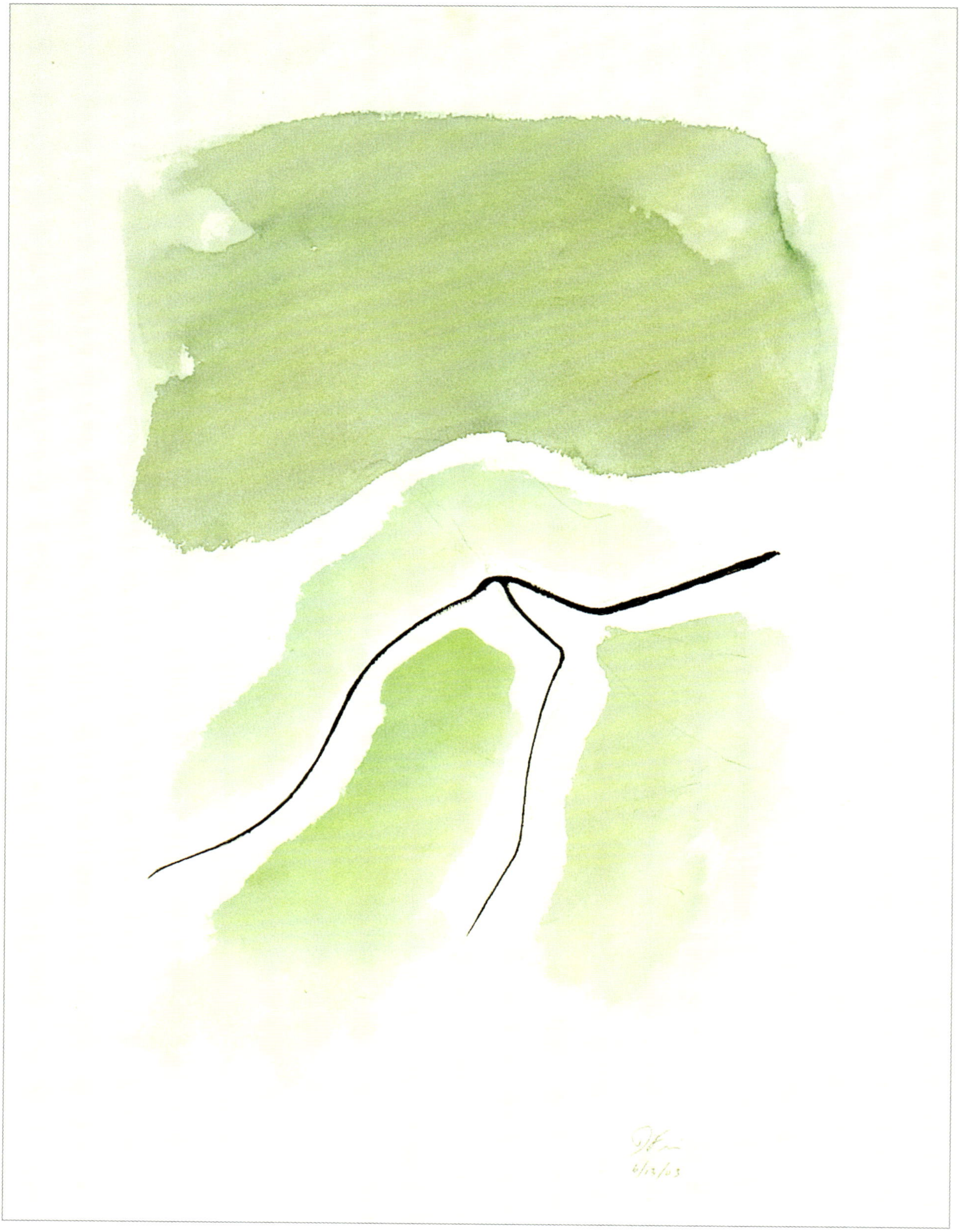

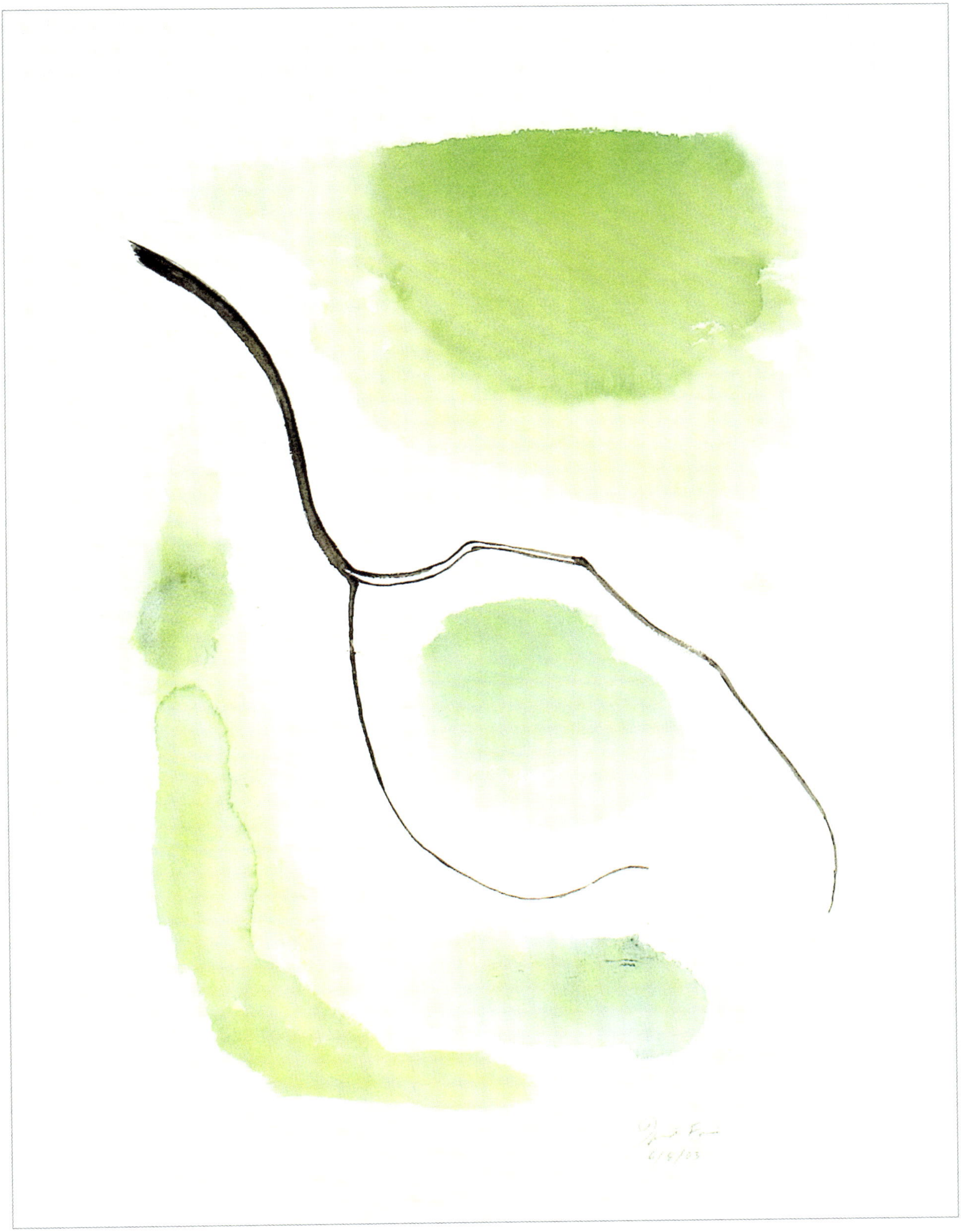

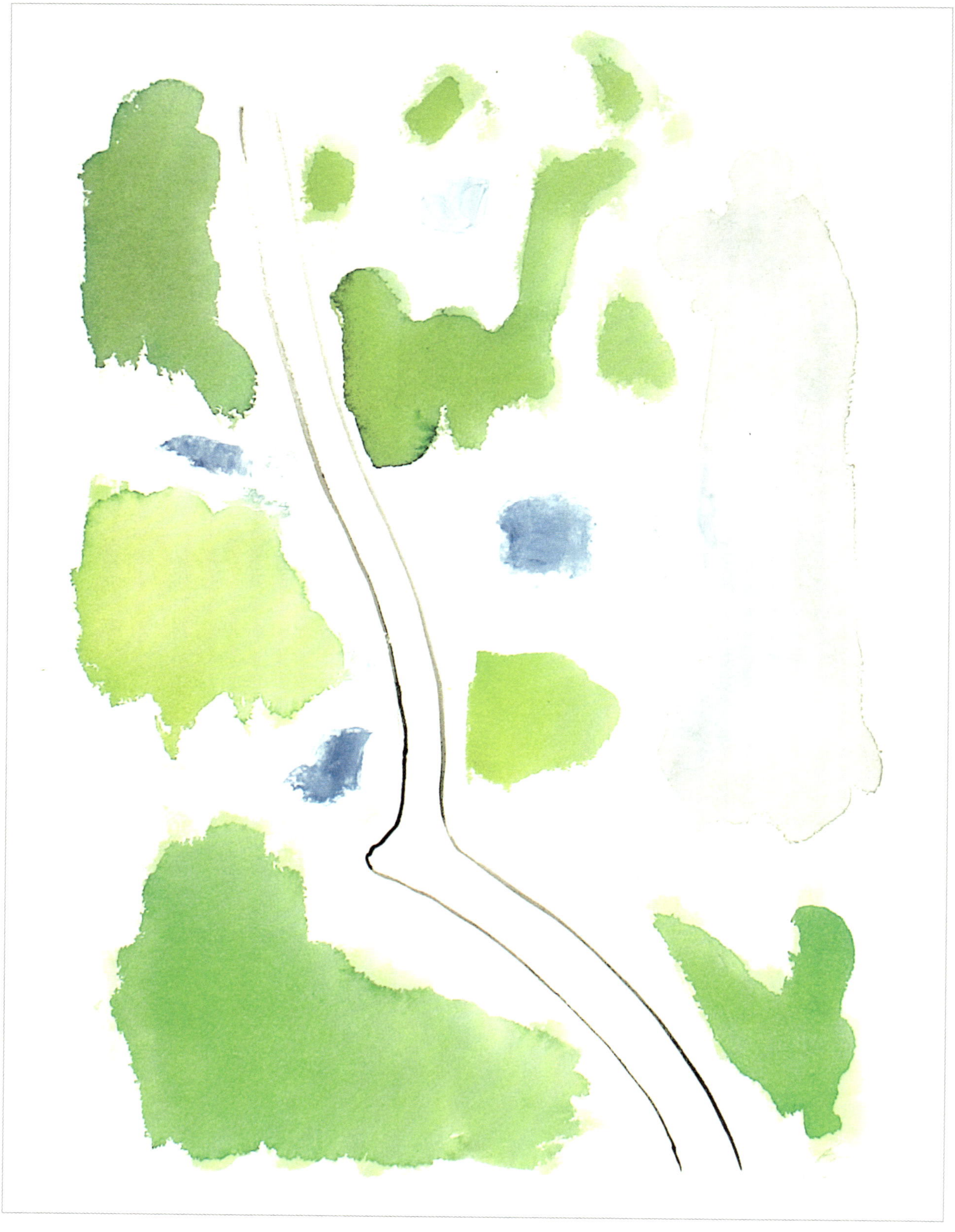

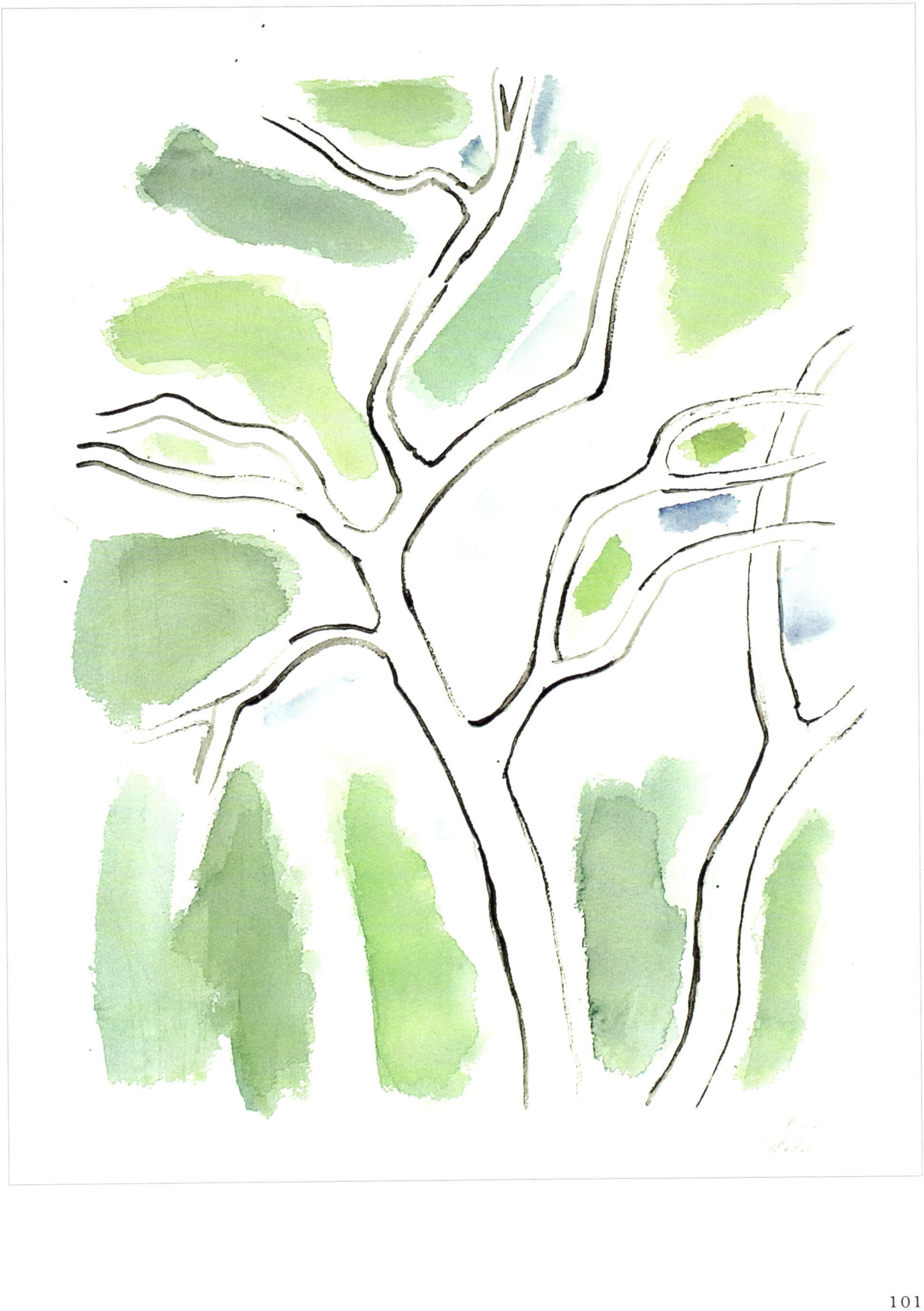

July

The maturing

of the season, brings

the height of life with fullness,

and complexity, and revelations;

with intense greens and strong lines

with blue—and sometimes gray—skies,

celebrating summer joys with new compositions.

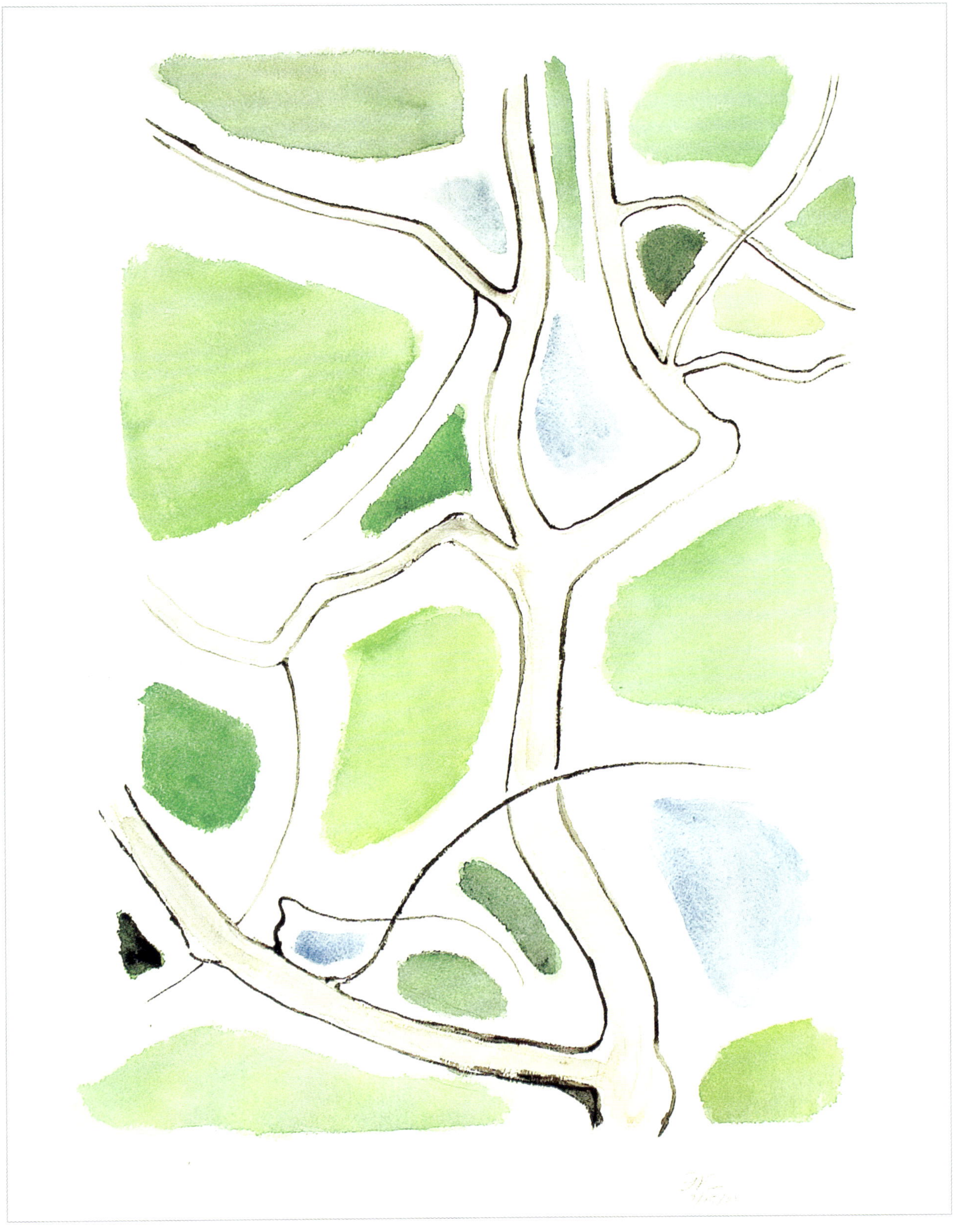

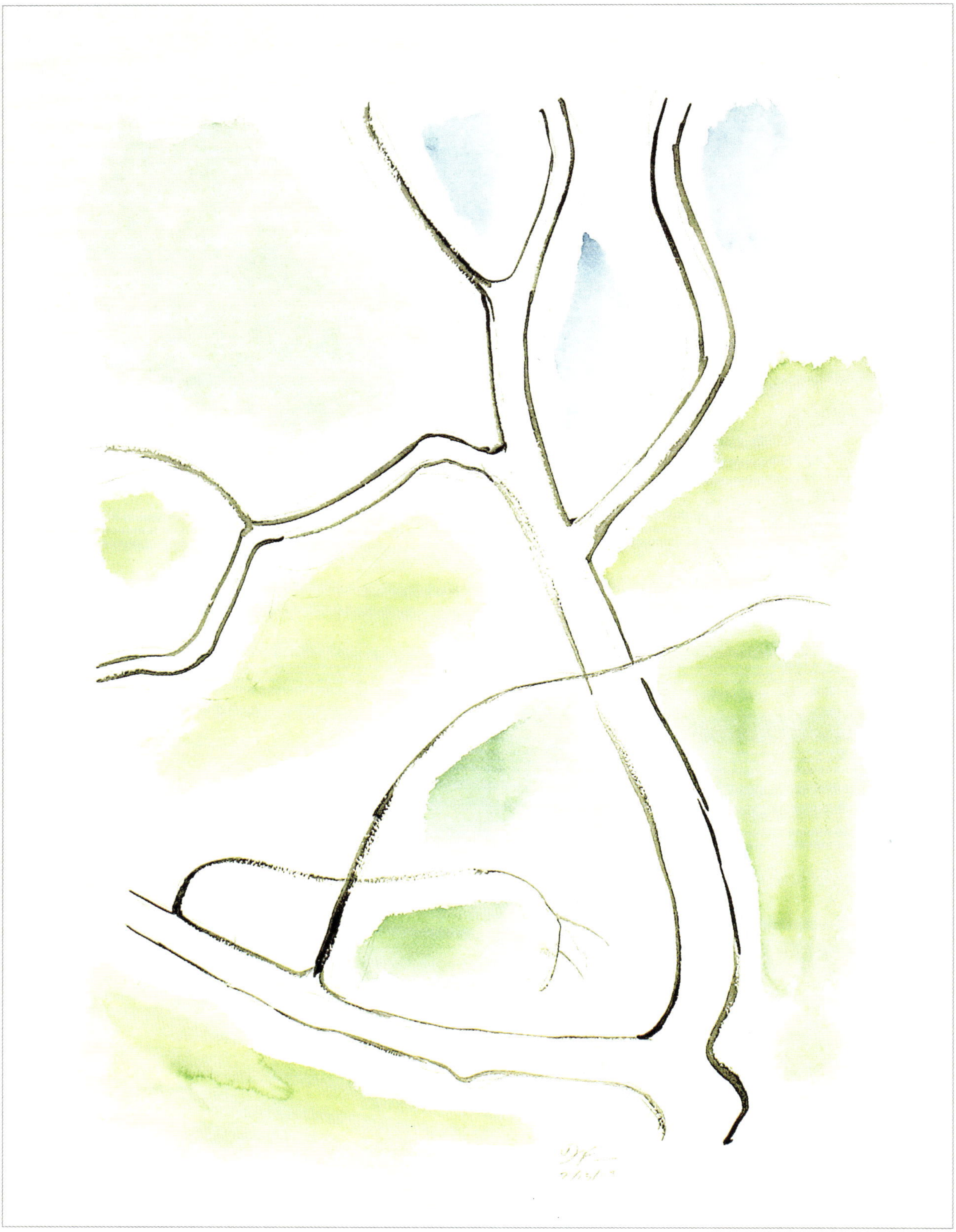

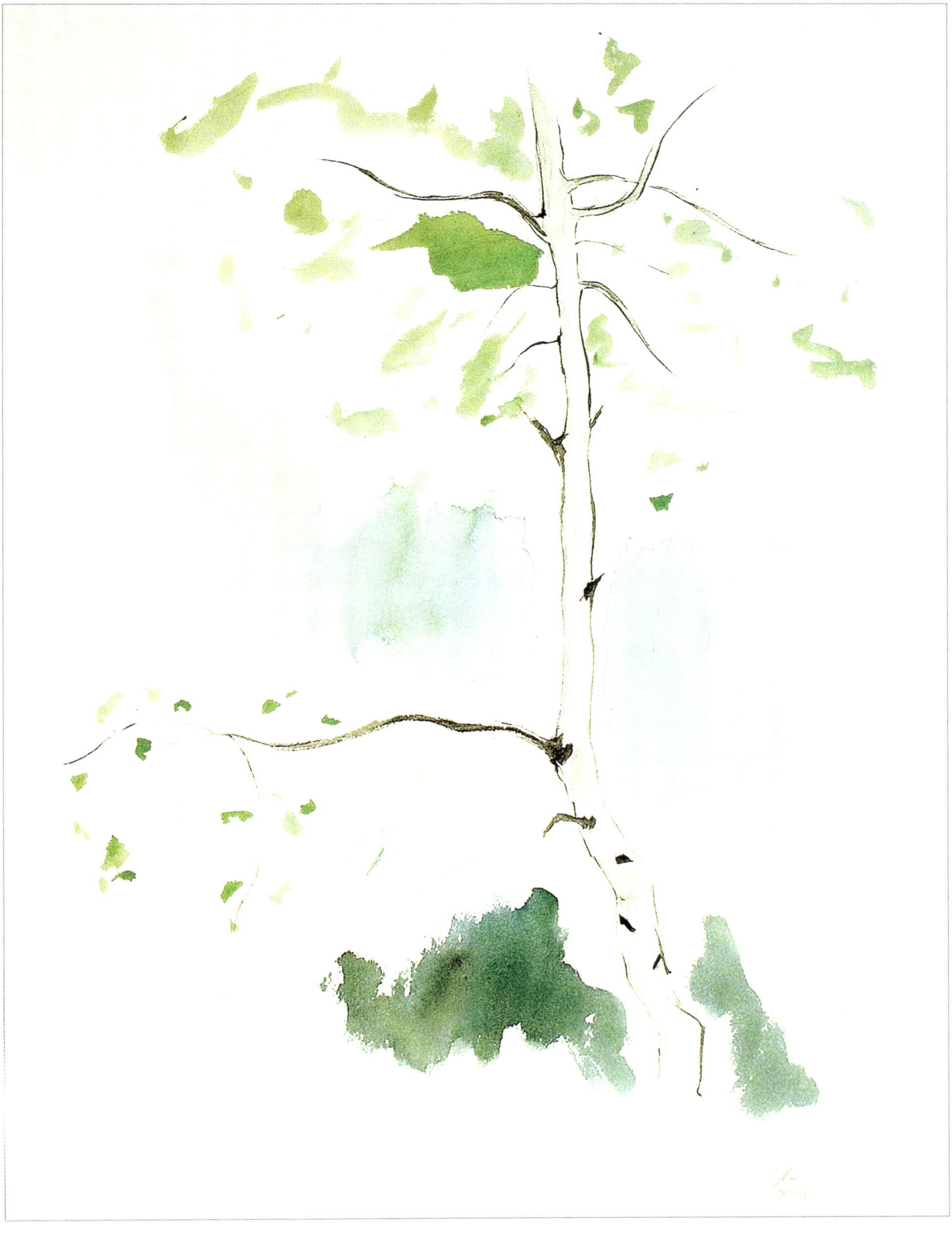

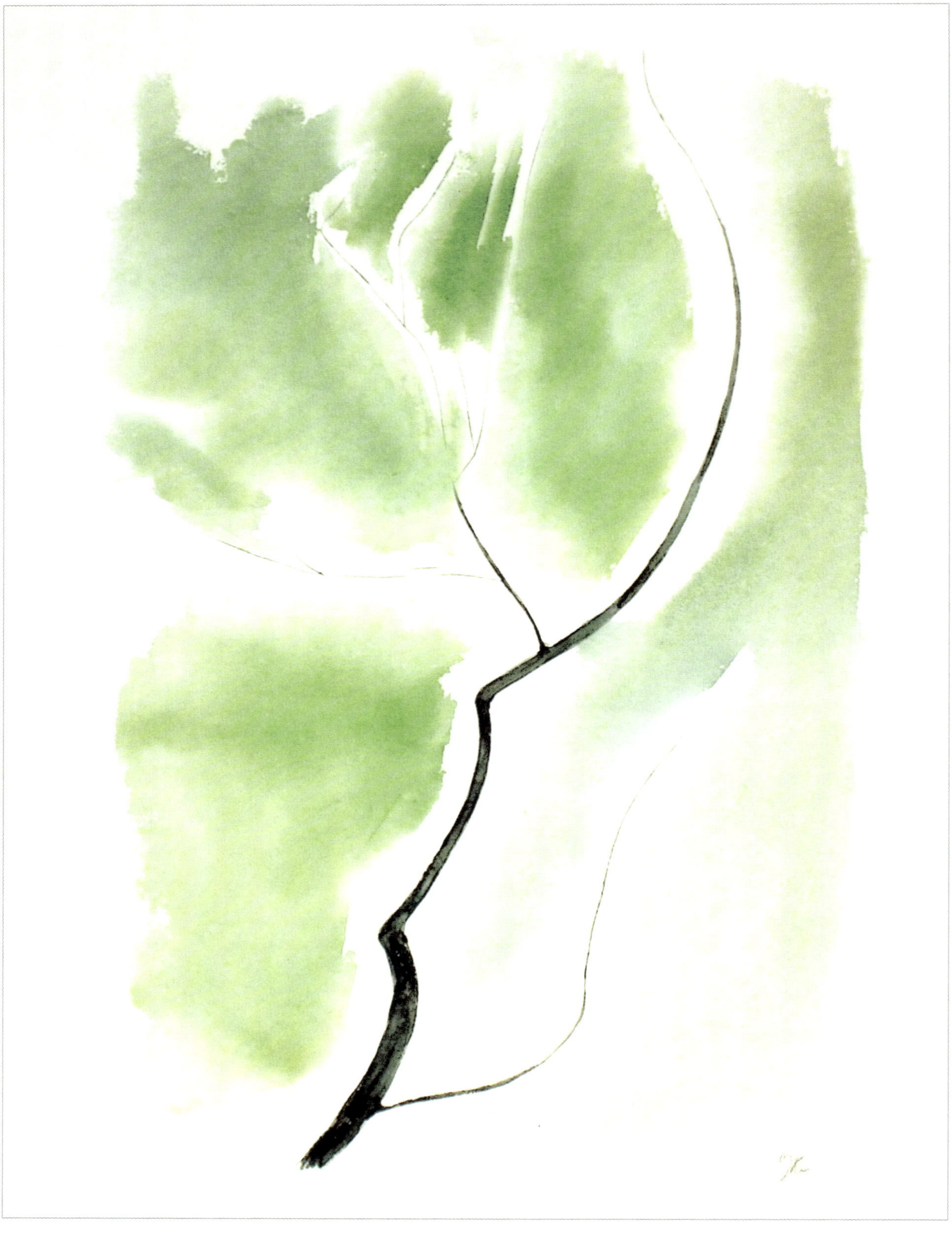

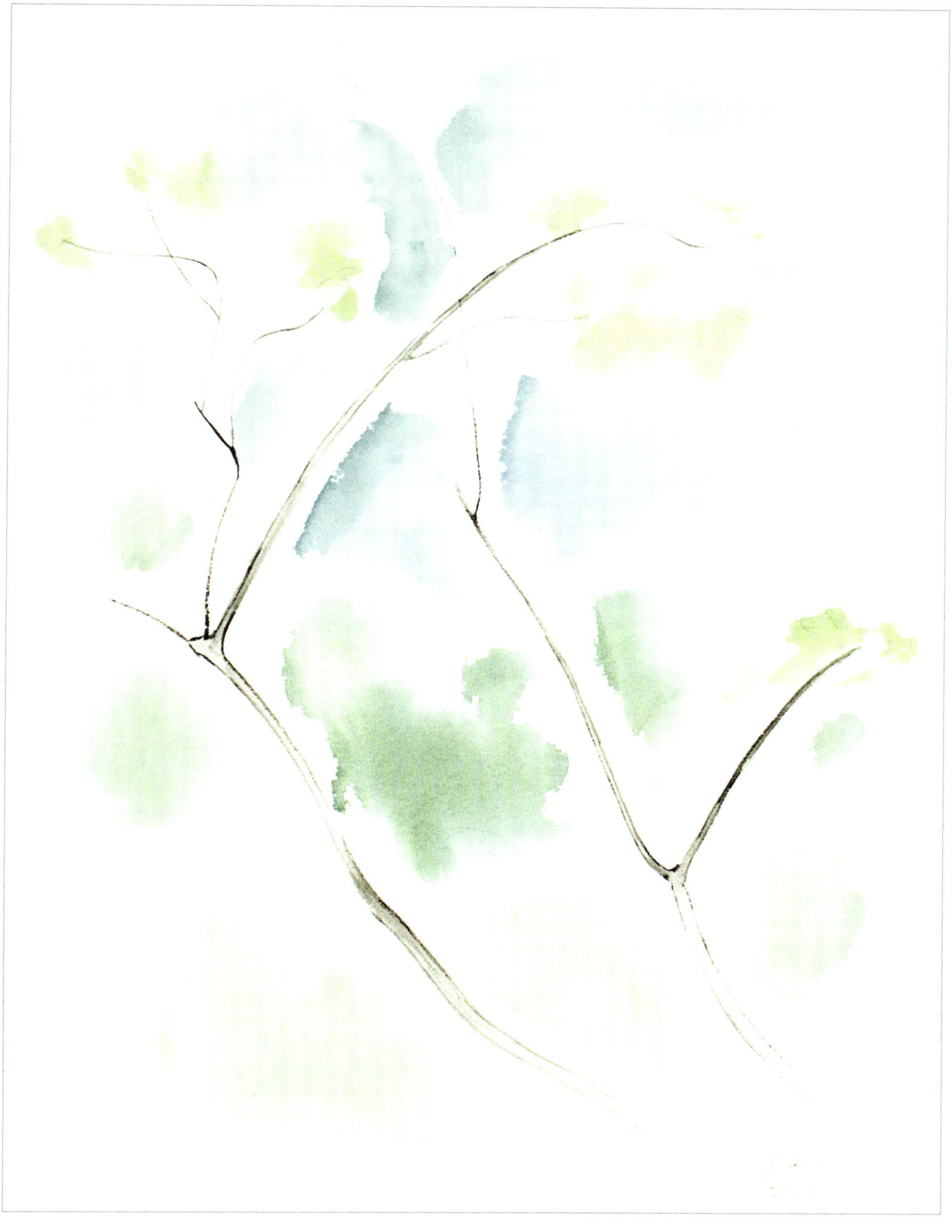

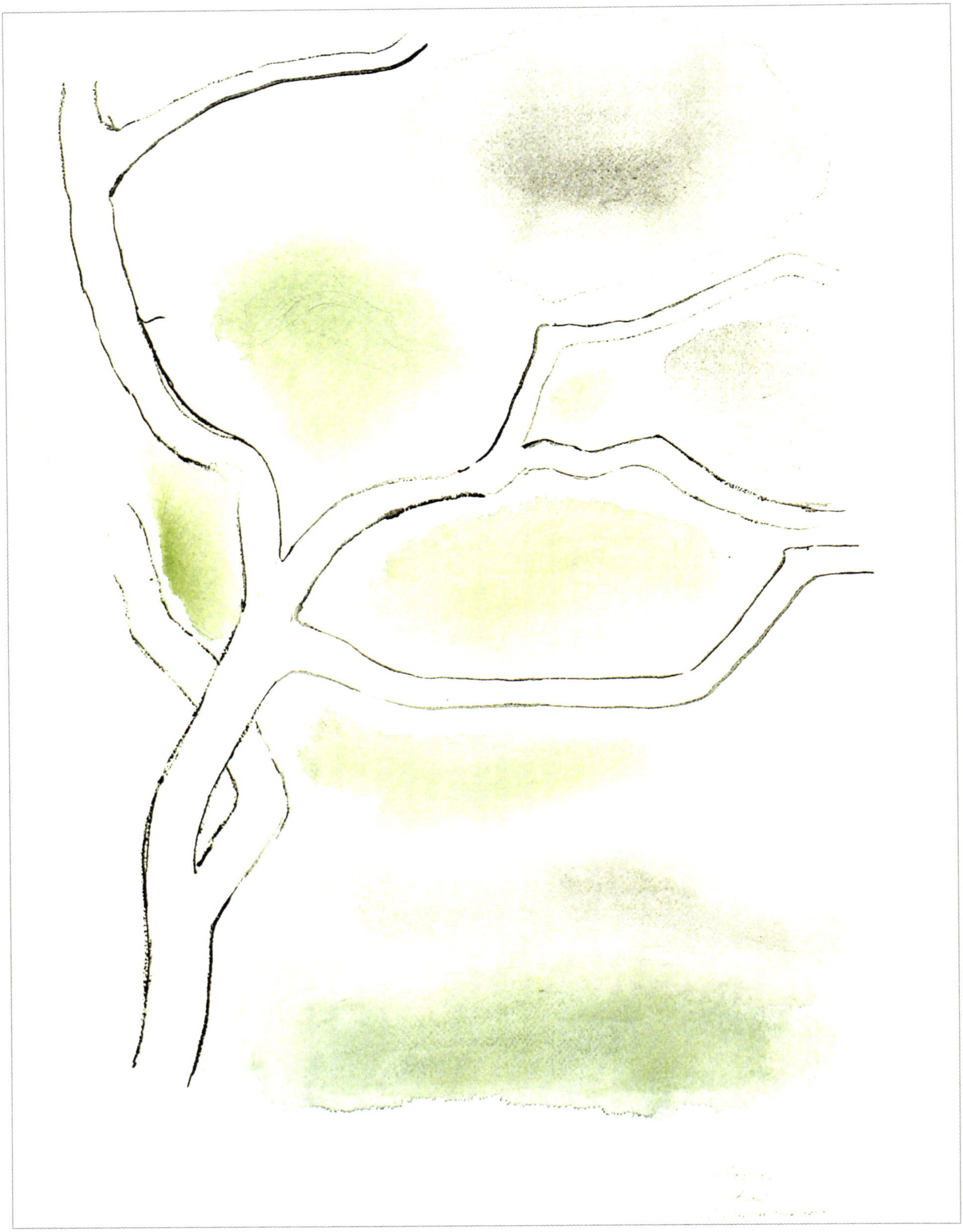

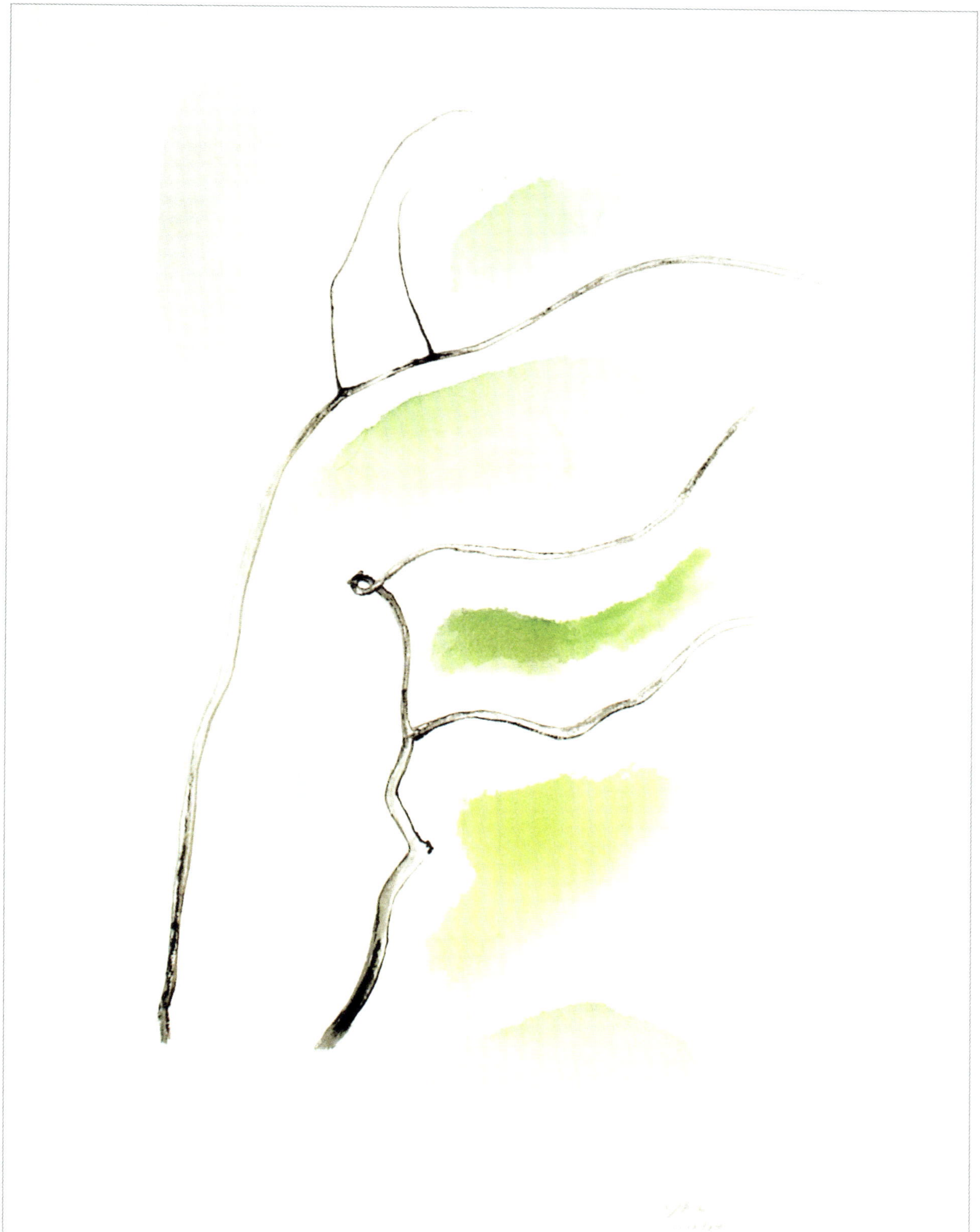

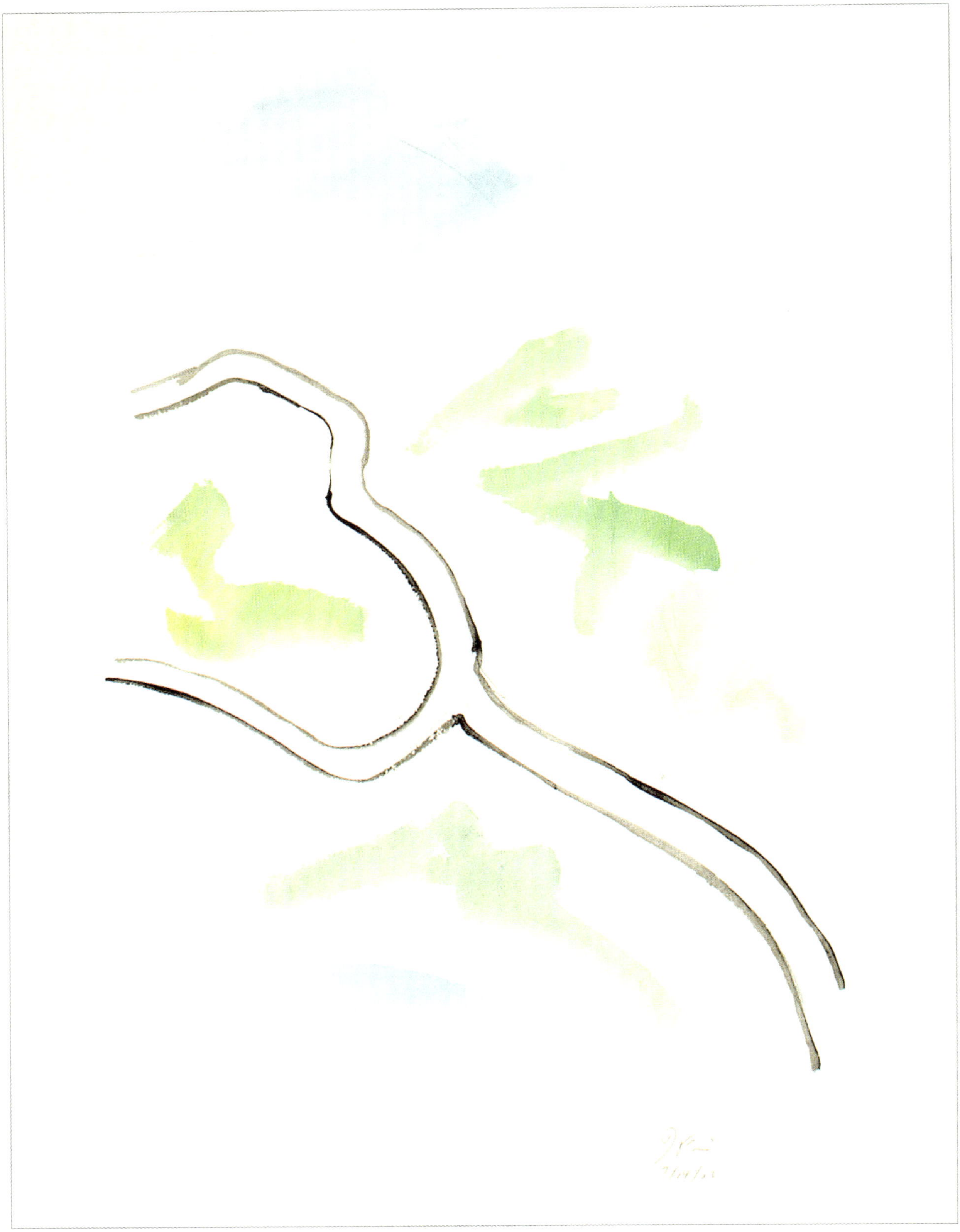

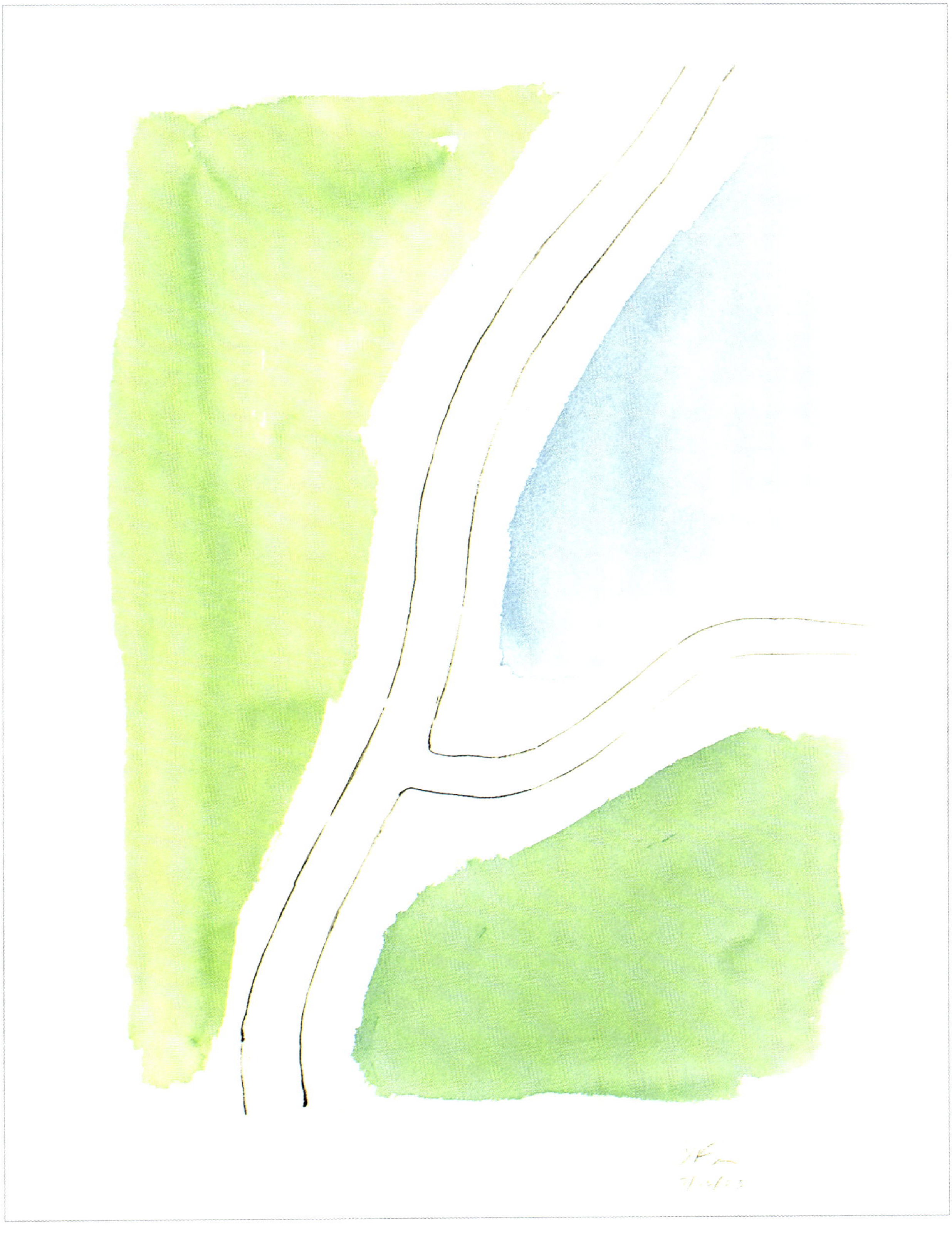

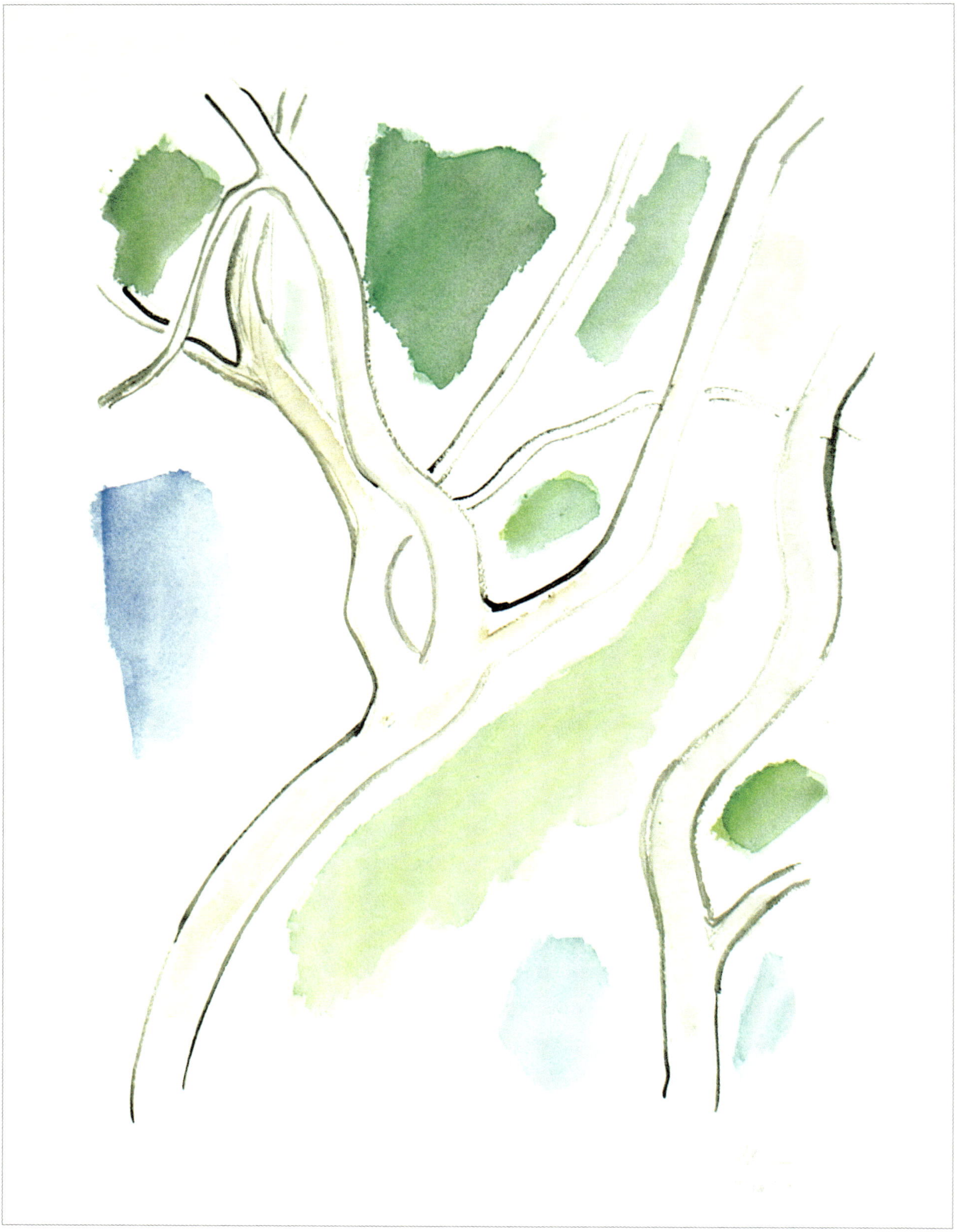

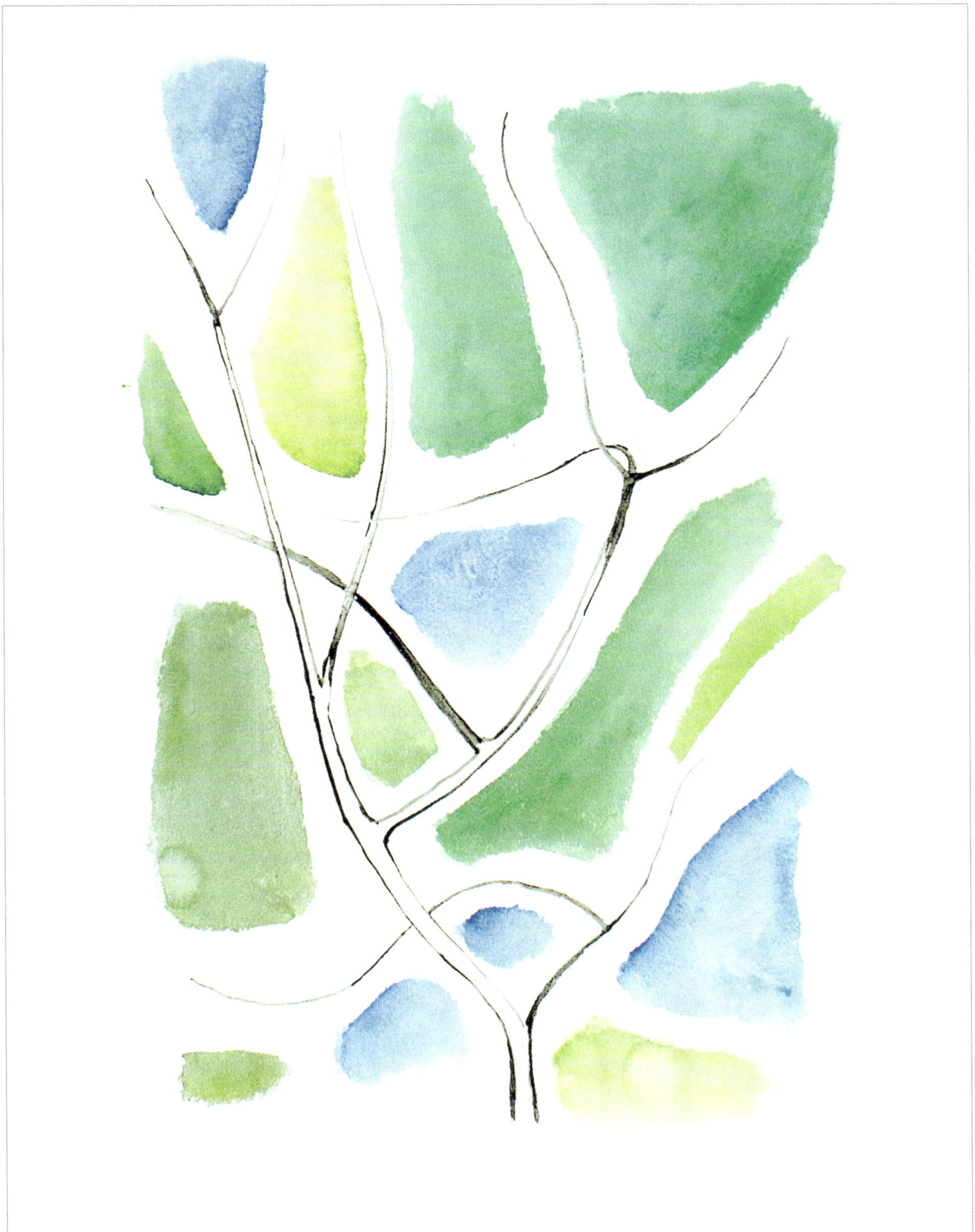

August

The mature life, brings confidence
that what we have is right
and full; the leaves
and branches
are what
they are
although a hint
of change is in the air,
with a touch of yellow here and there.

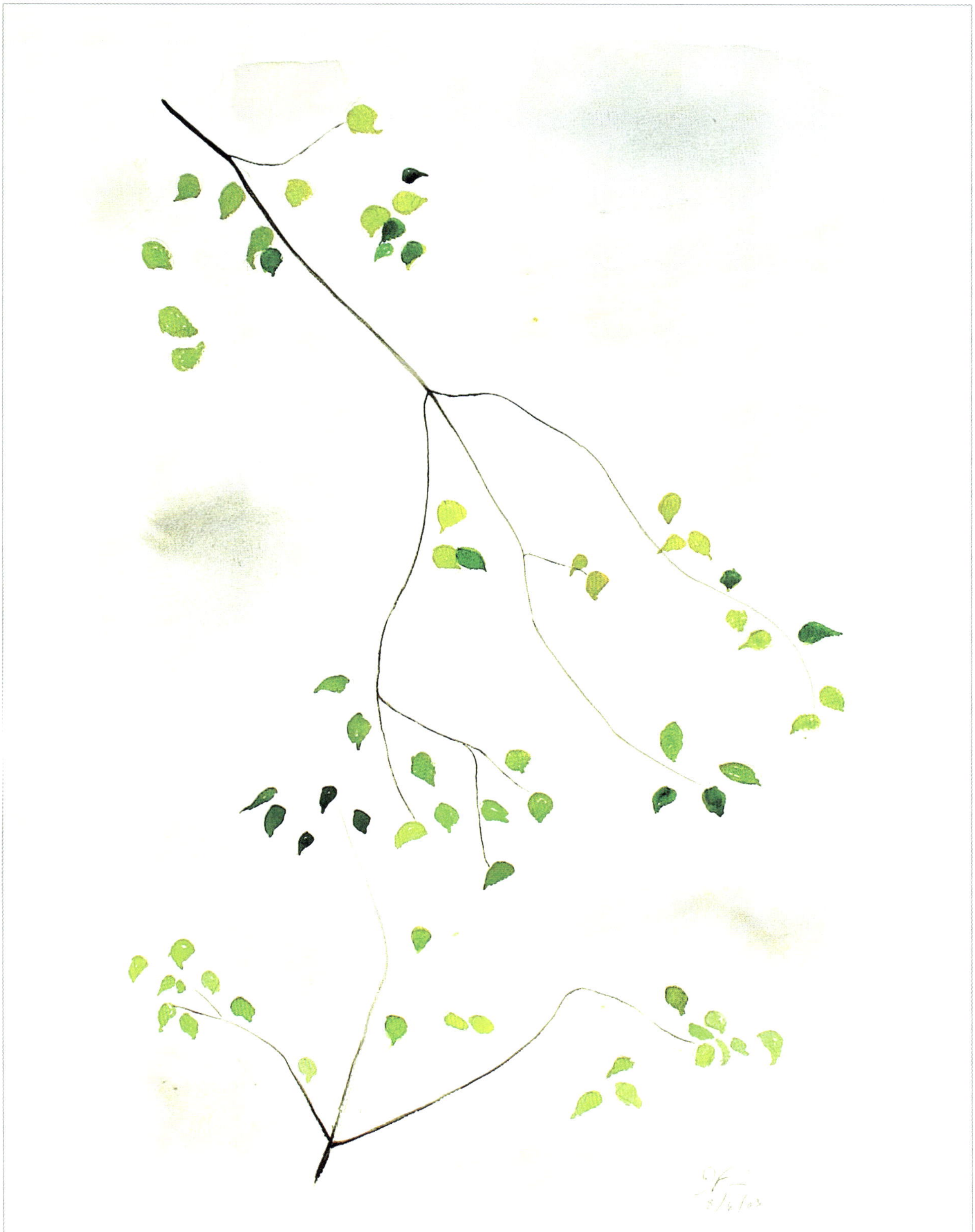

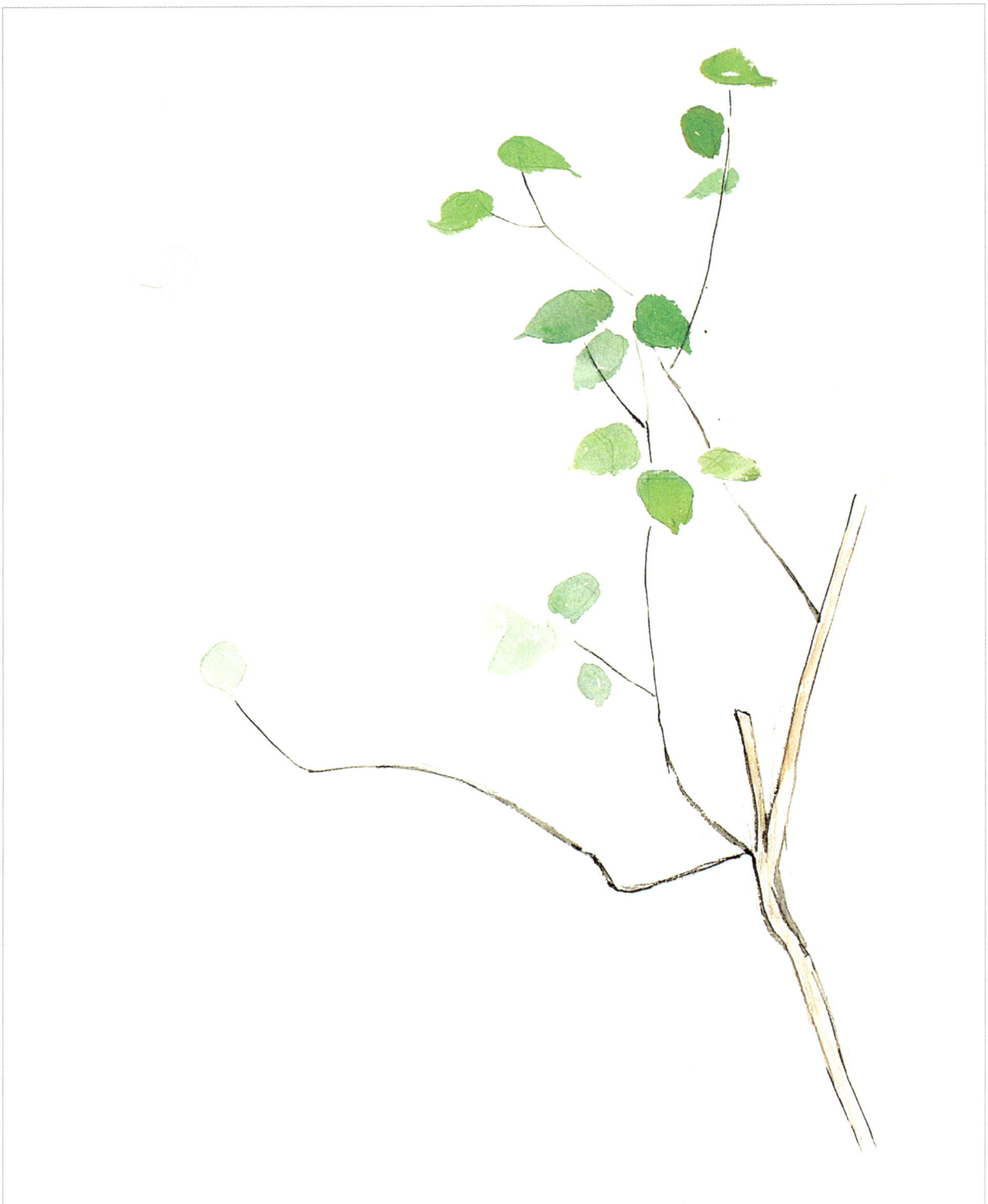

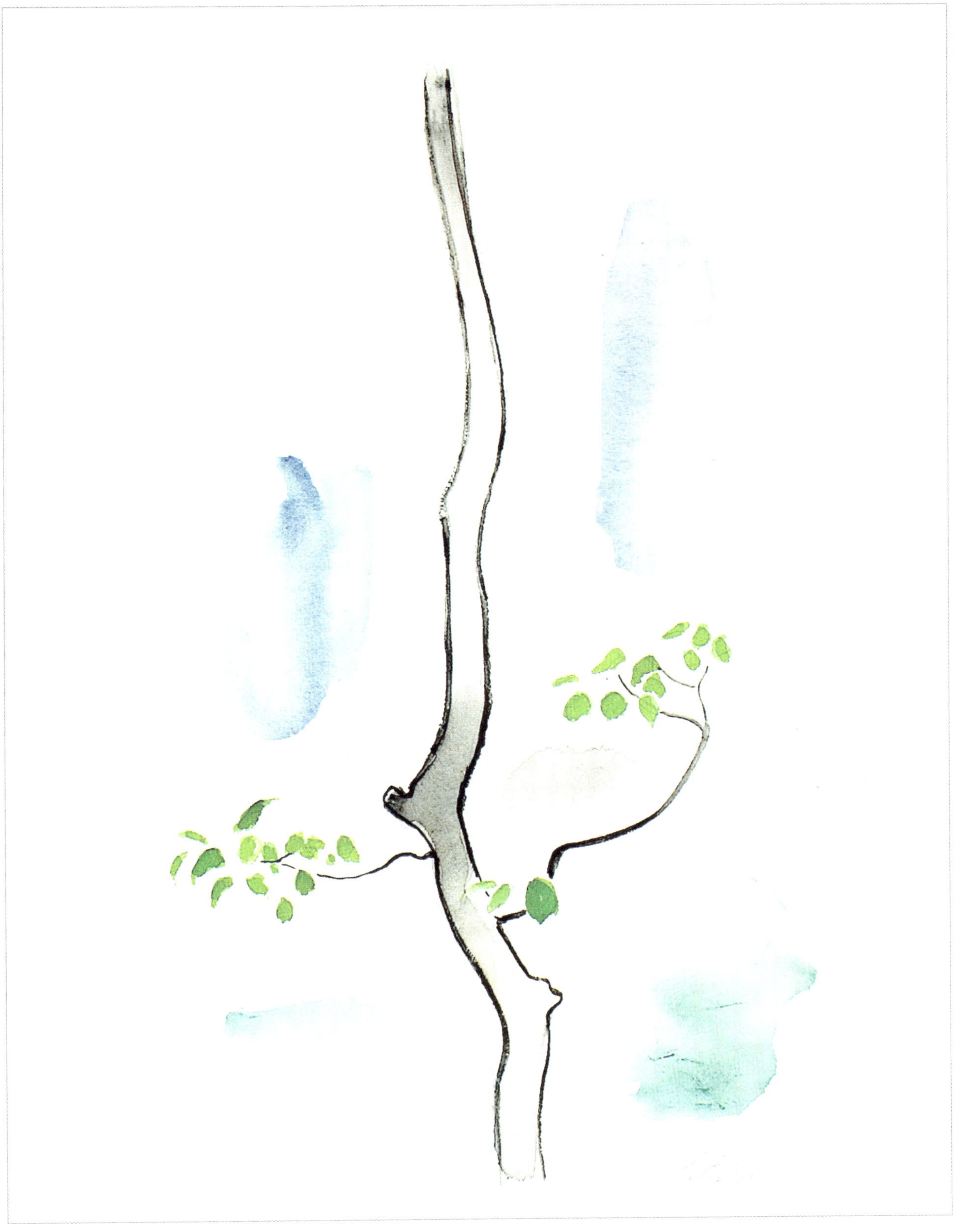

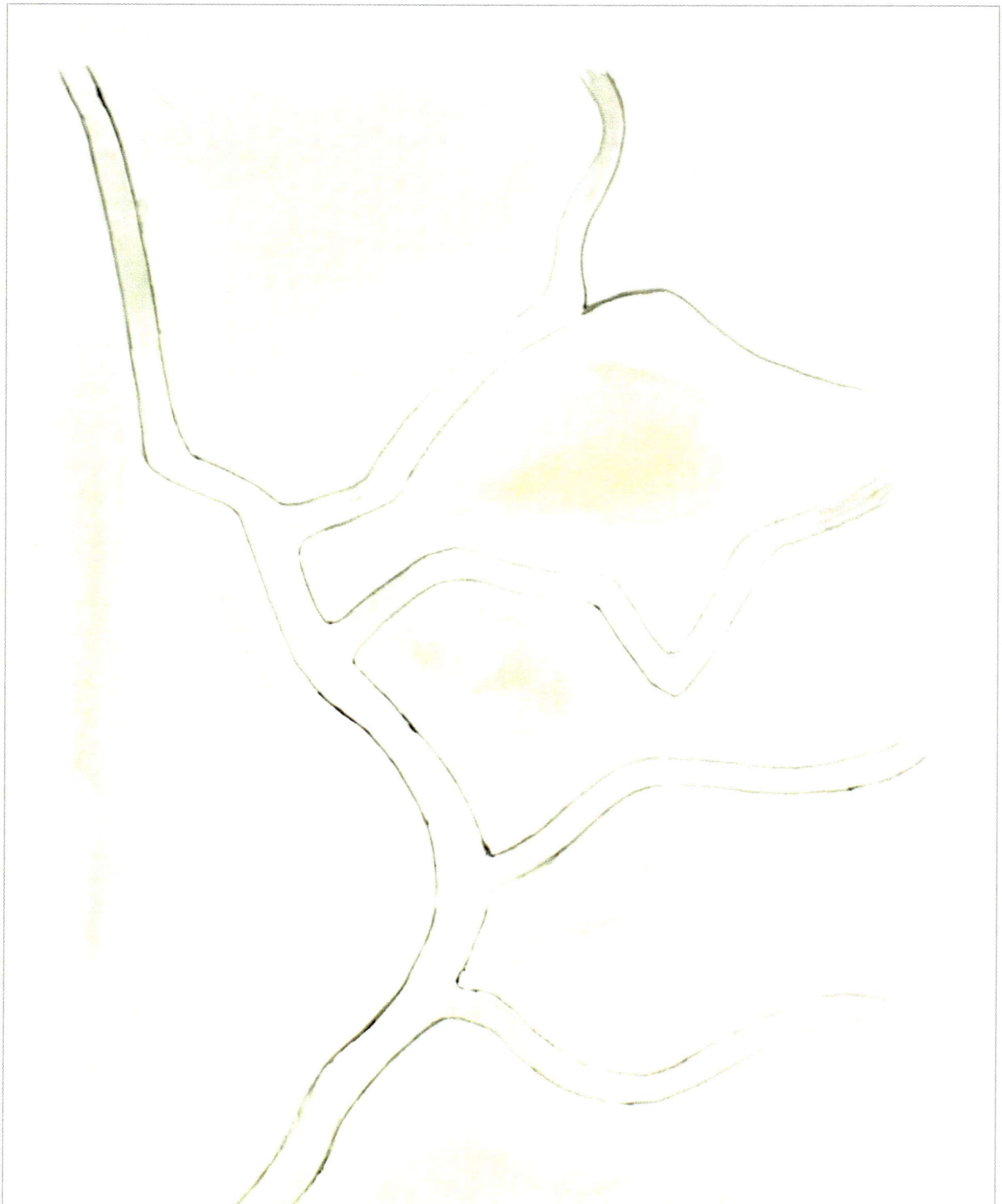

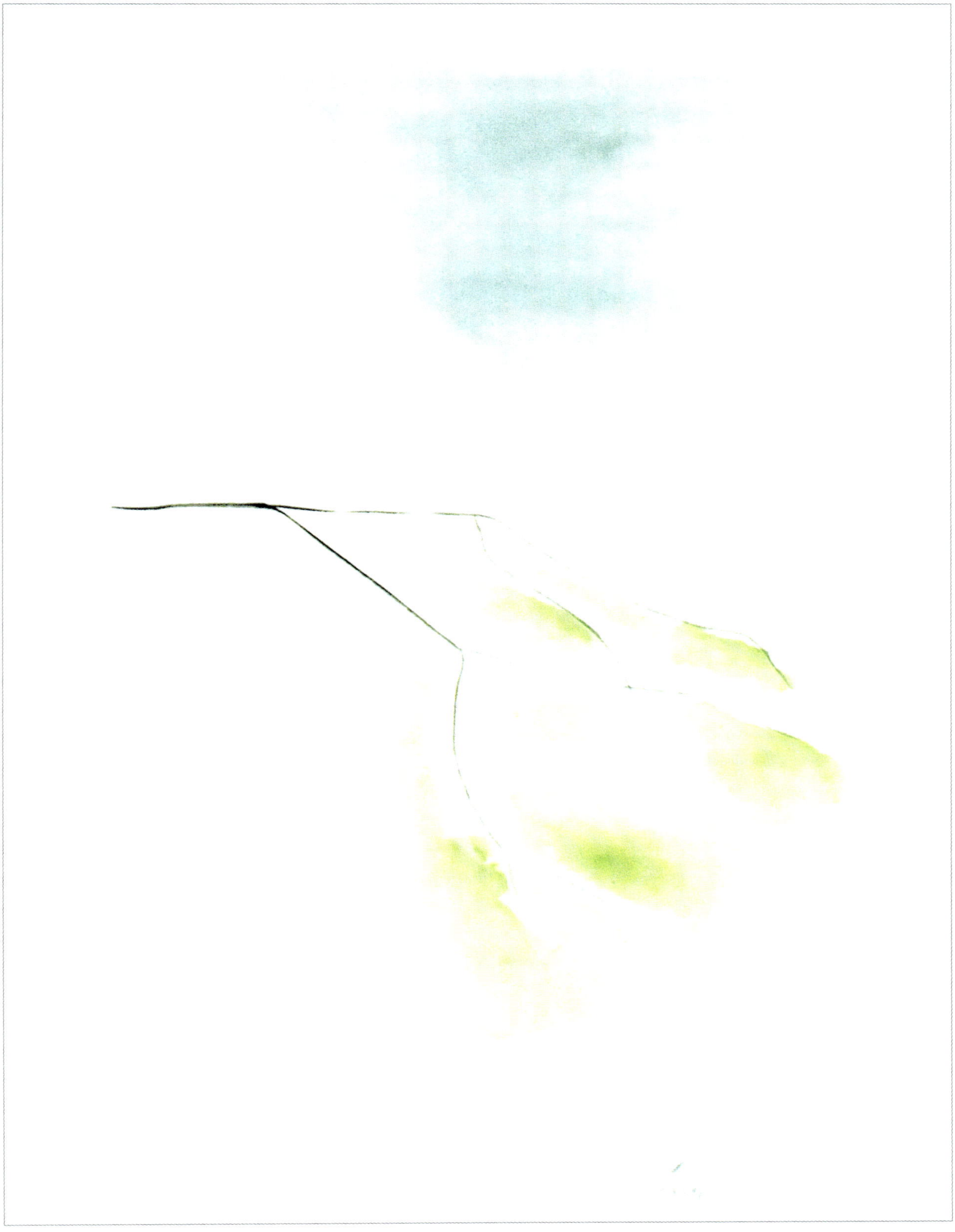

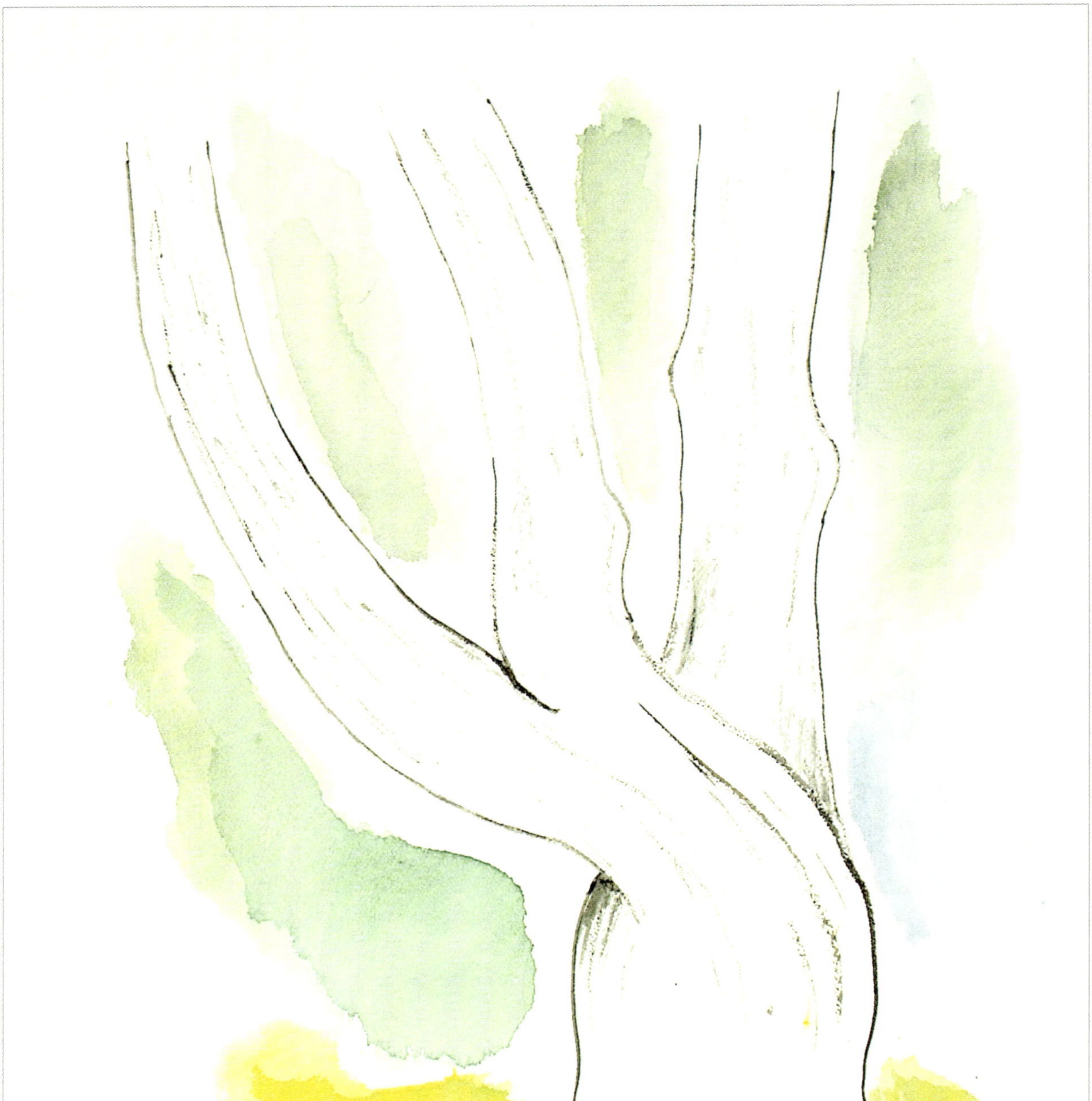

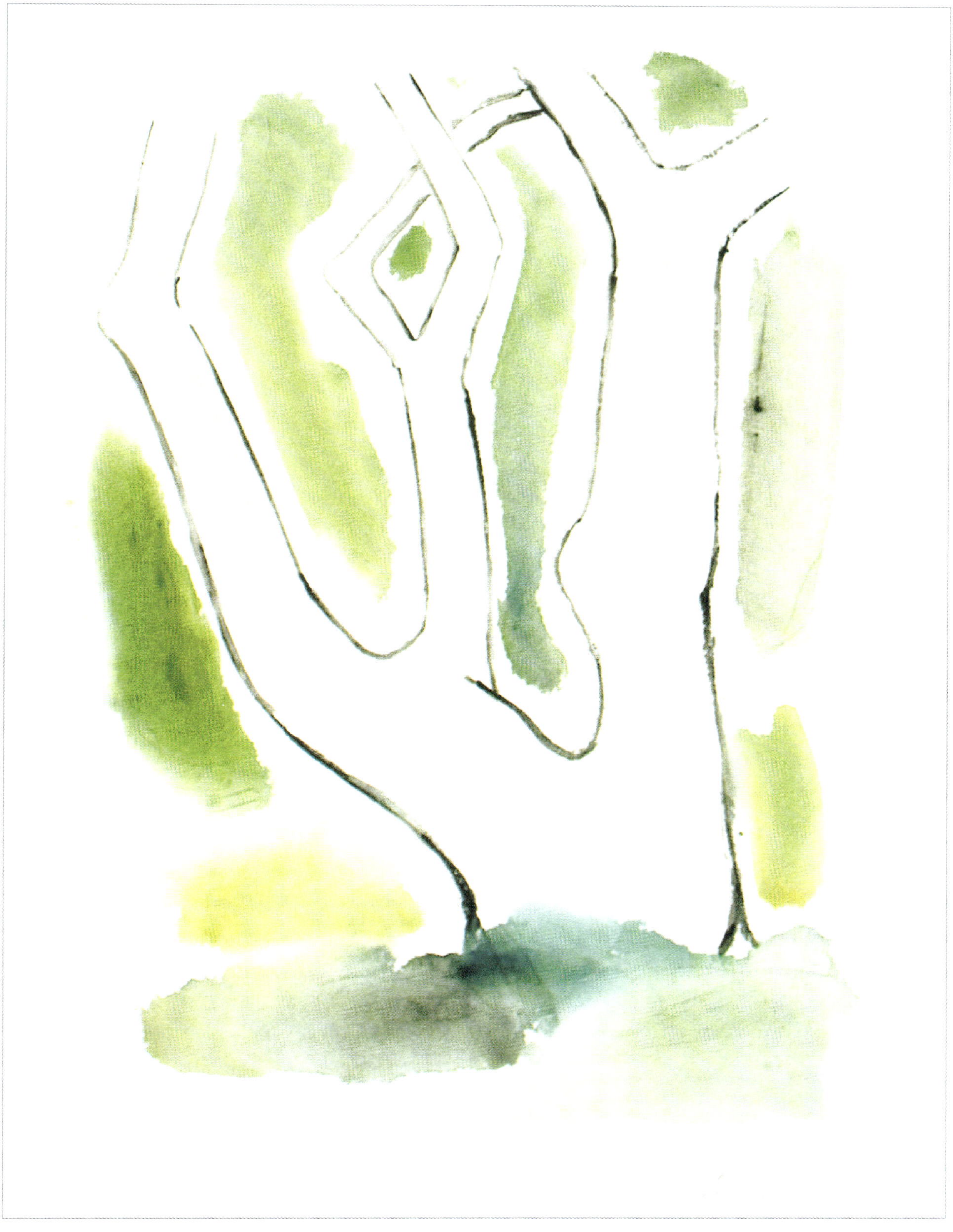

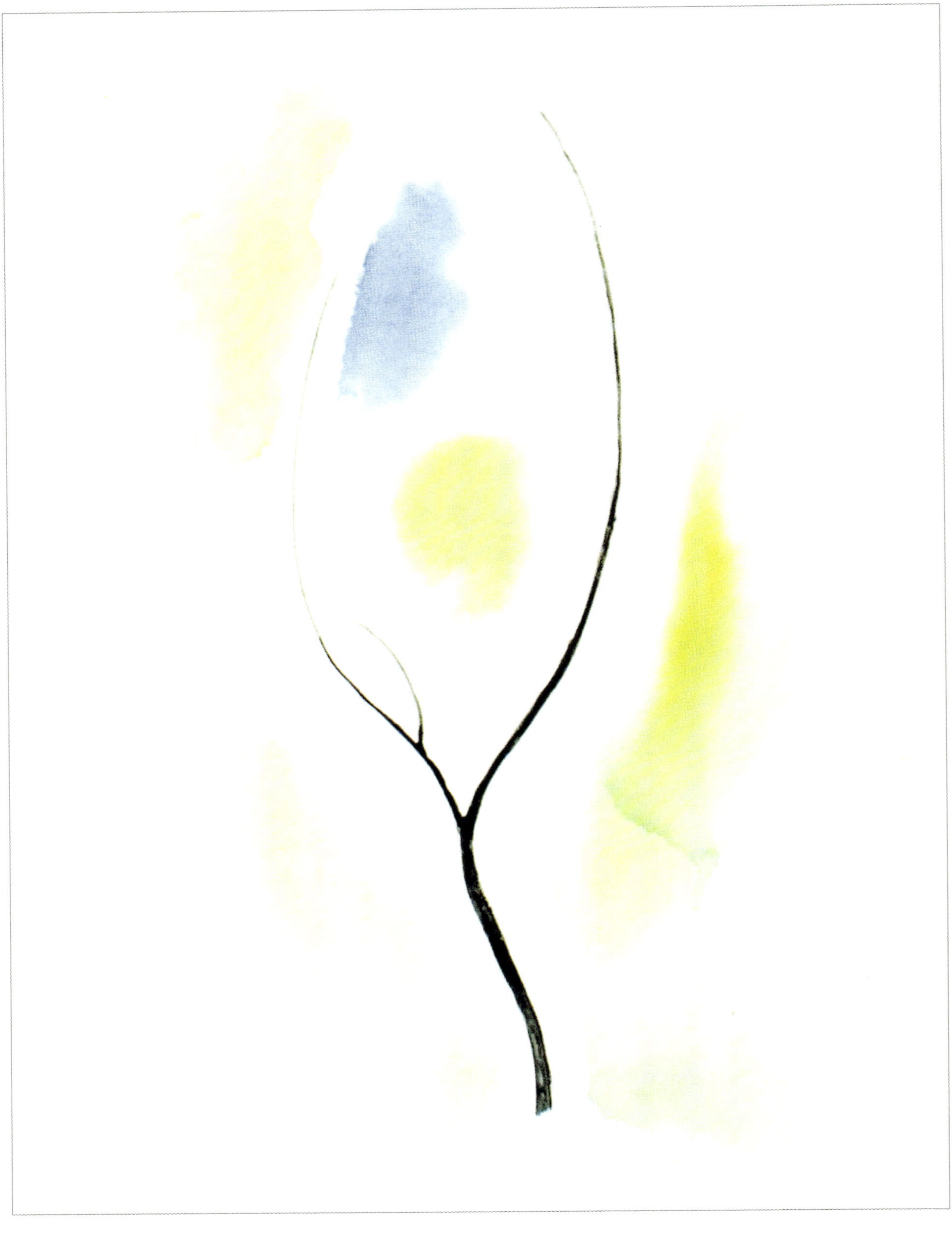

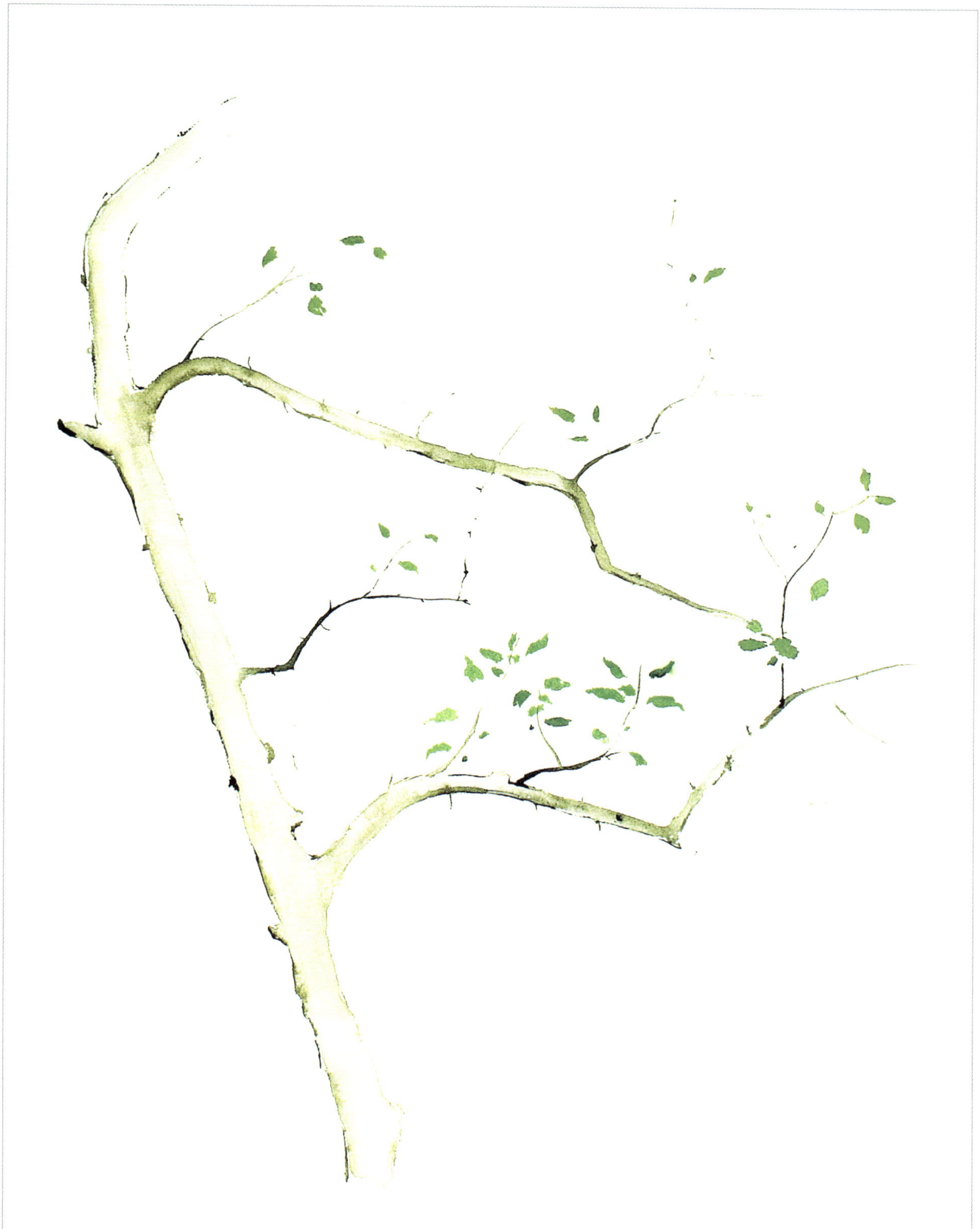

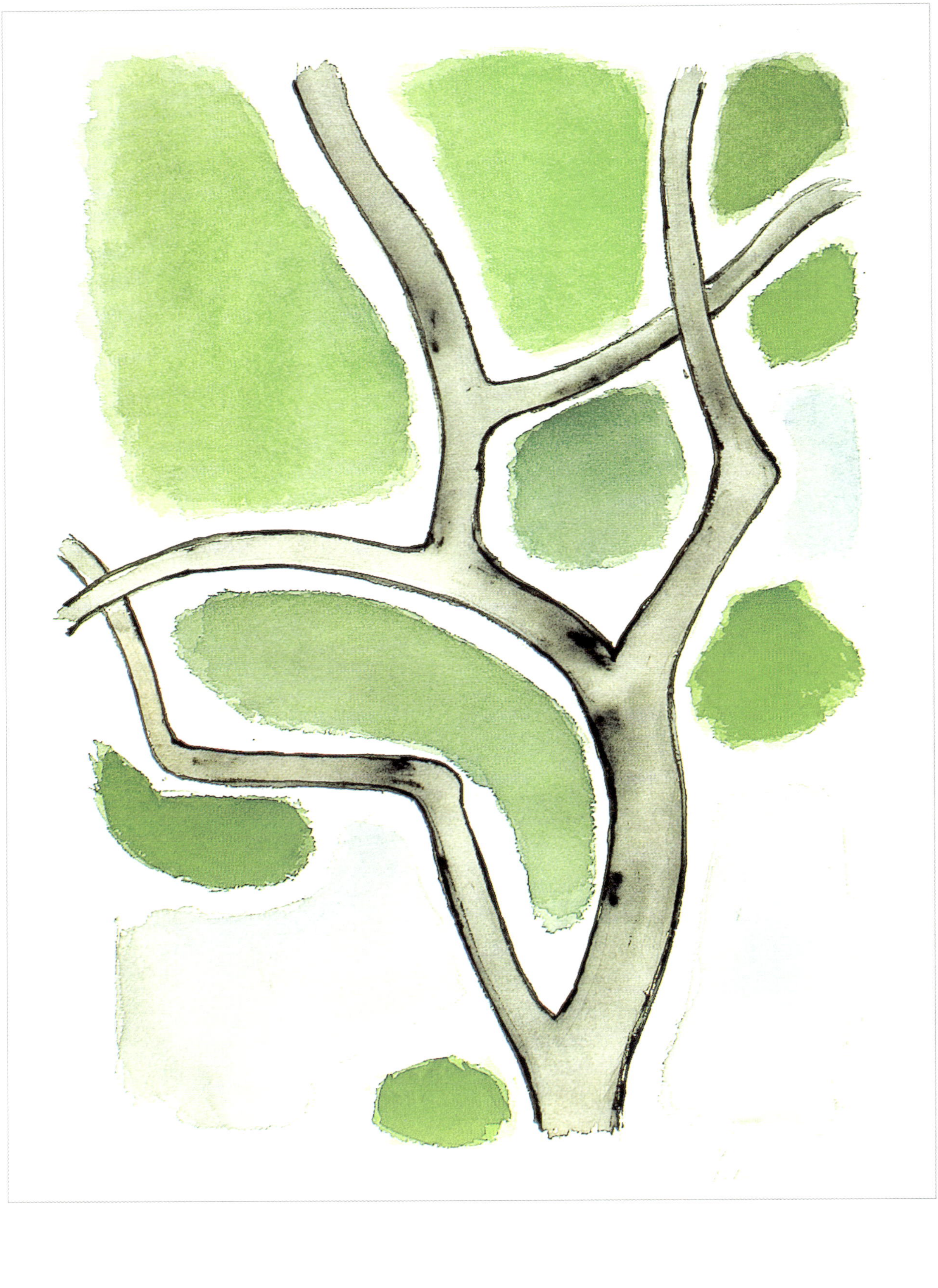

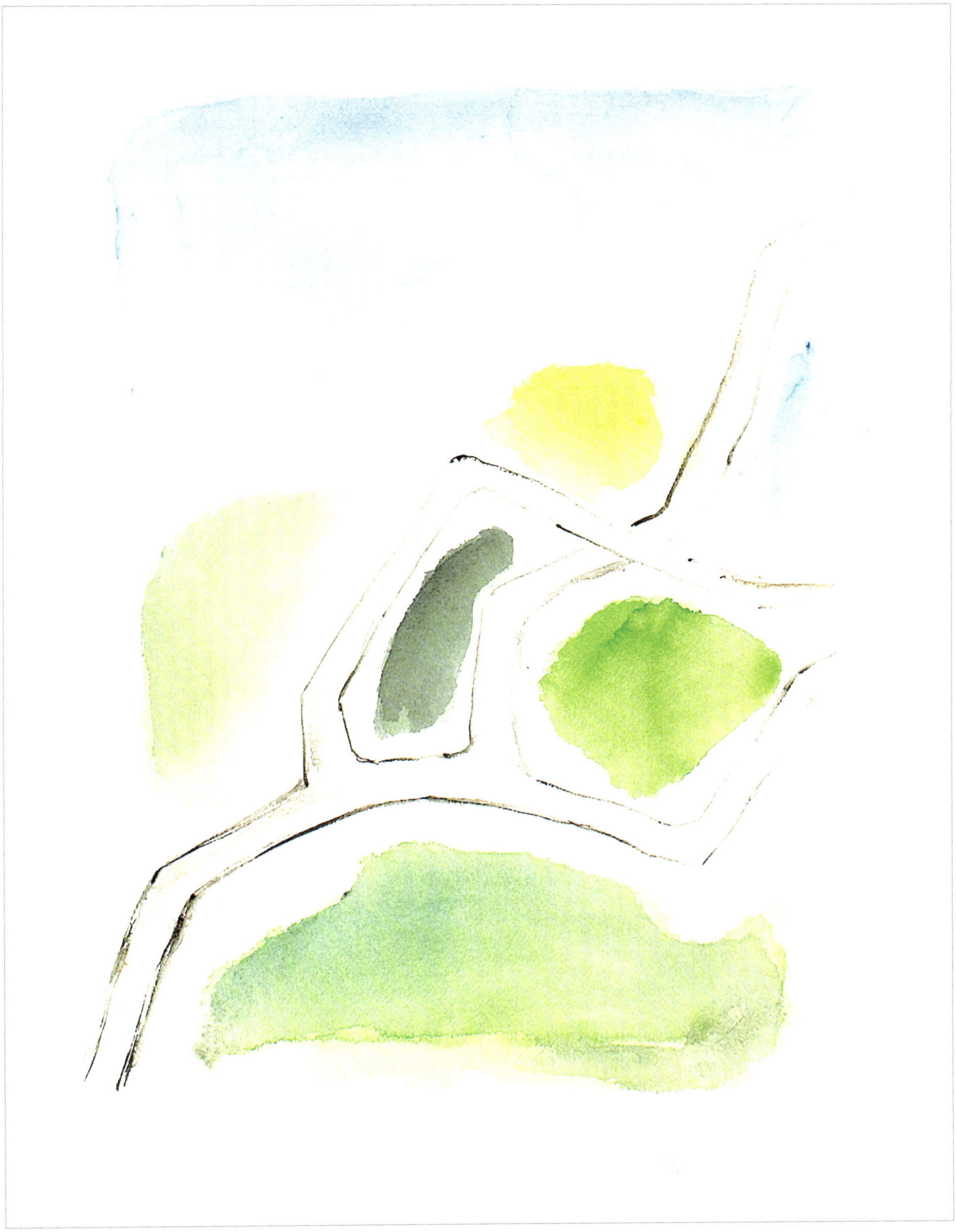

September

Orange and dark green have now arrived
to enrich the colors of the leaves,
but we sense that the end
is not so far away.
The trees
stand straight,
facing the future with courage,
happy with life and colors that still
fill the air and remain tightly on branches.

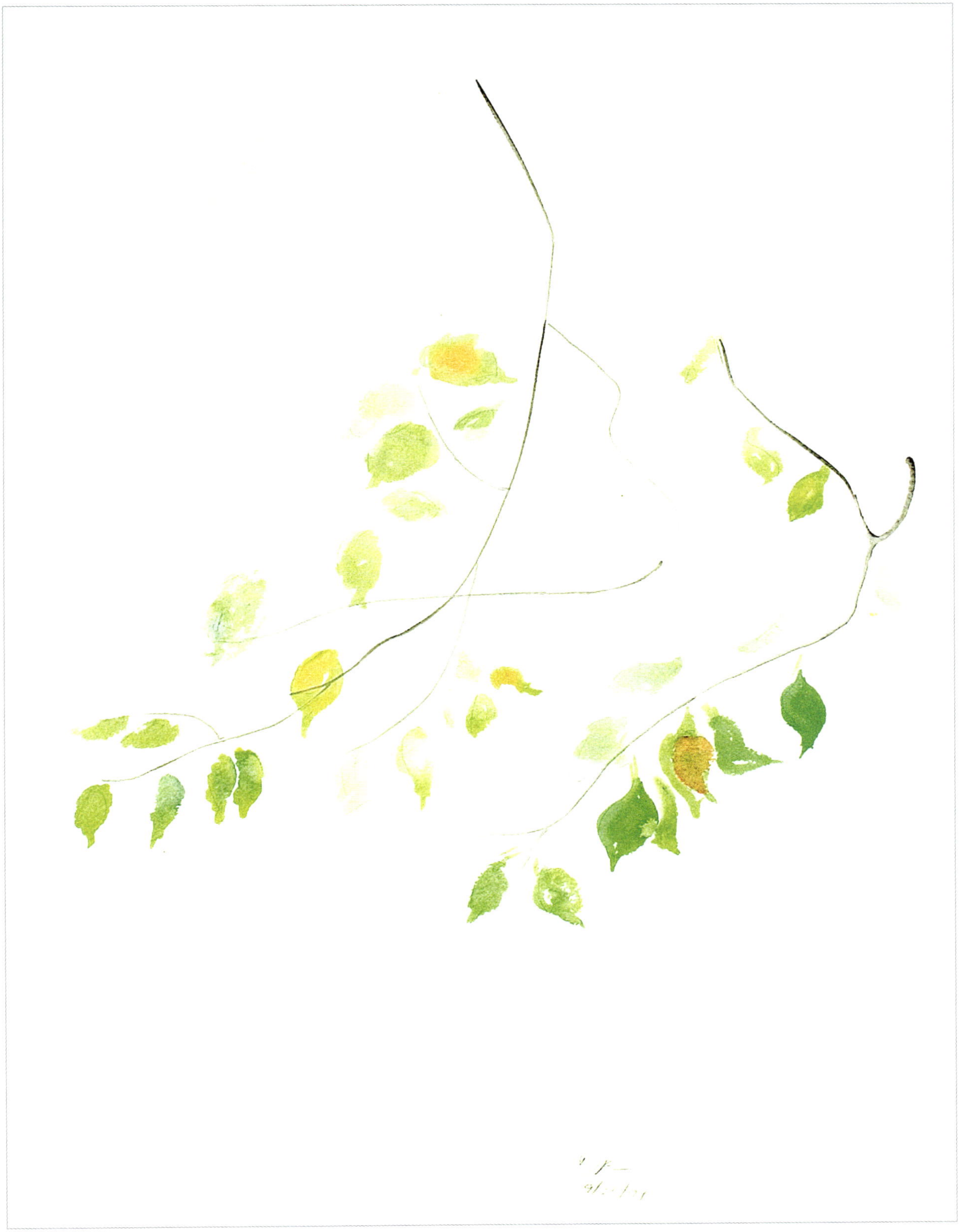

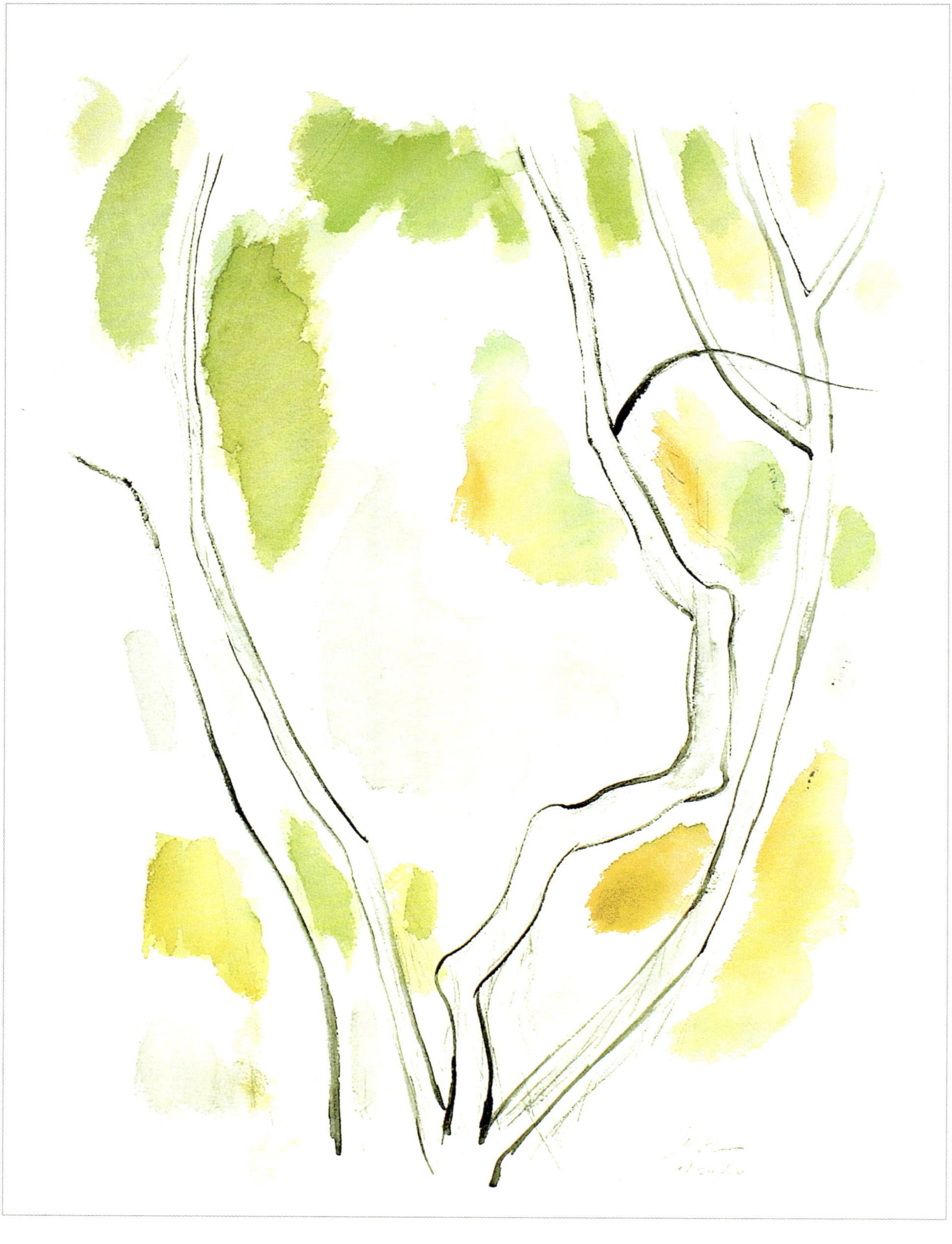

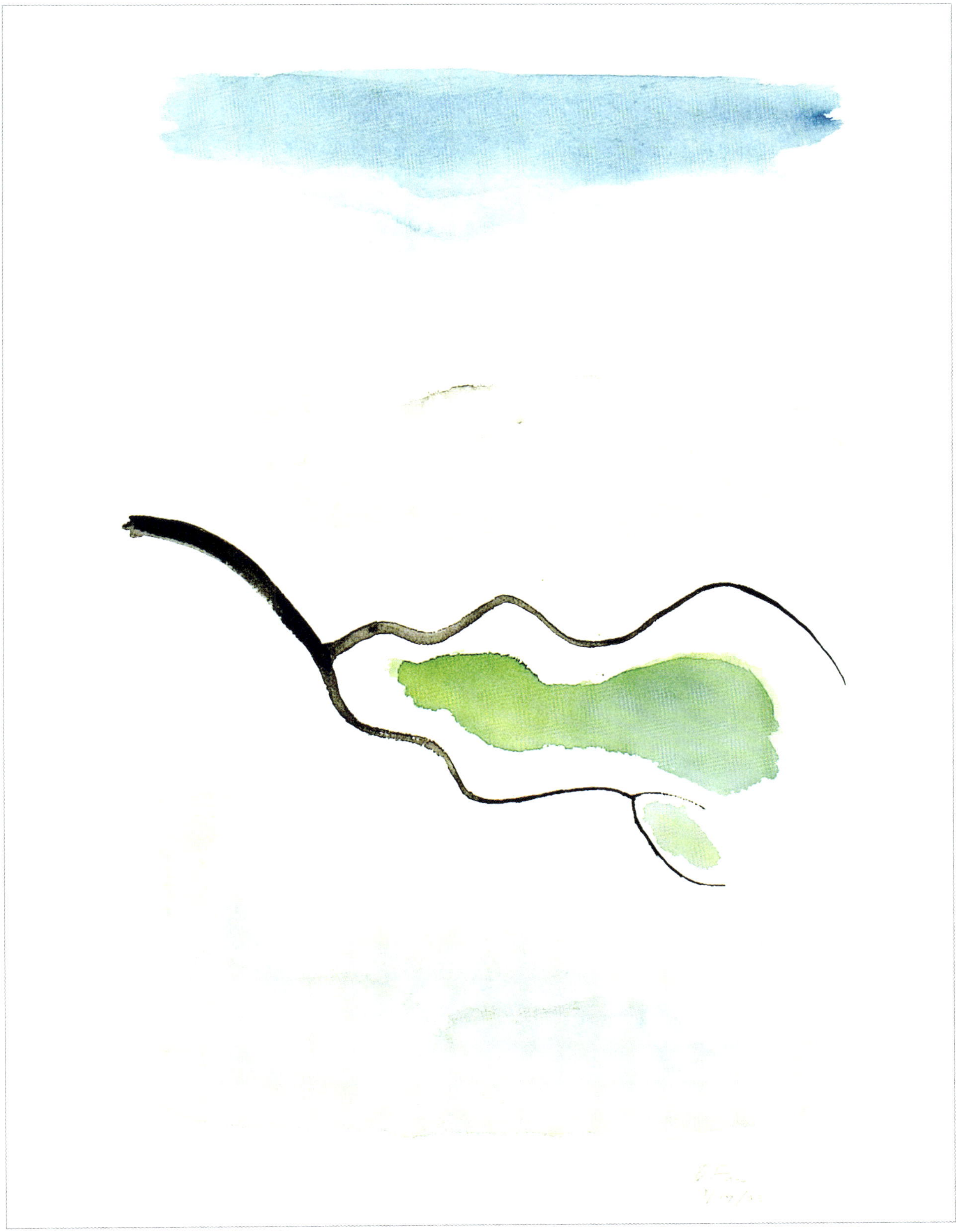

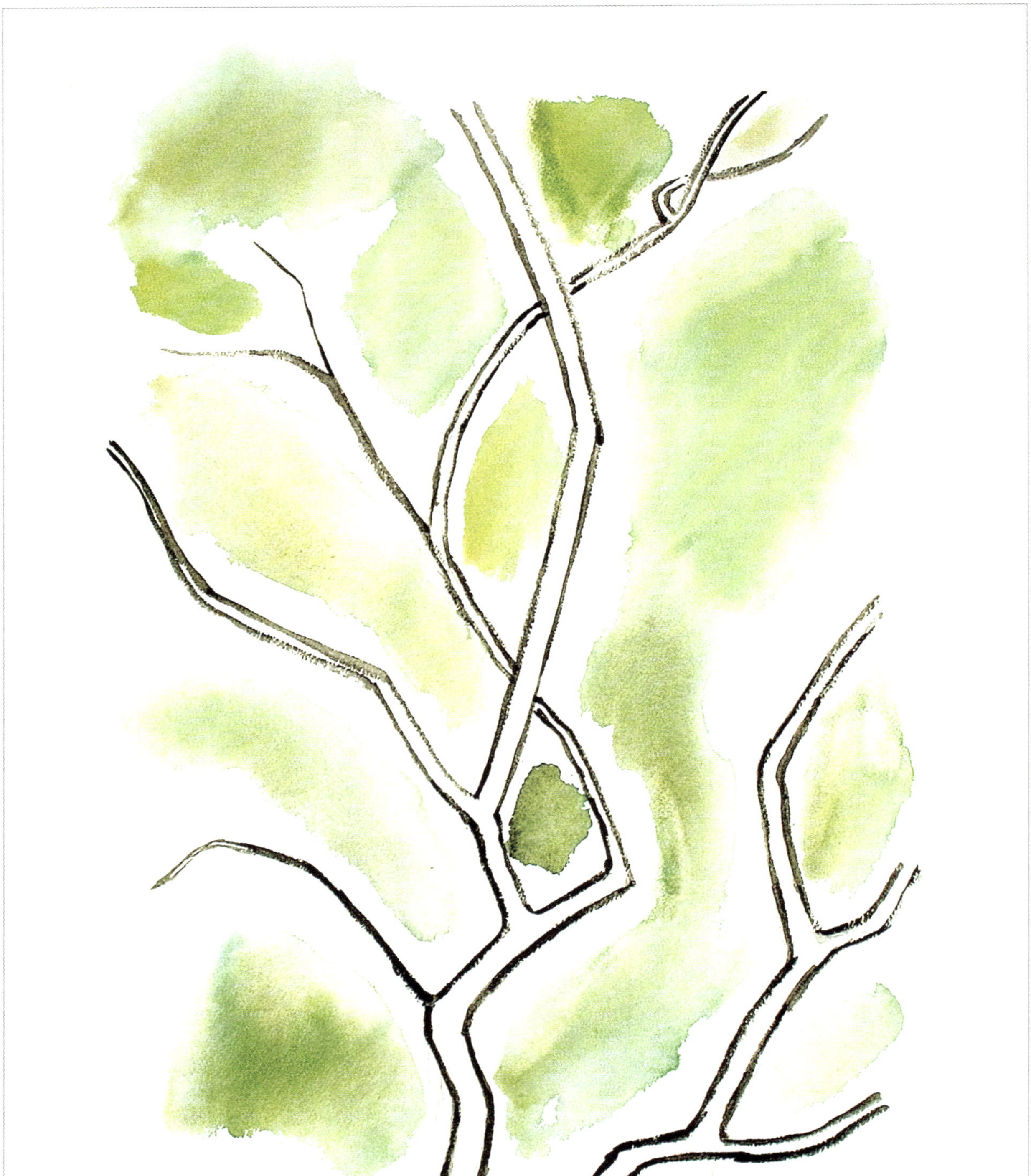

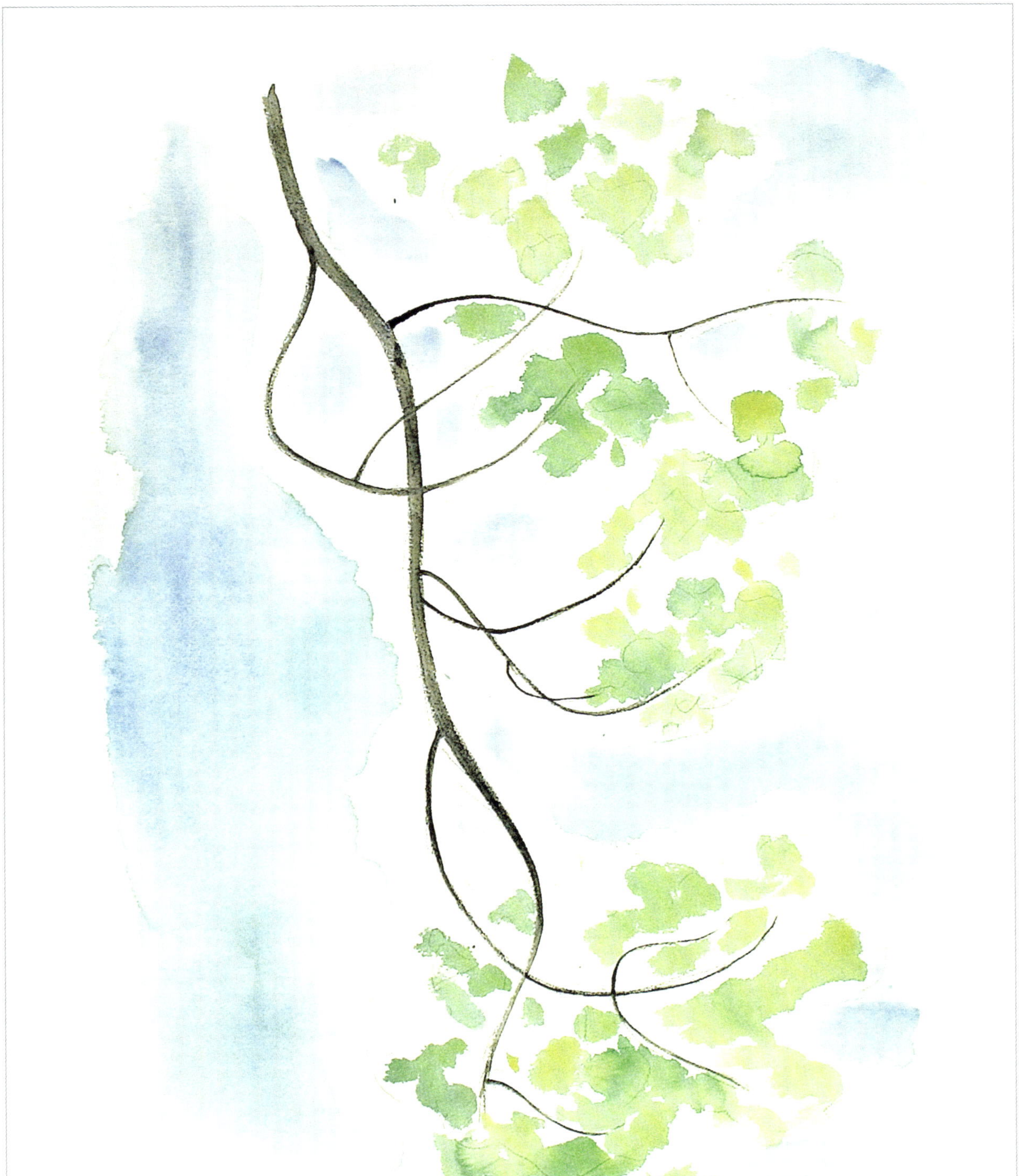

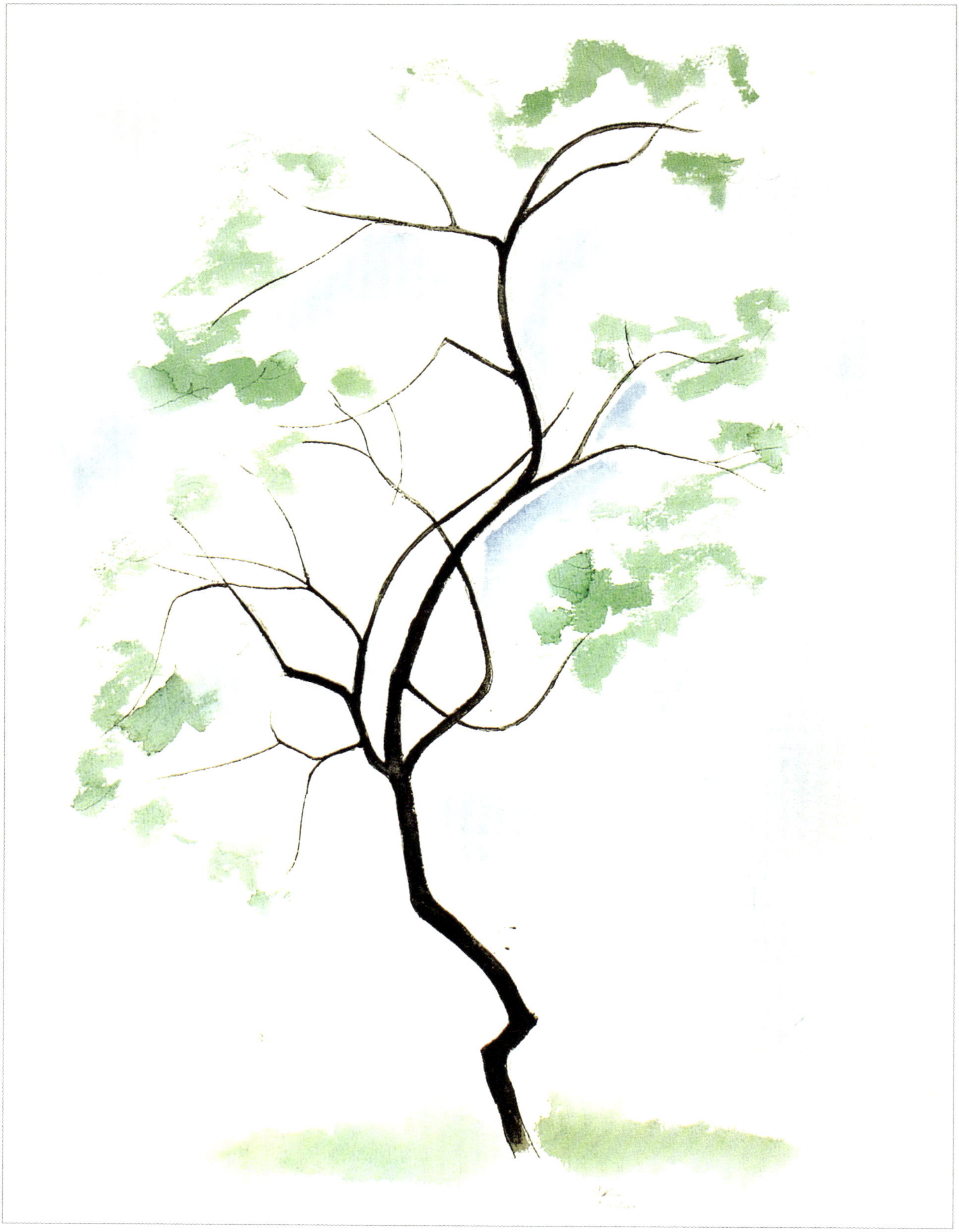

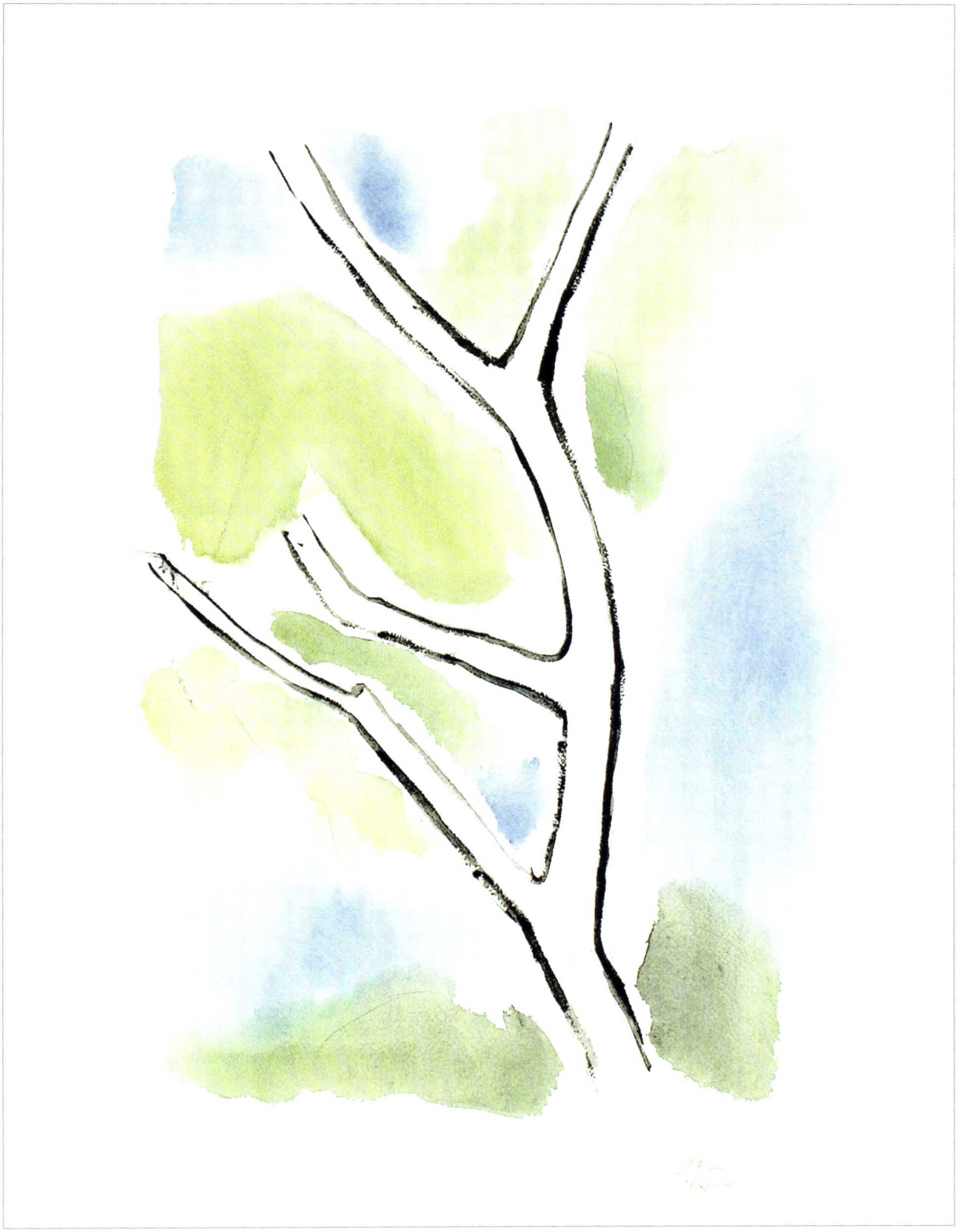

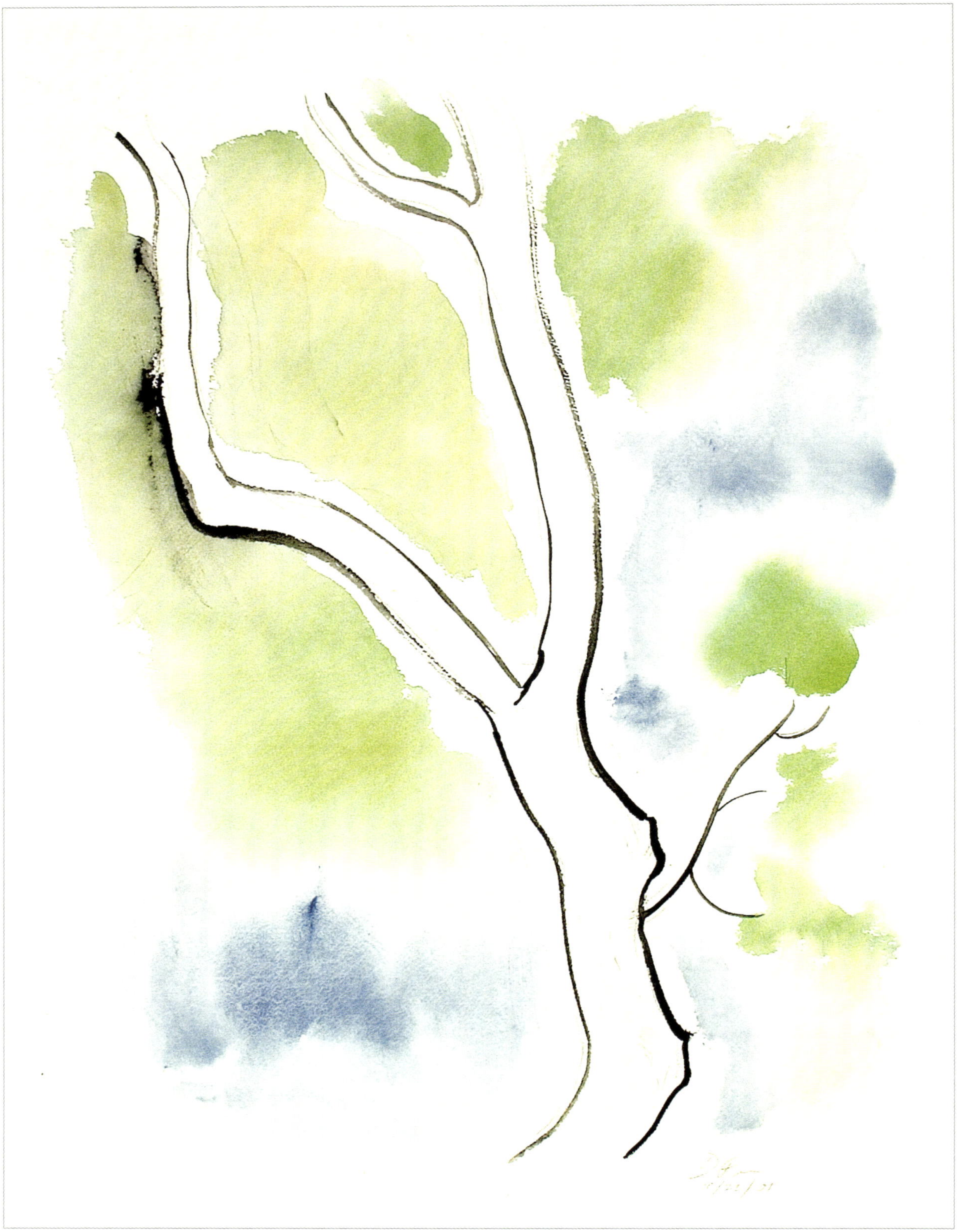

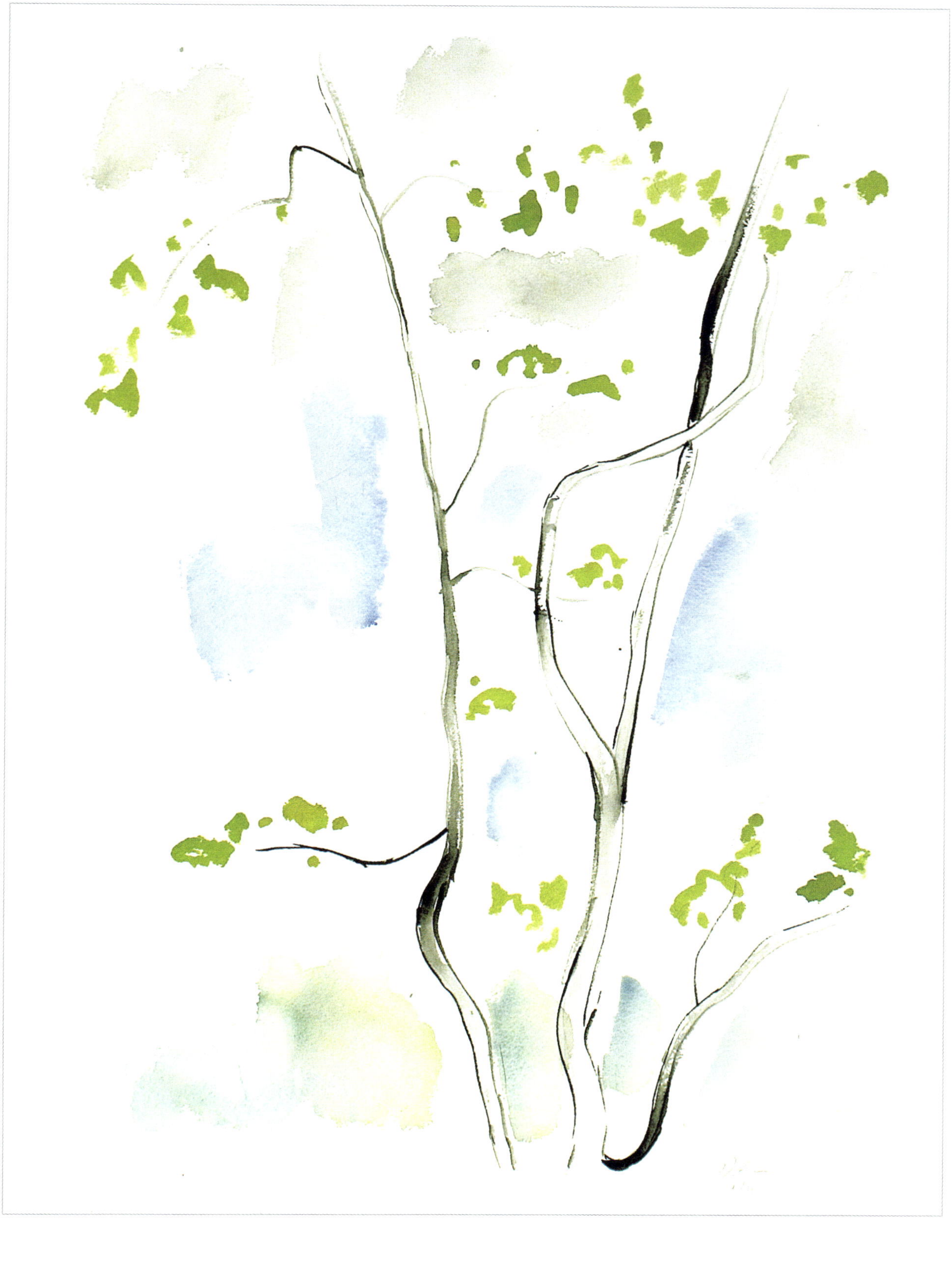

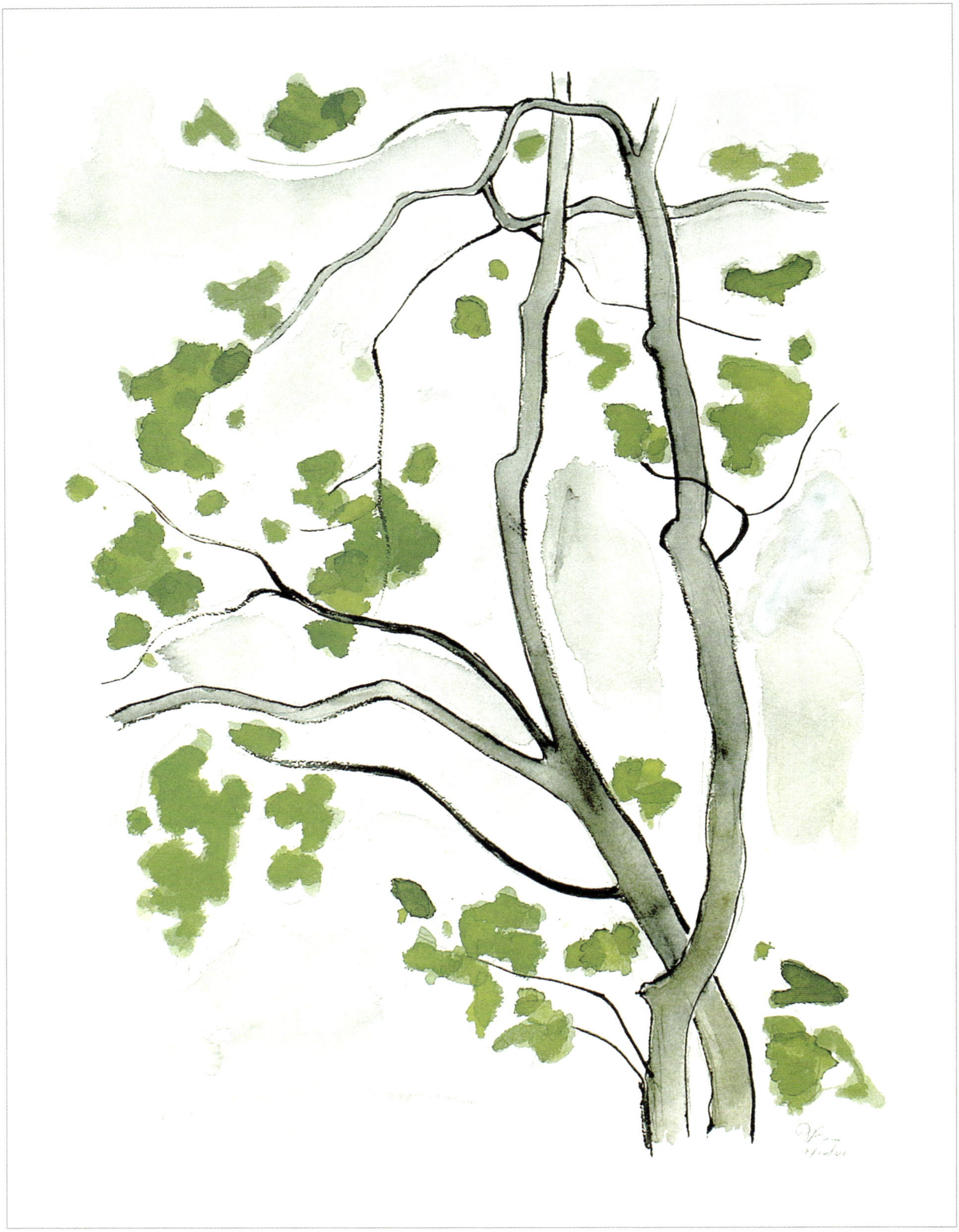

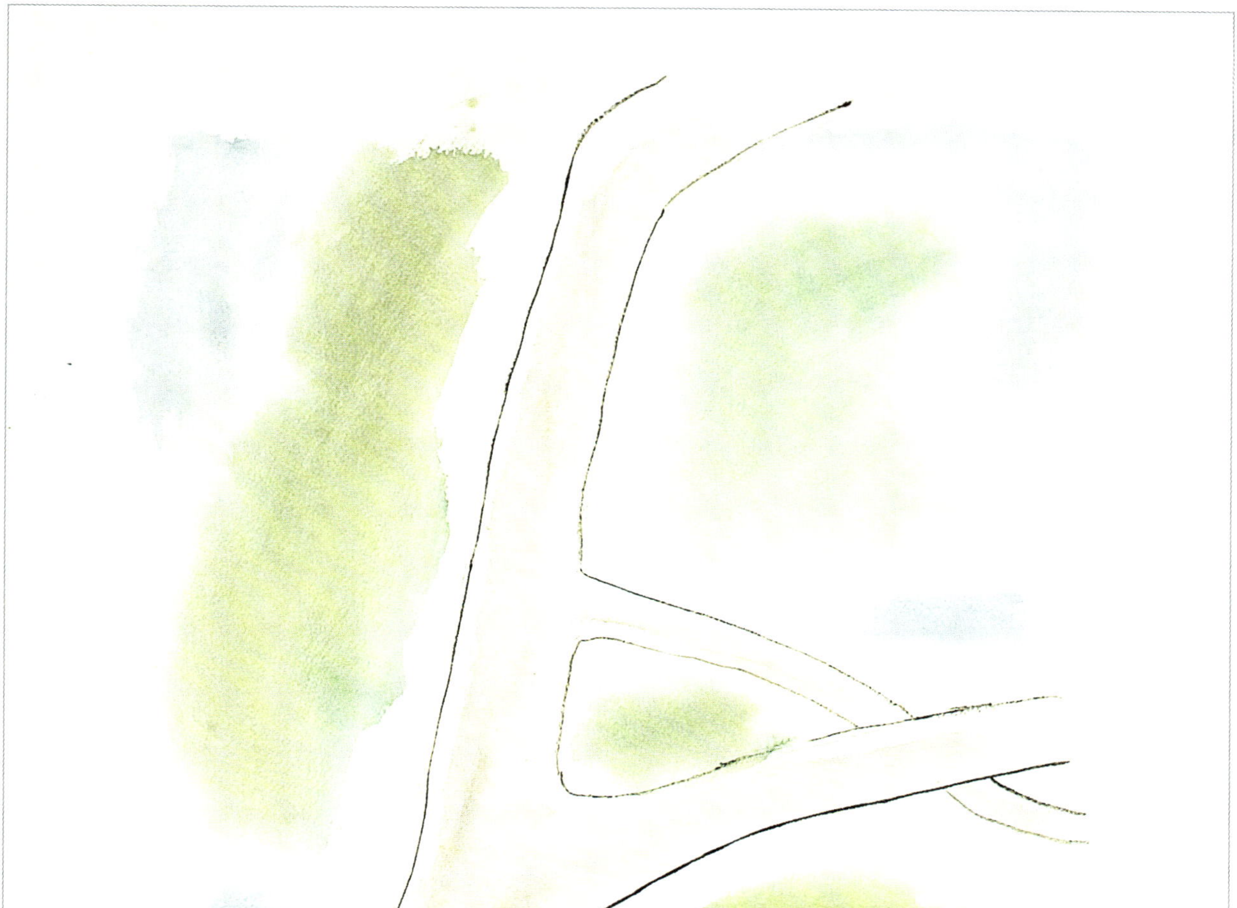

October

The trees are brave, like all of life, as
the yellow-gold fills the sky.
Every day the happy
colors stir the
heart and mind,
even though the leaves
of the trees—like us—must know
that they—as we—cannot live forever.

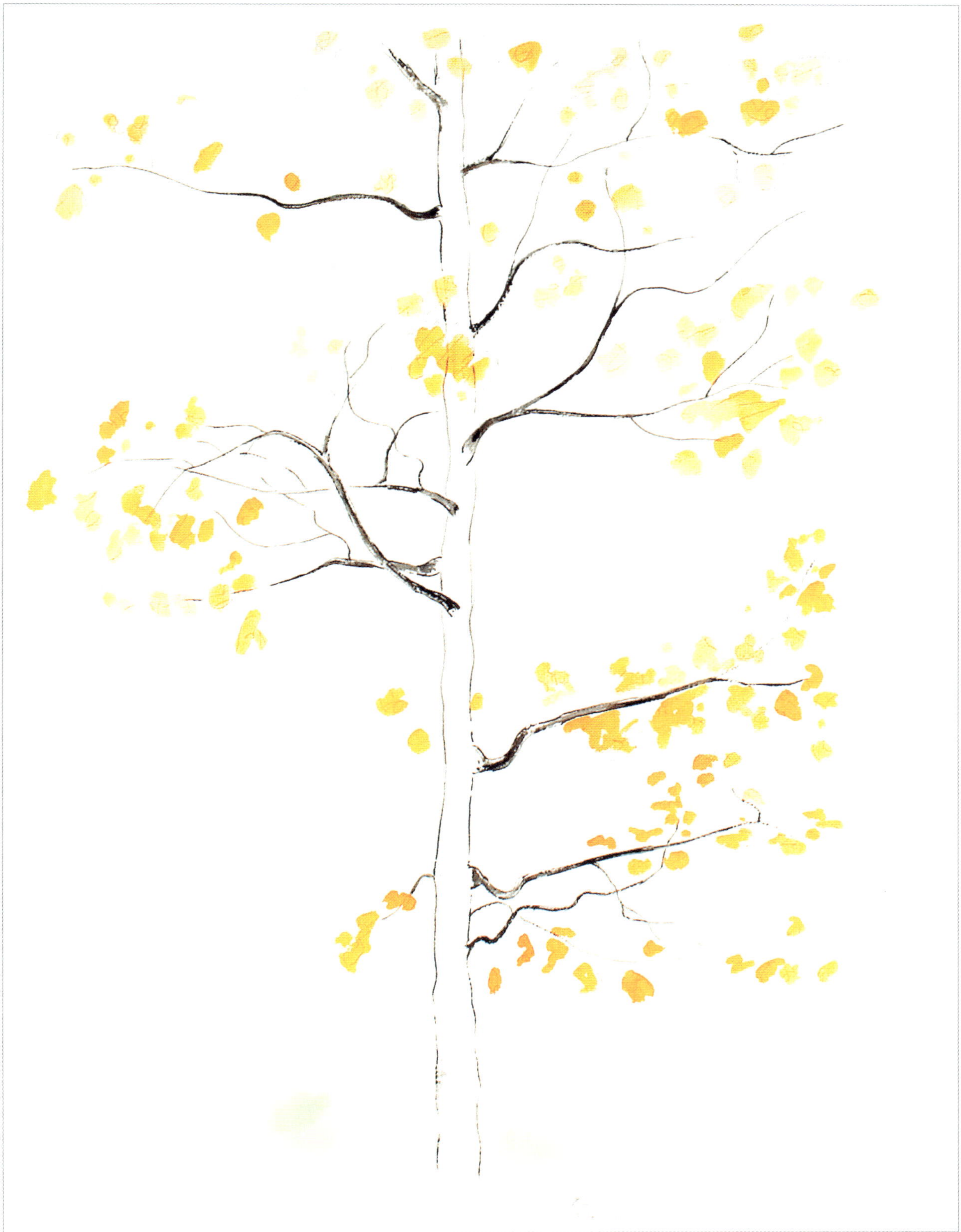

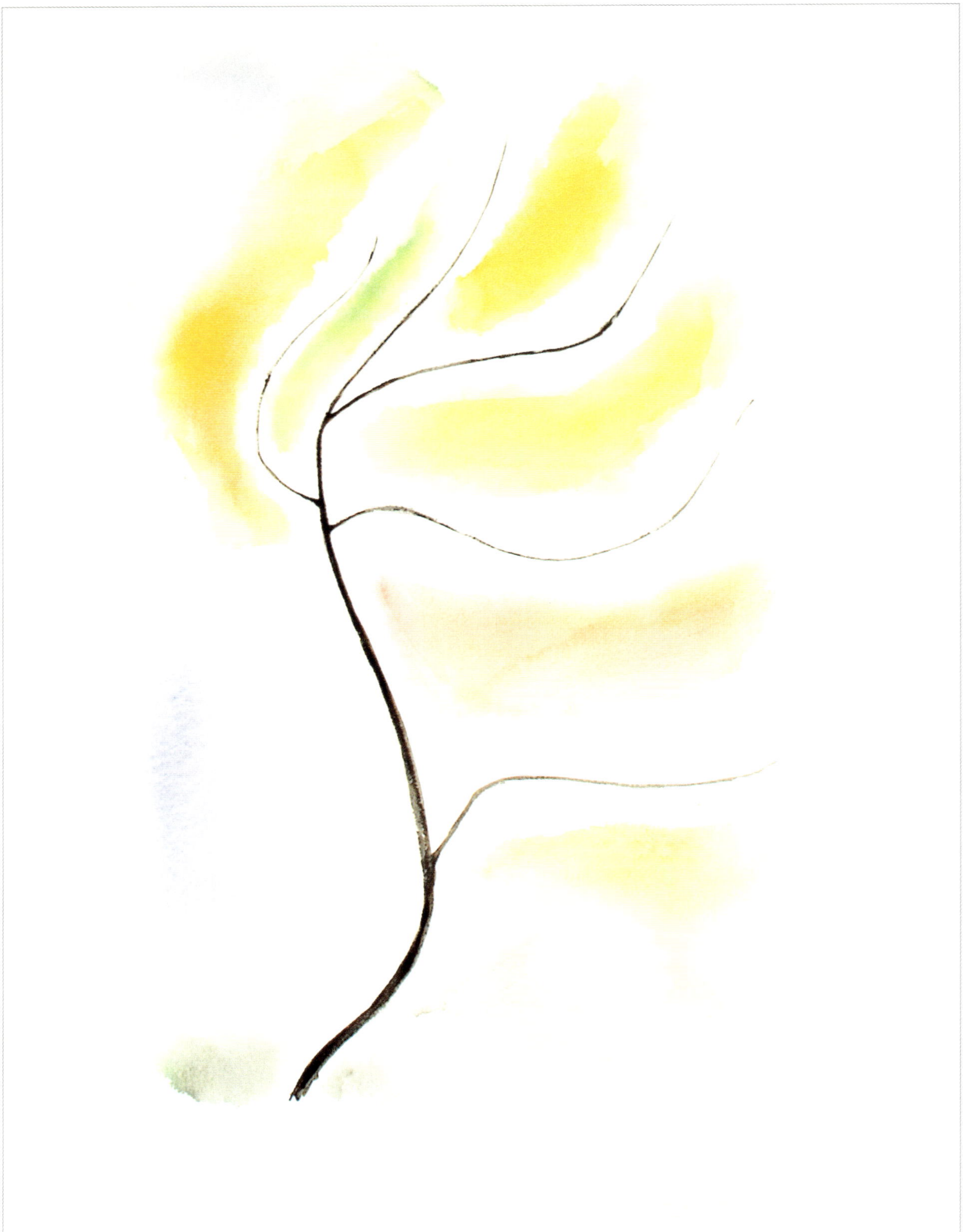

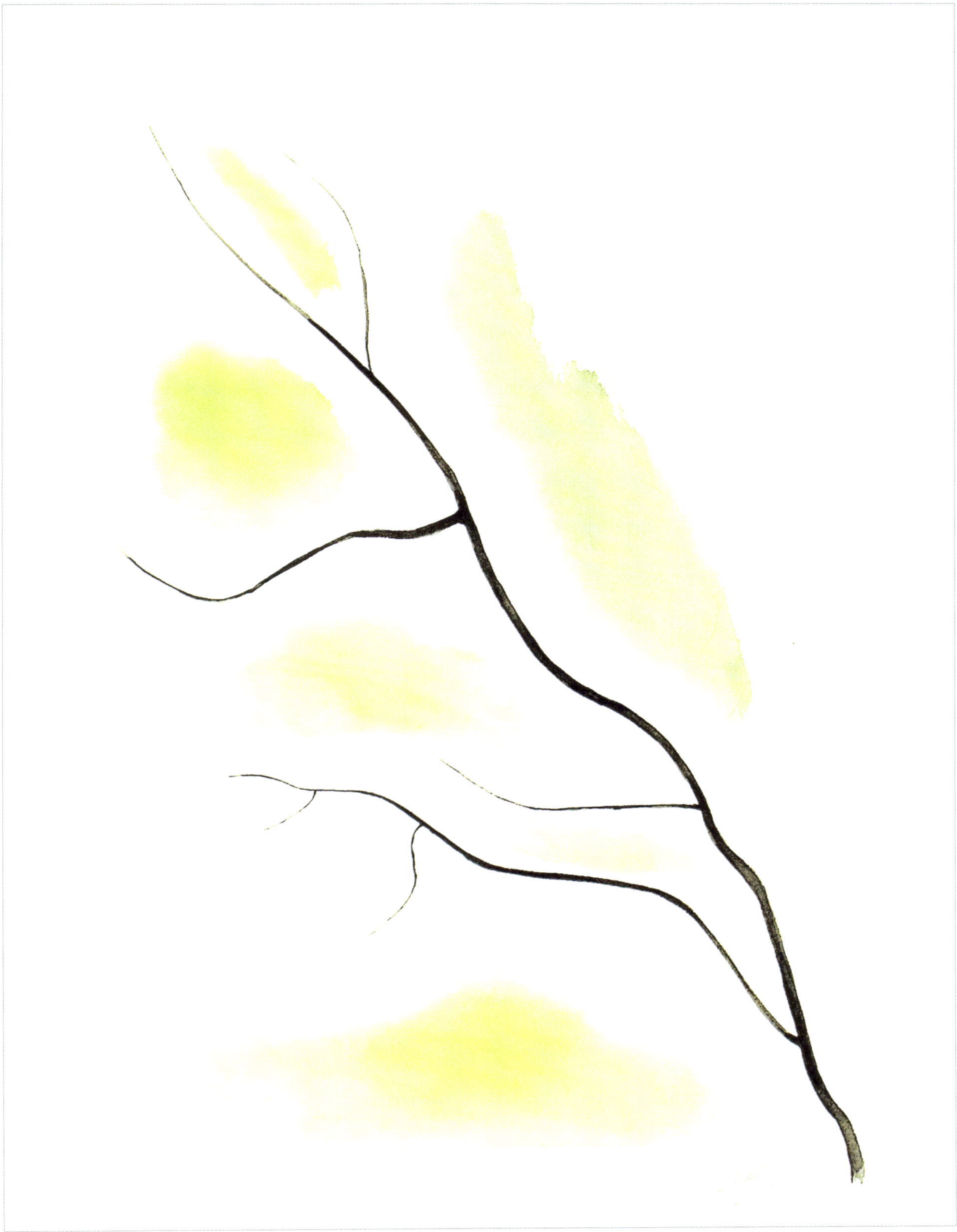

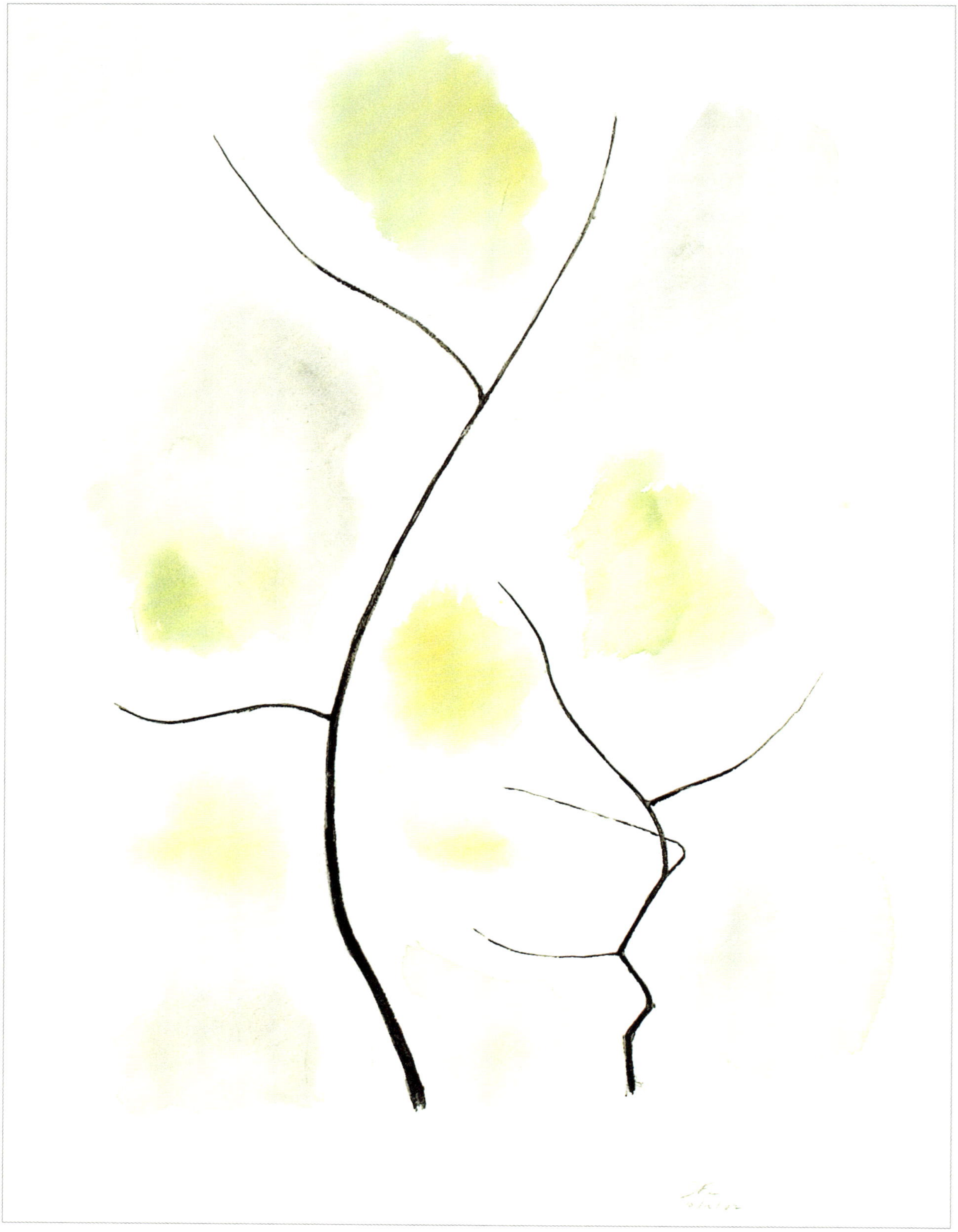

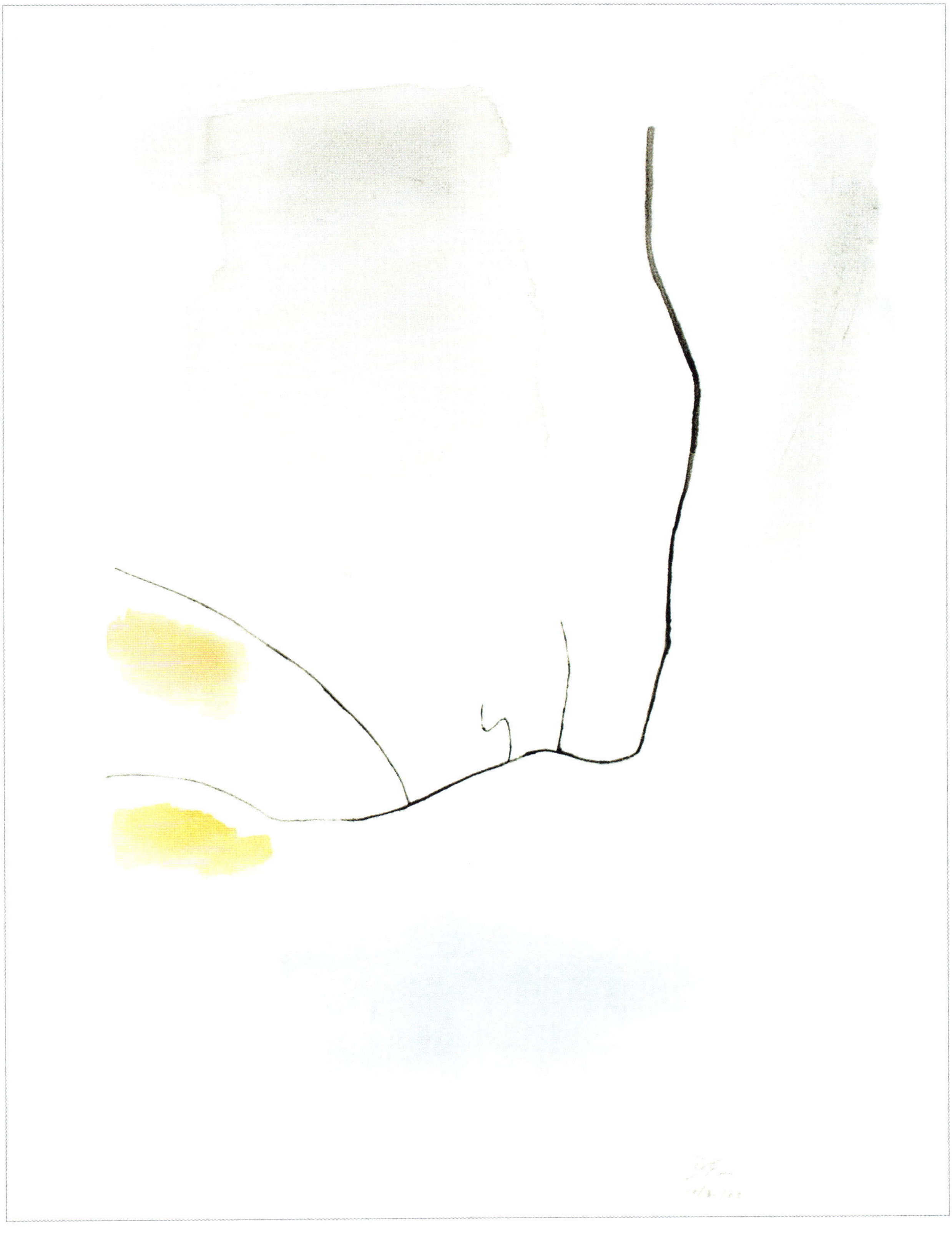

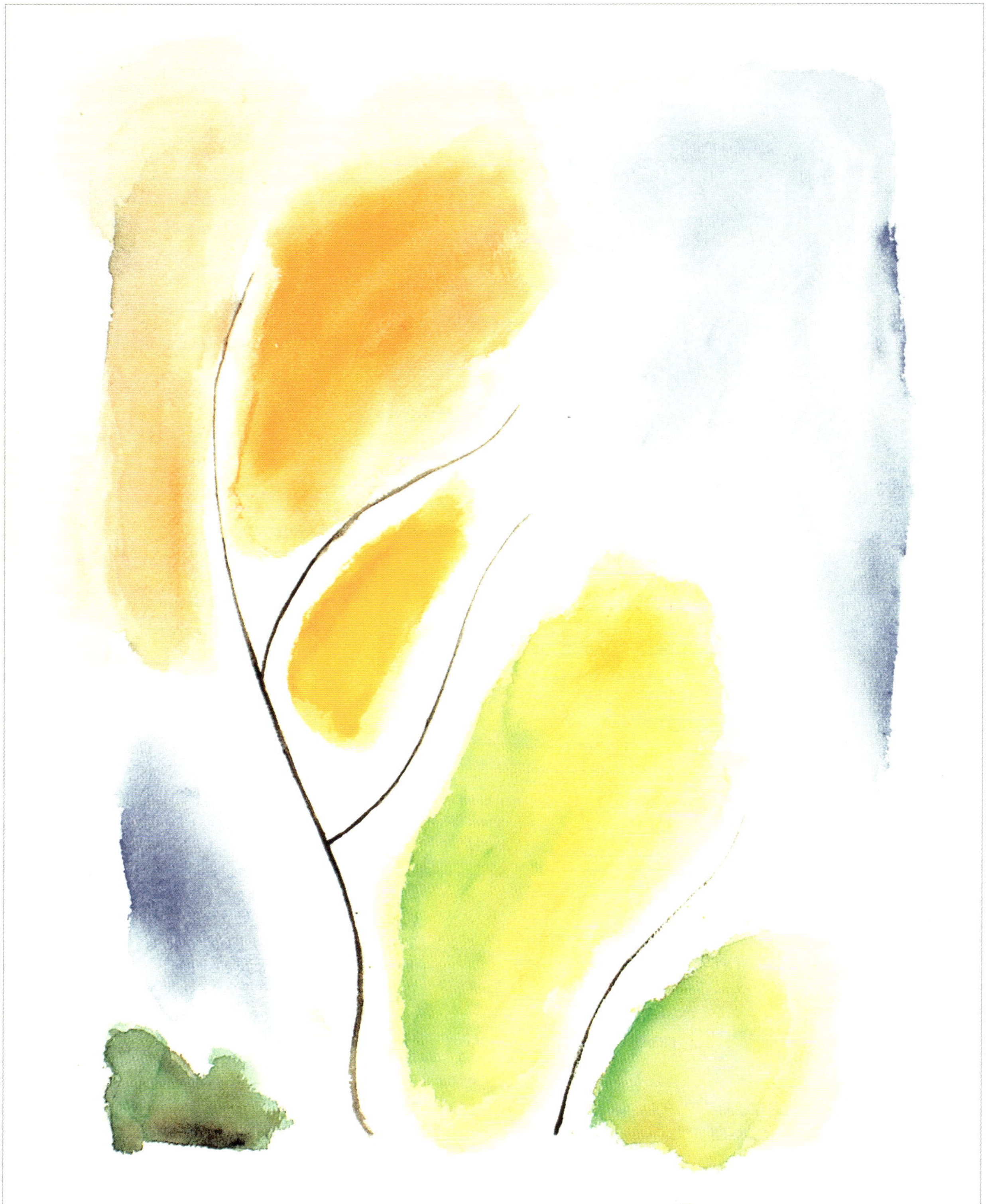

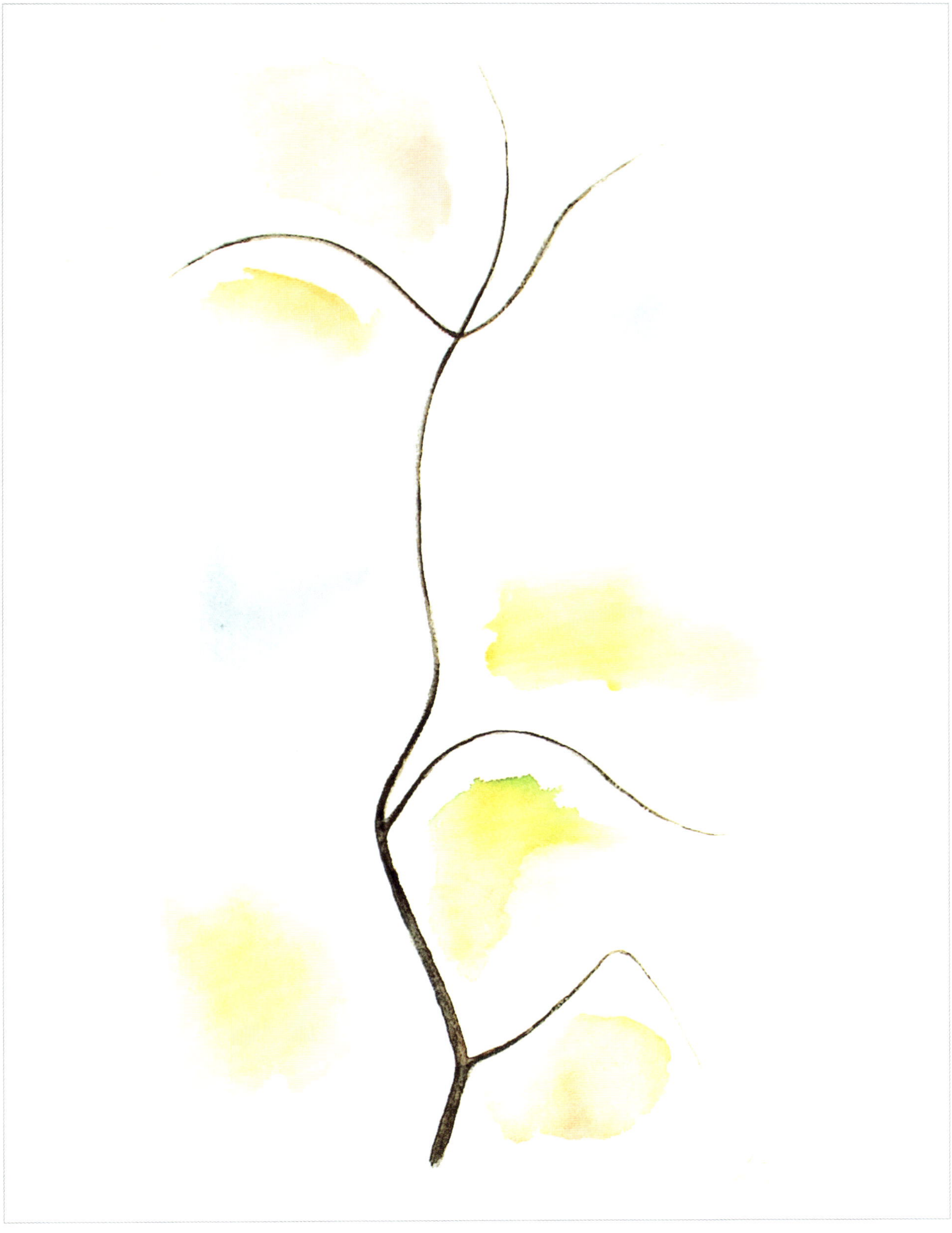

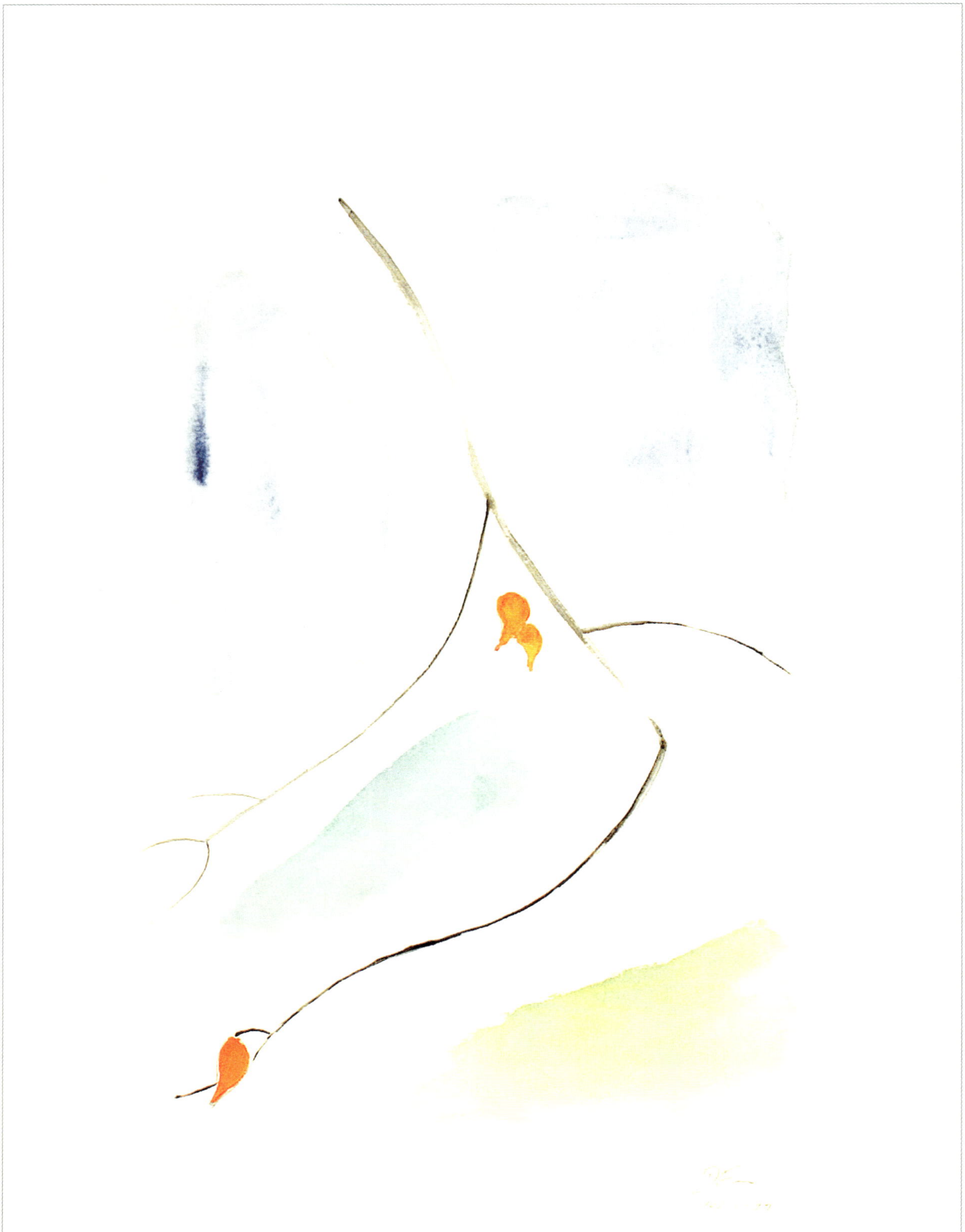

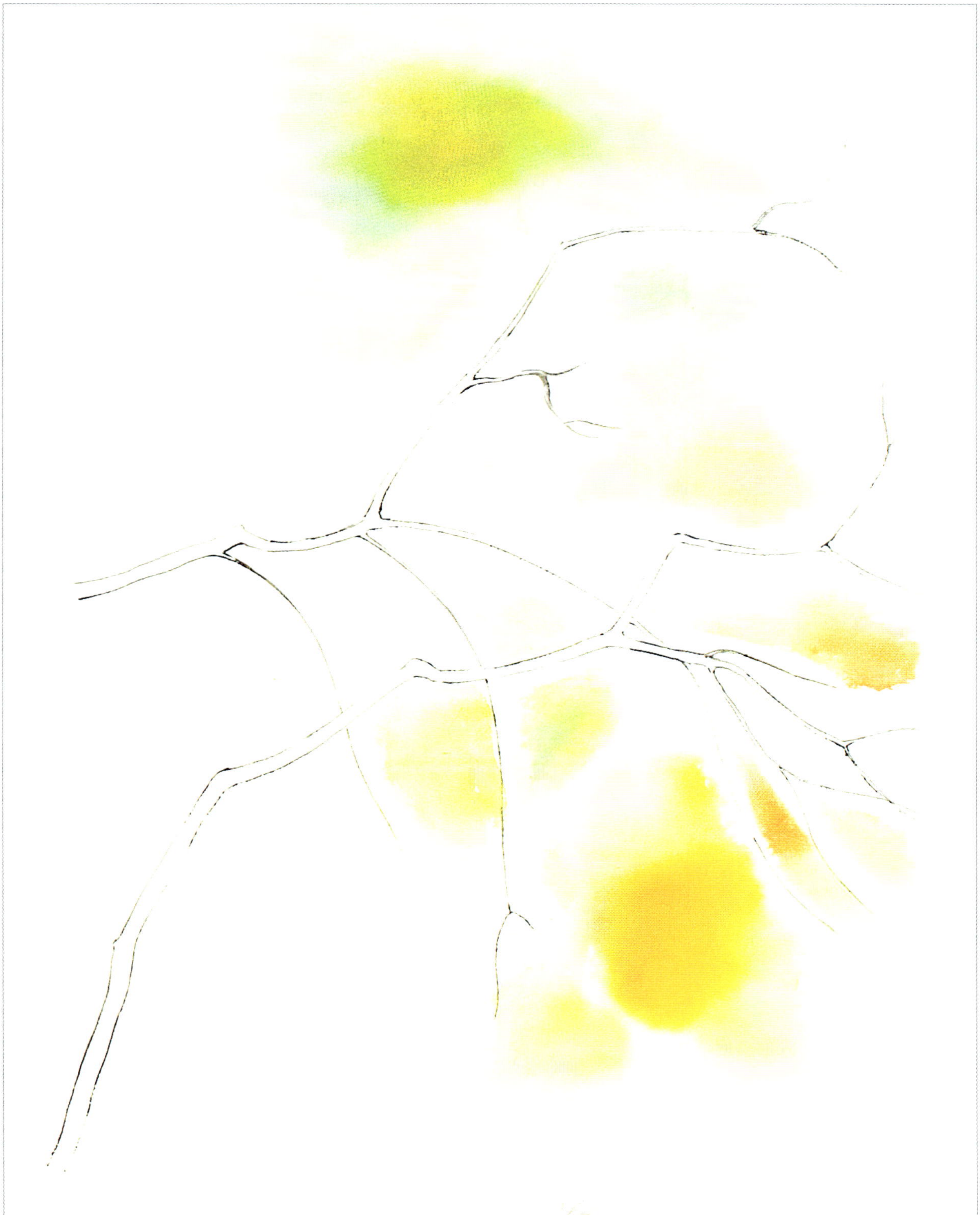

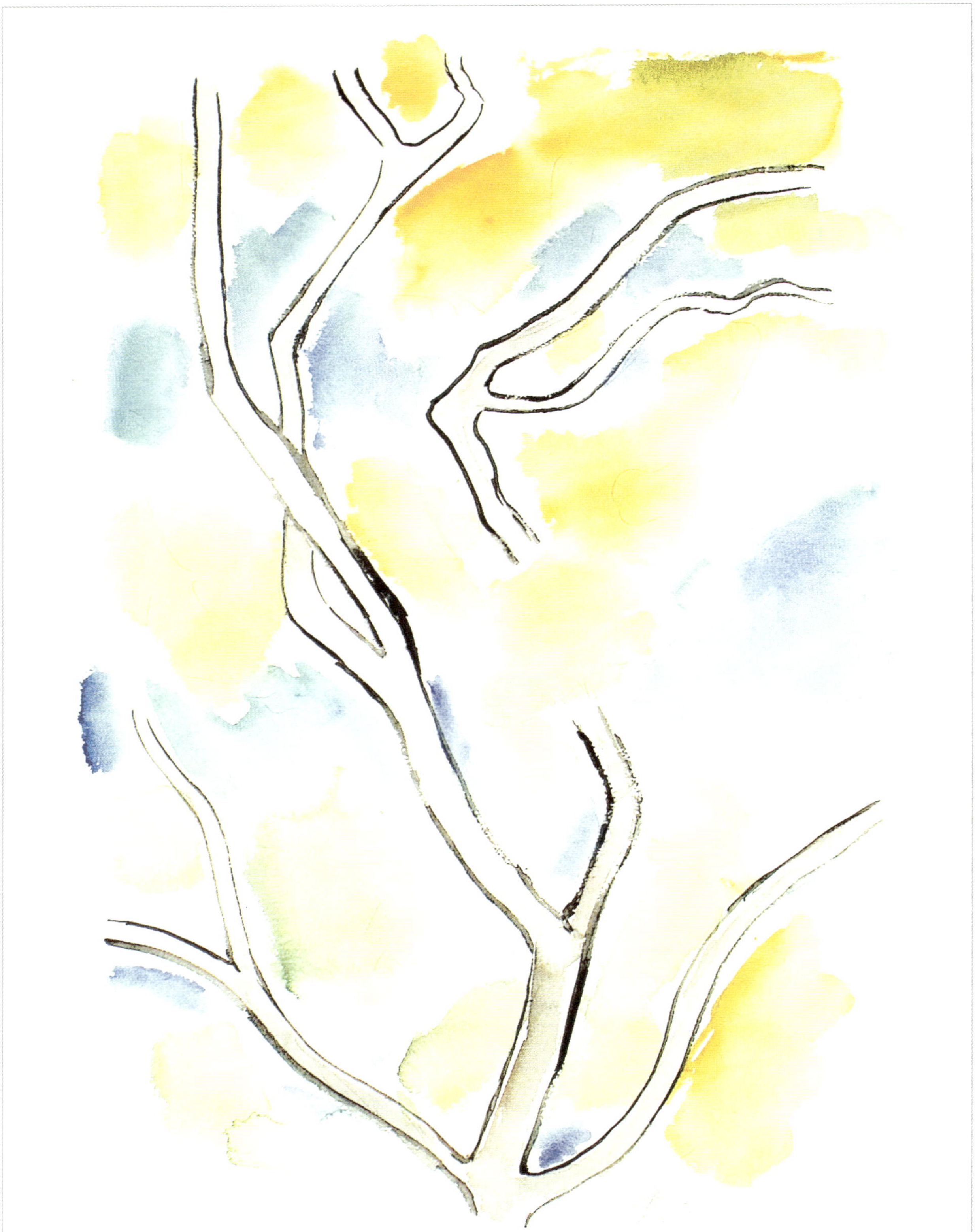

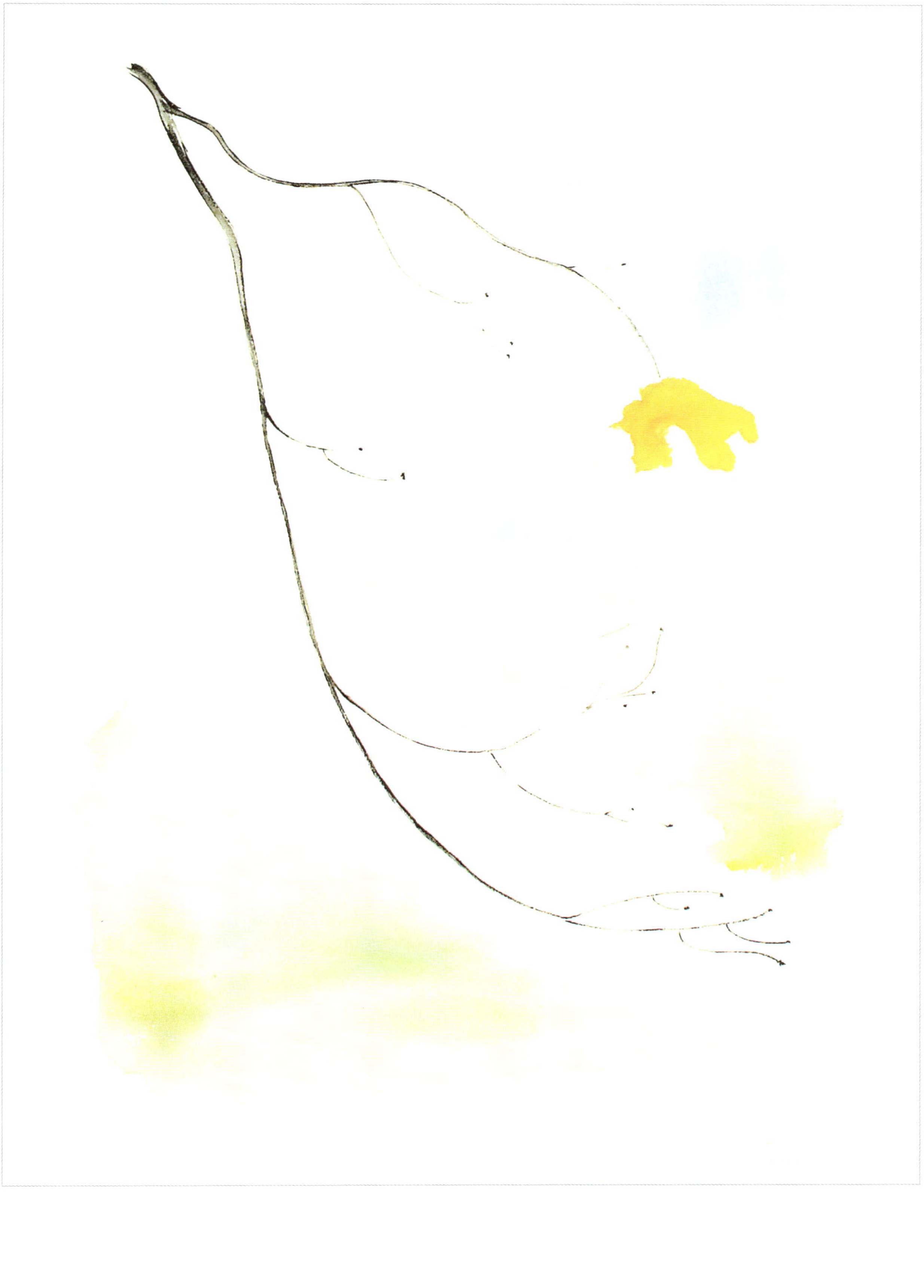

November

They have not gone away yet. There is still
foliage out there, remnants of our
summer joy. The trees are
standing tall,
ready
to face,
without regret,
or complaints, about
what lies ahead. They know that
they (as we) have much to be grateful for.

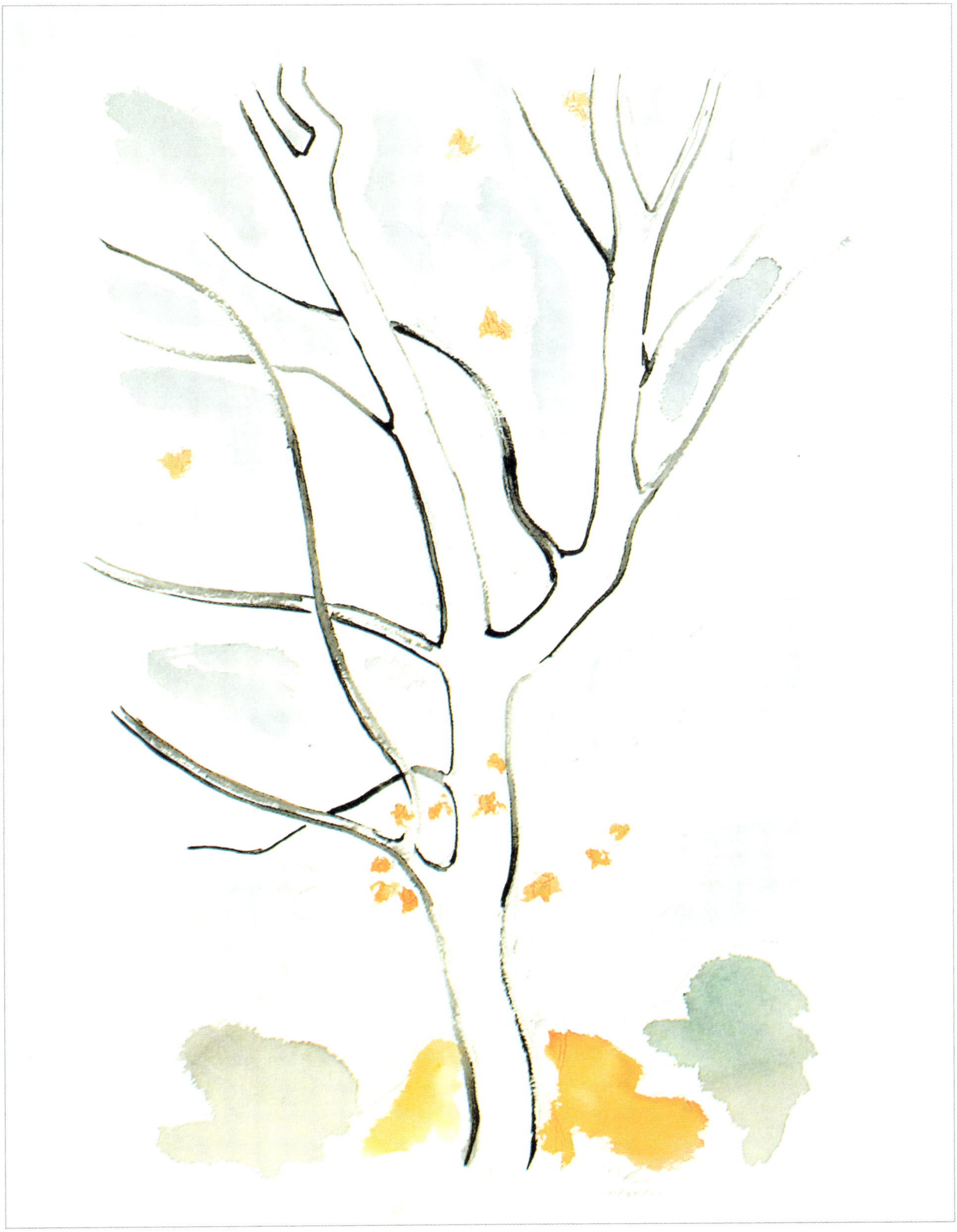

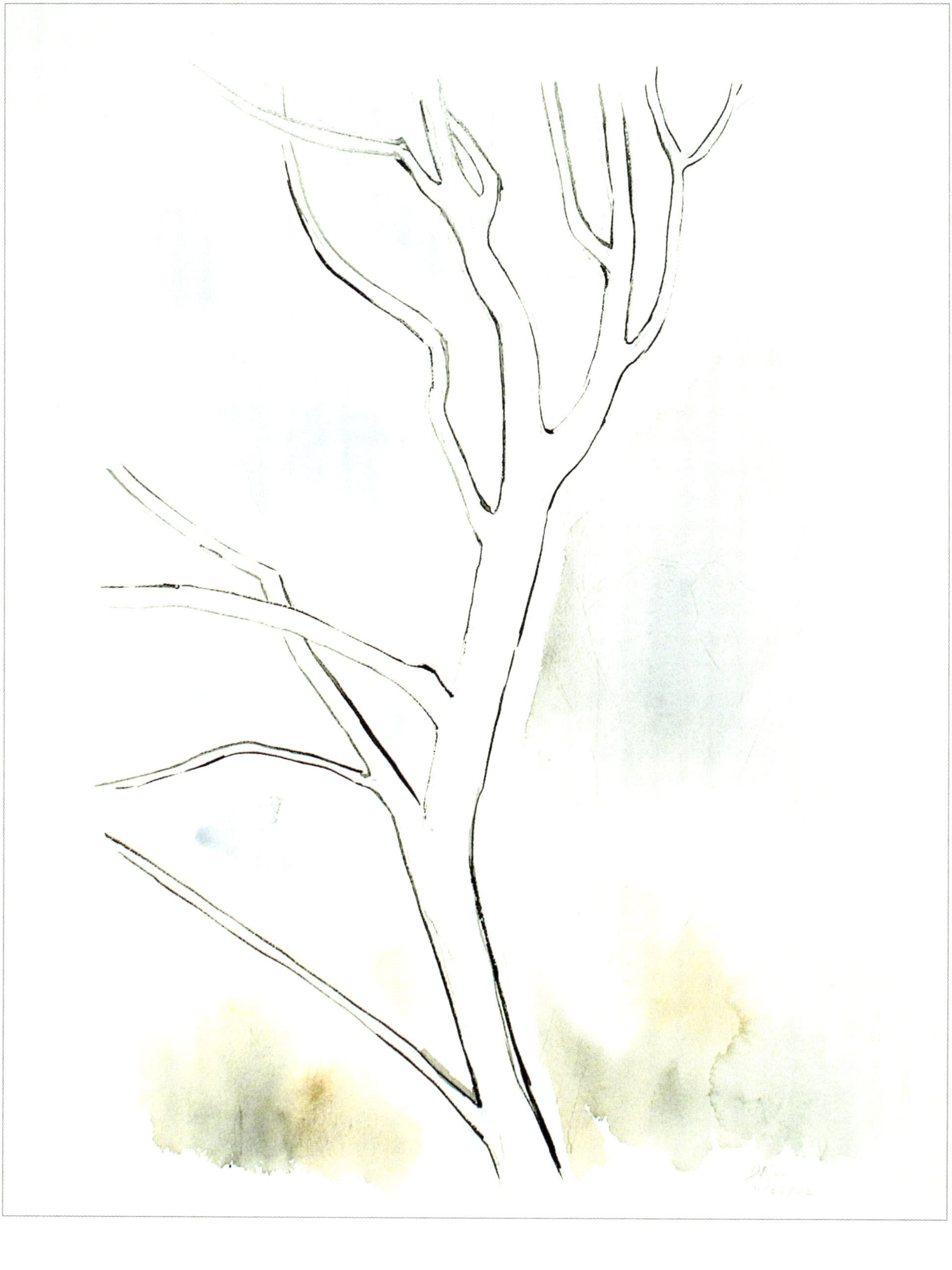

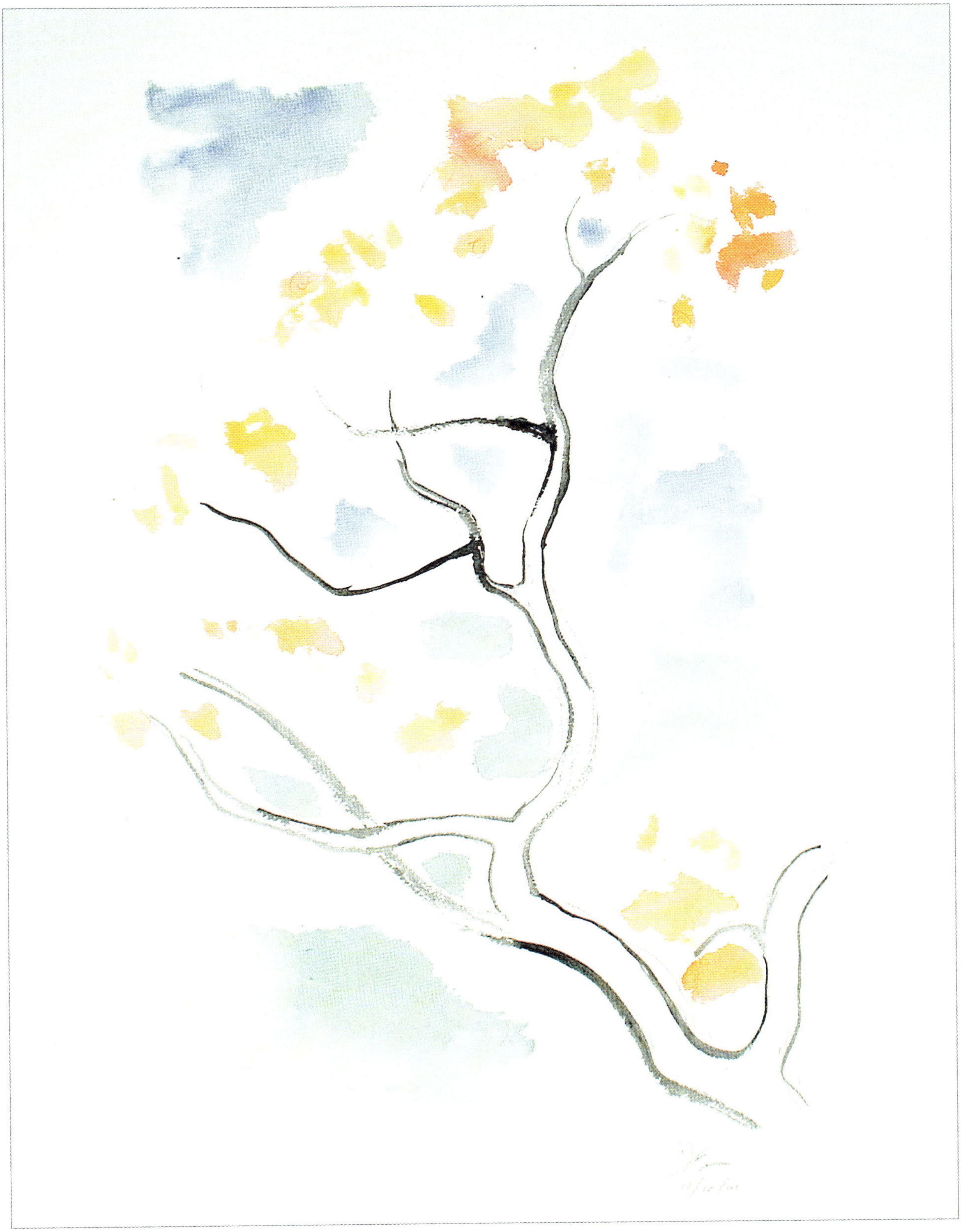

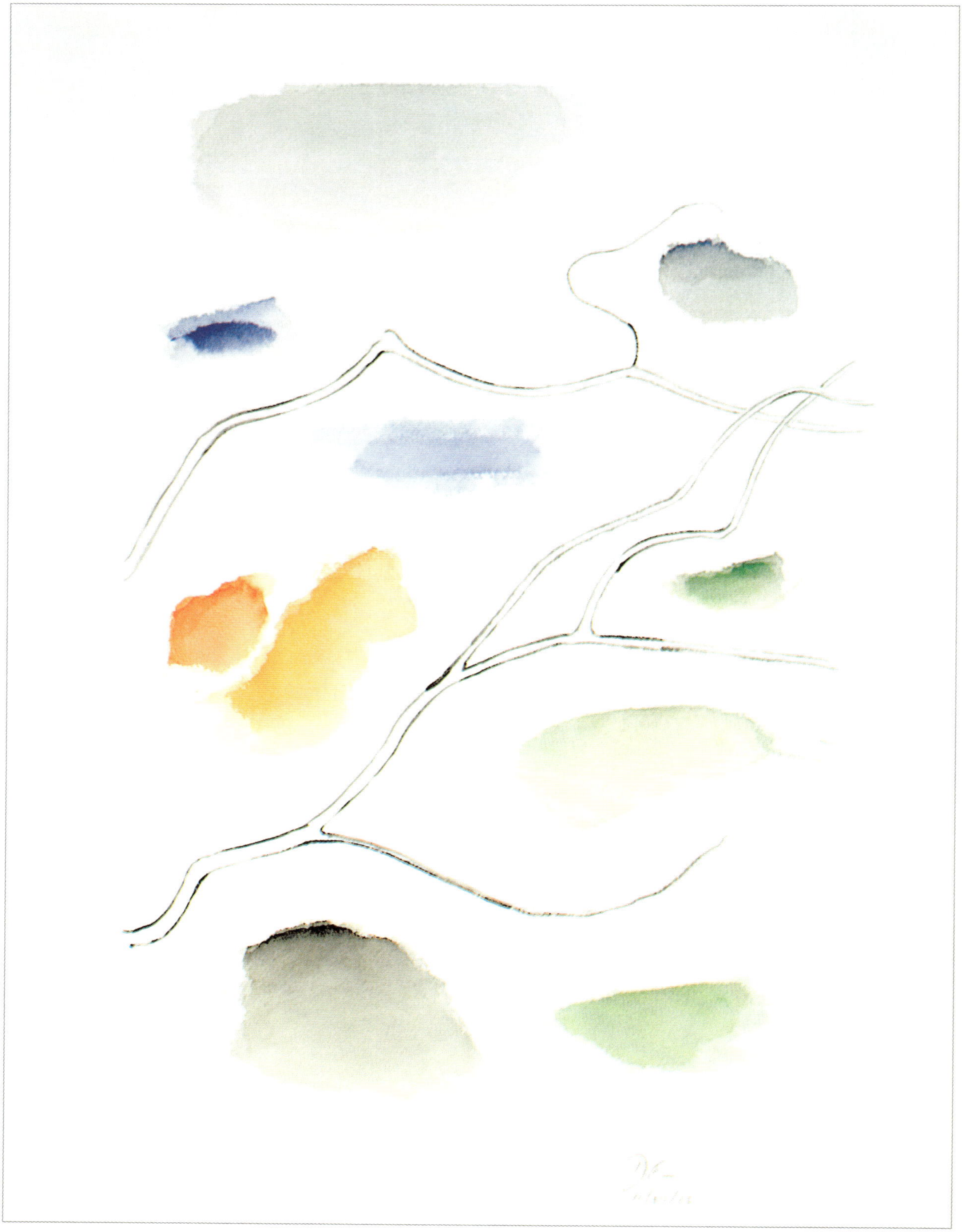

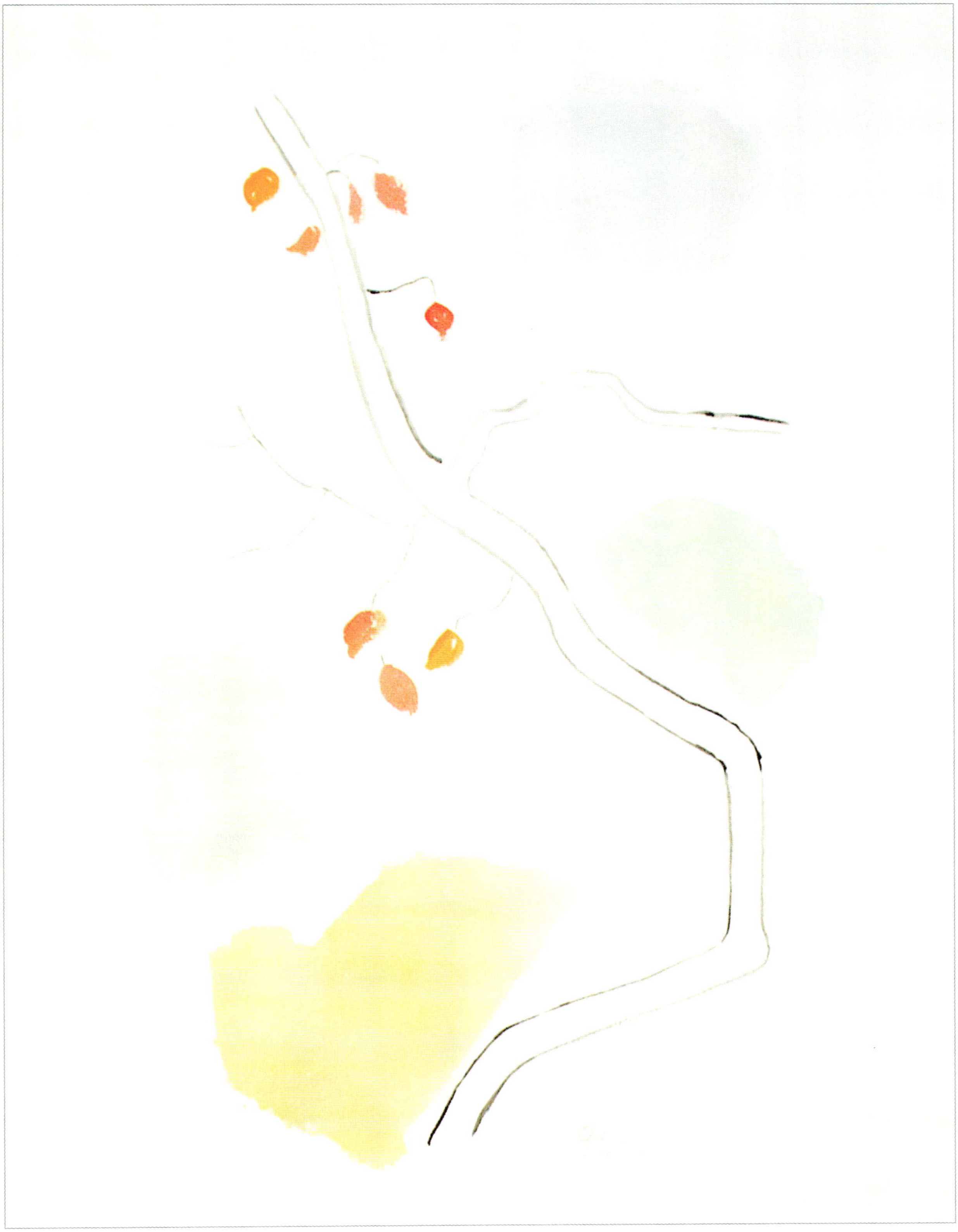

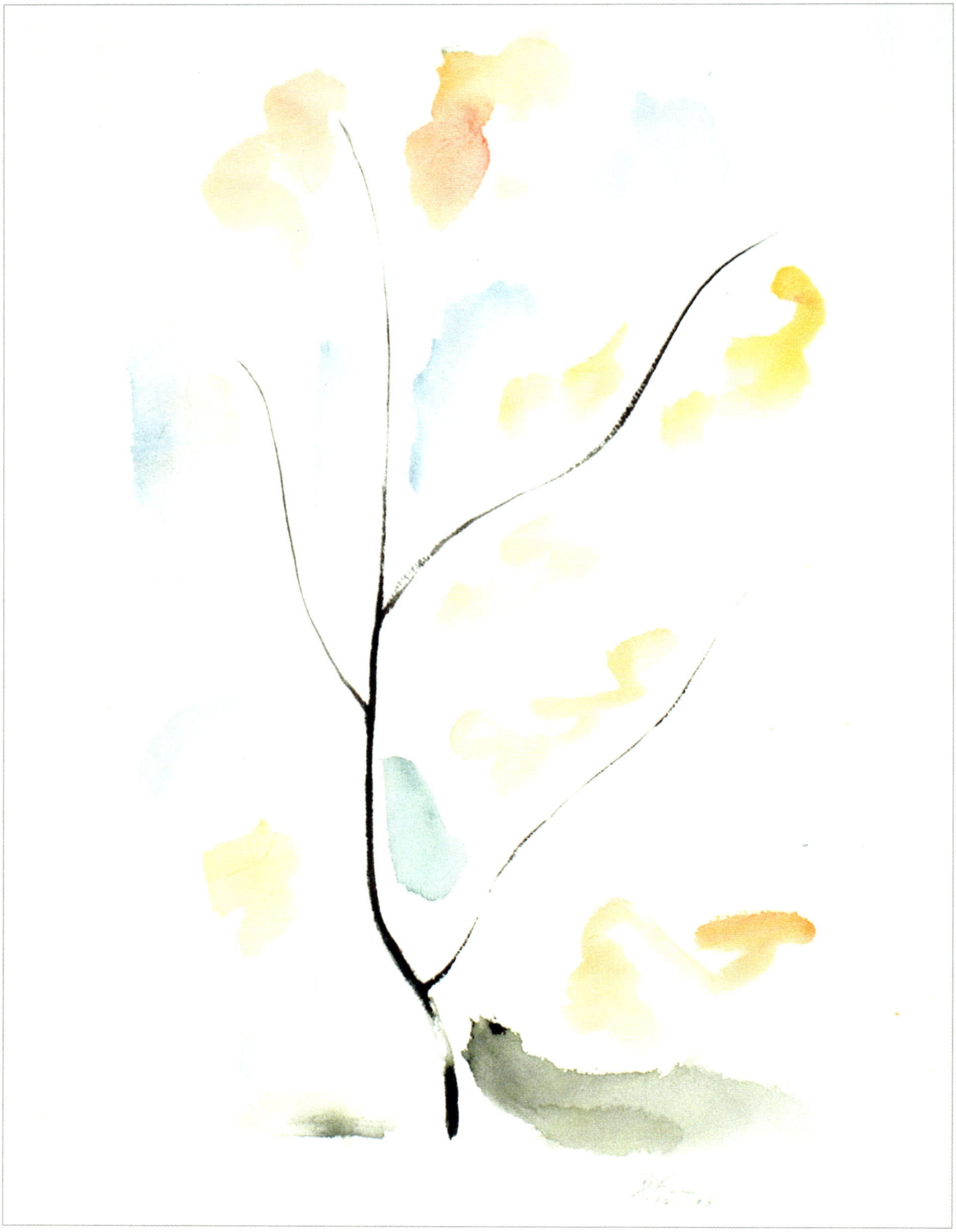

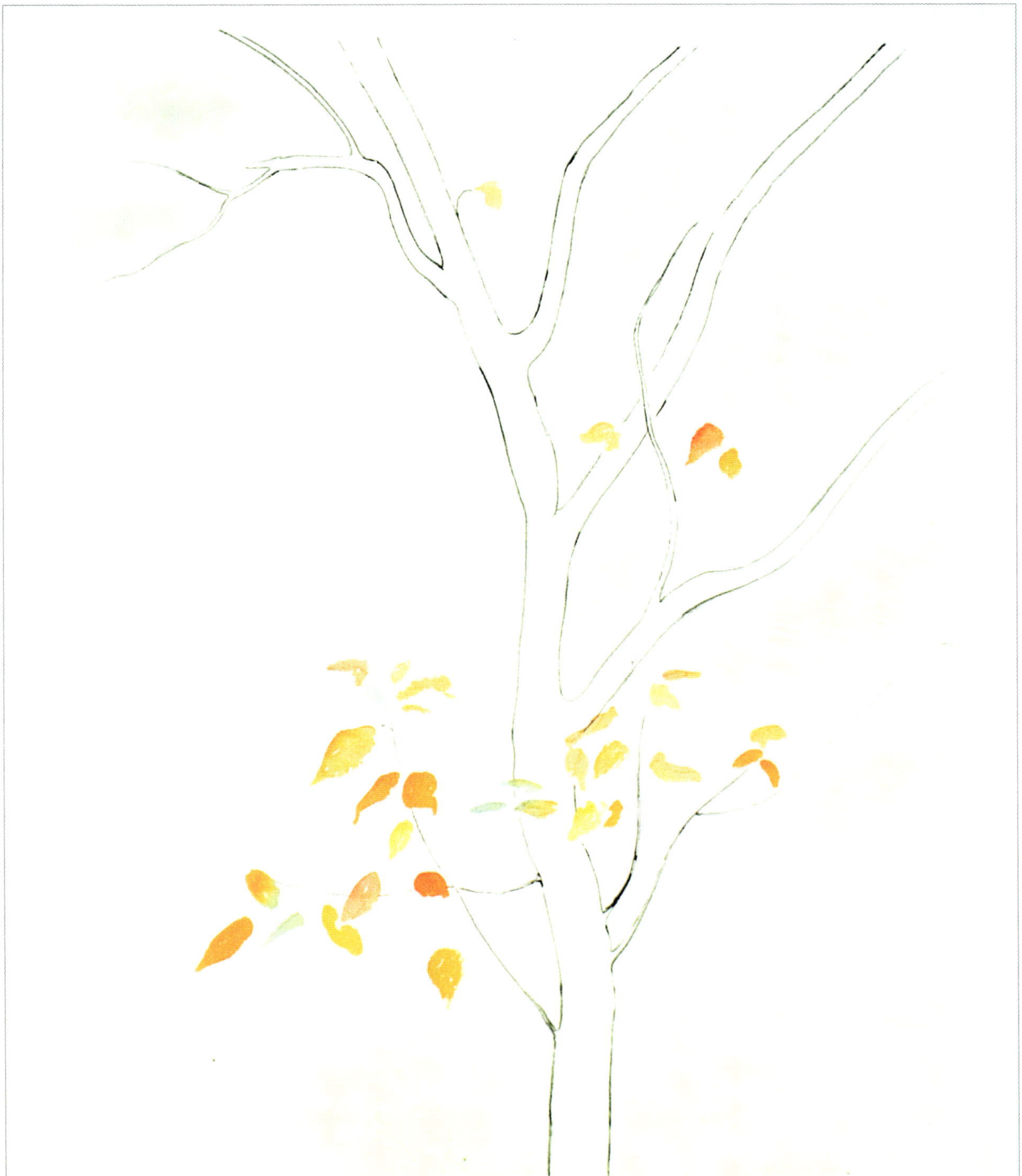

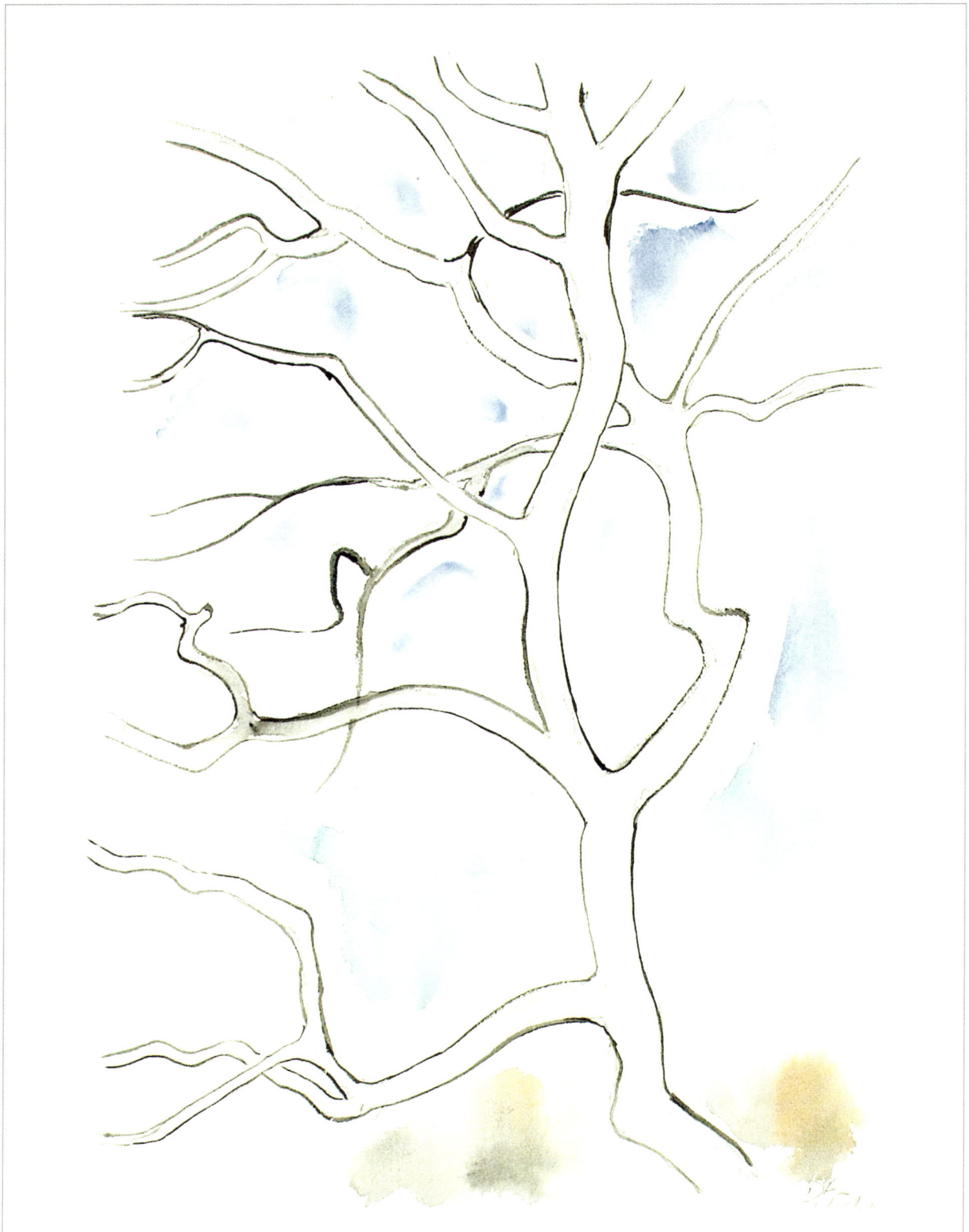

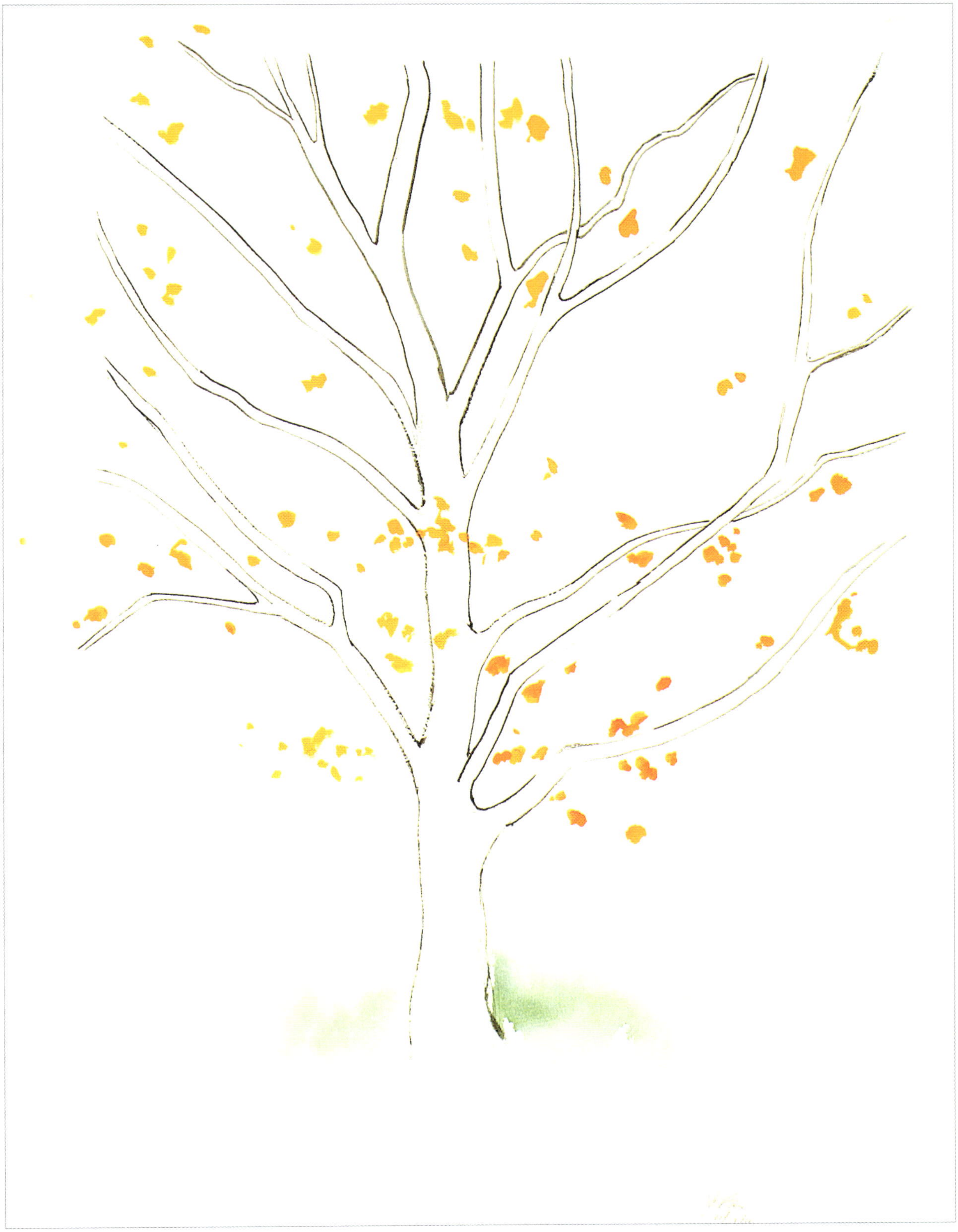

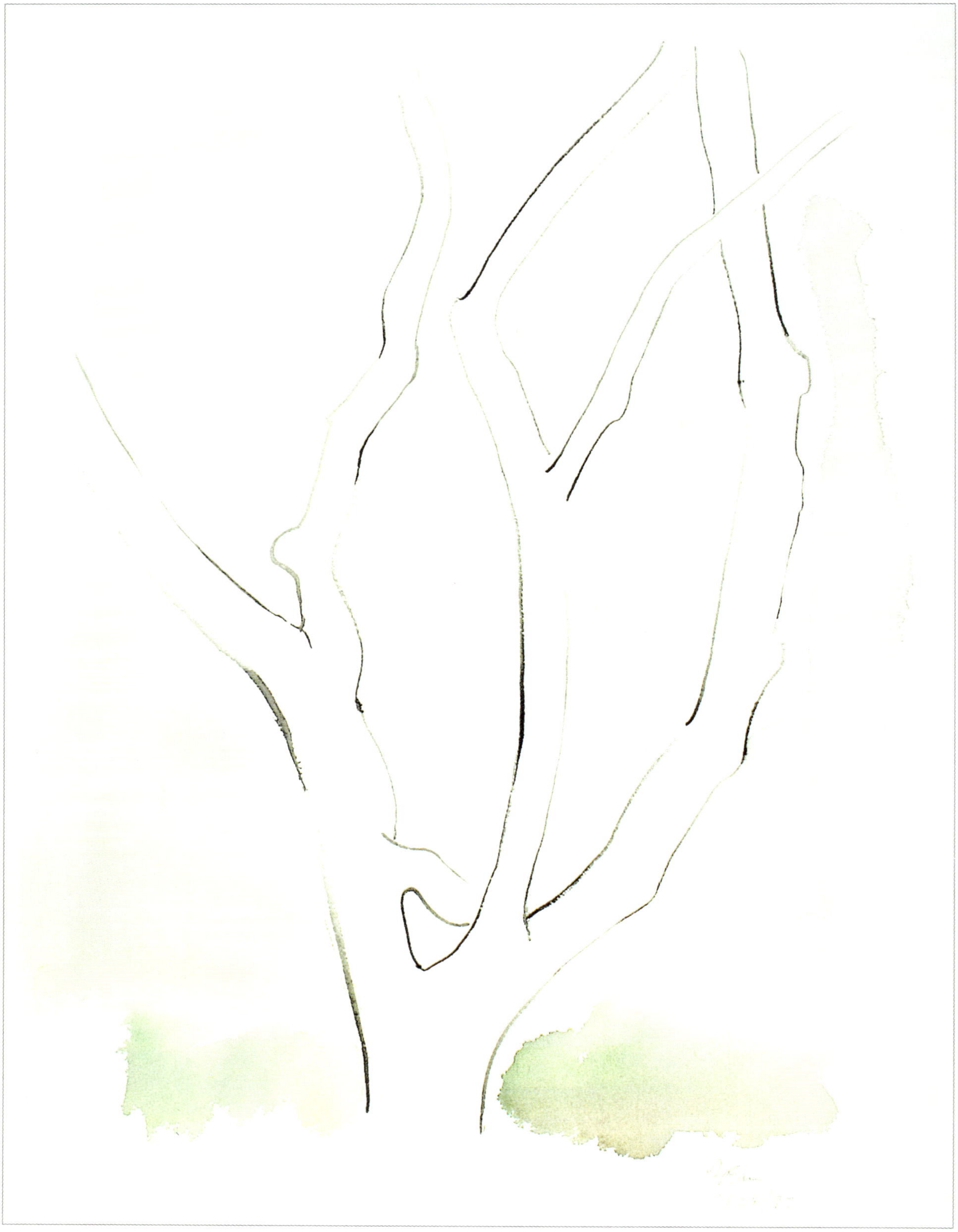

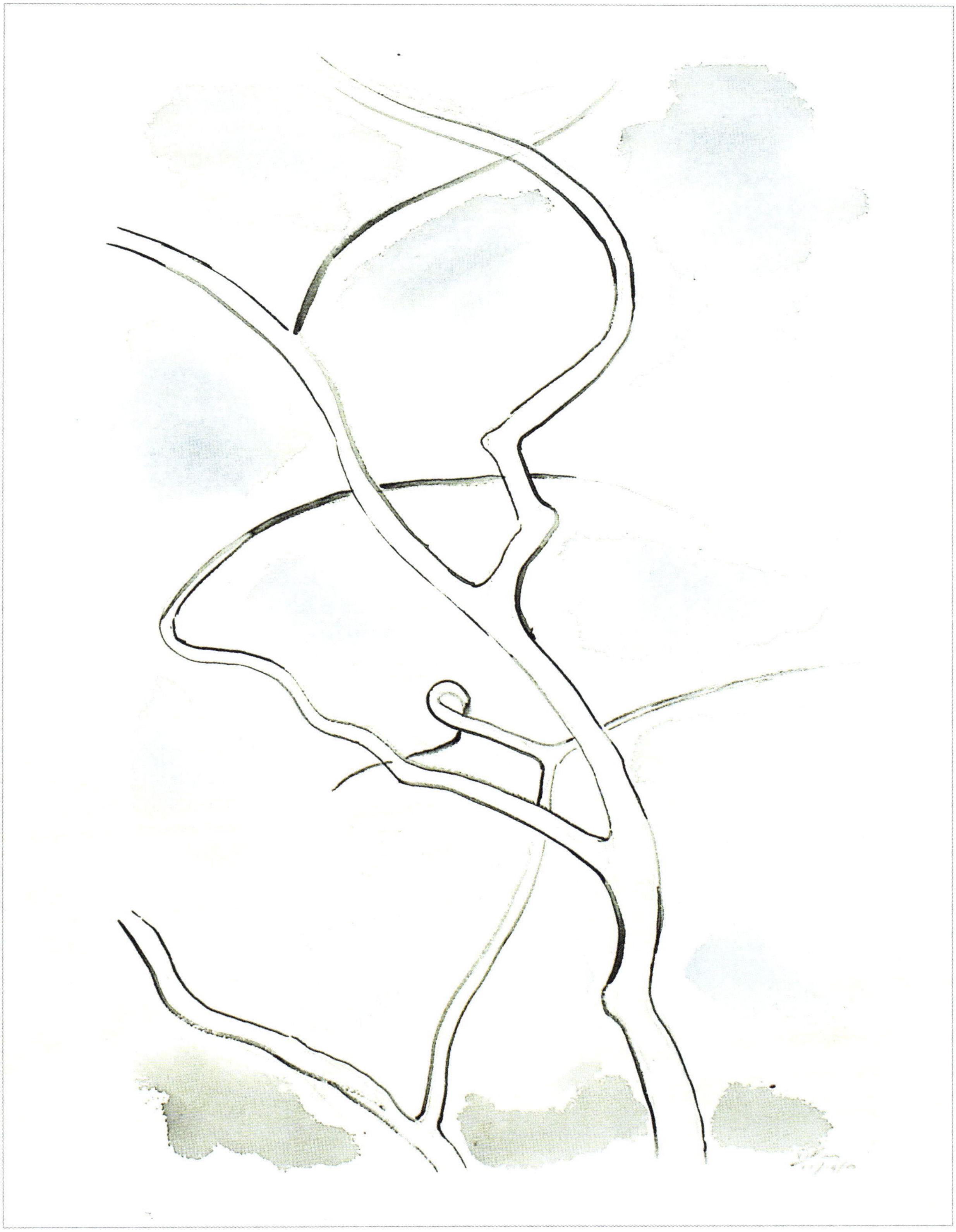

December

Now the inevitable end has come. How can we
be sad when life has been so rich? What we
see in the branches of the trees
is the final ending of
the lives of leaves;
but they, like us,
can be comforted knowing
that spring will come again and new
buds will come to celebrate the joys of life,
as when our lives end, newborns will take our place.

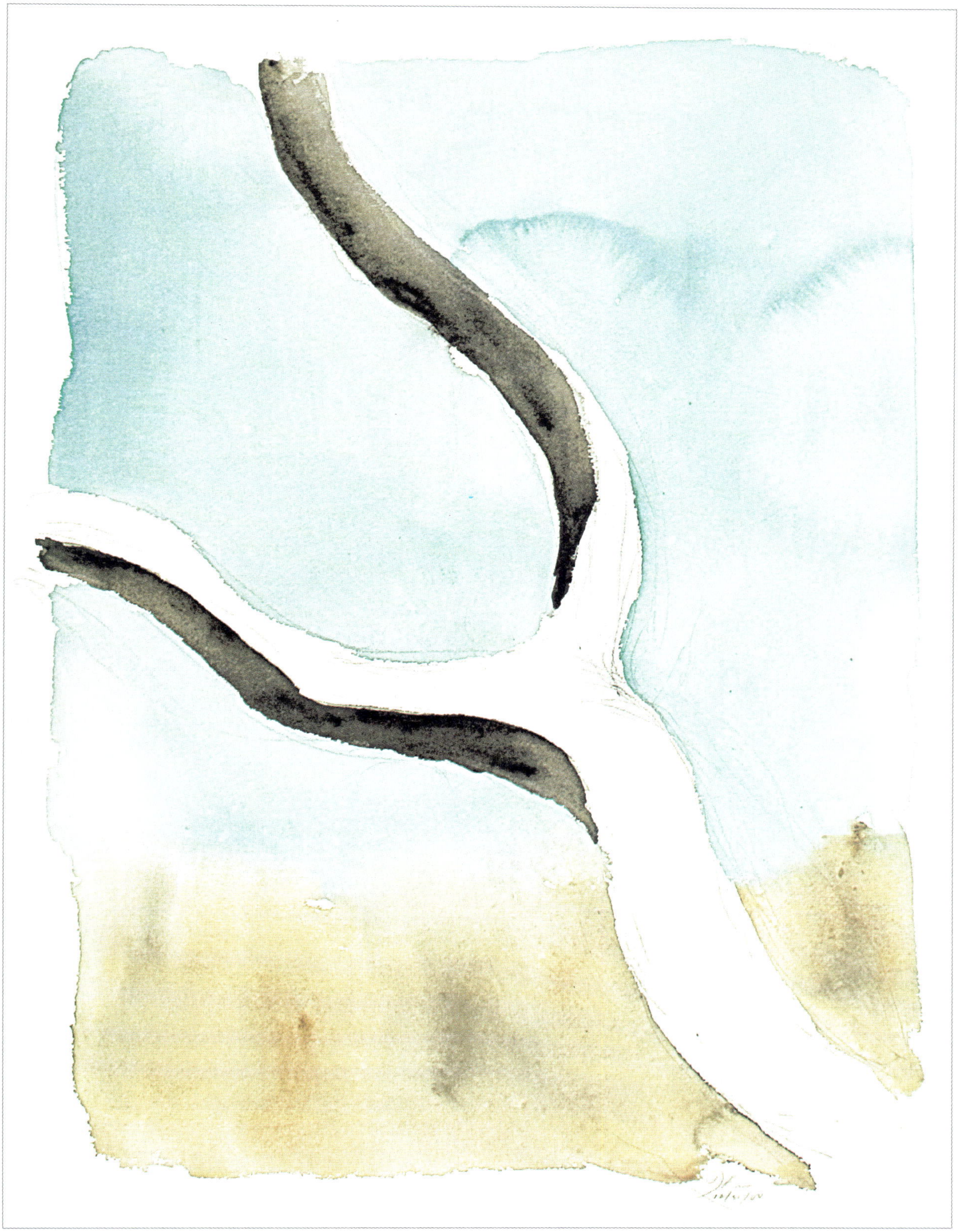

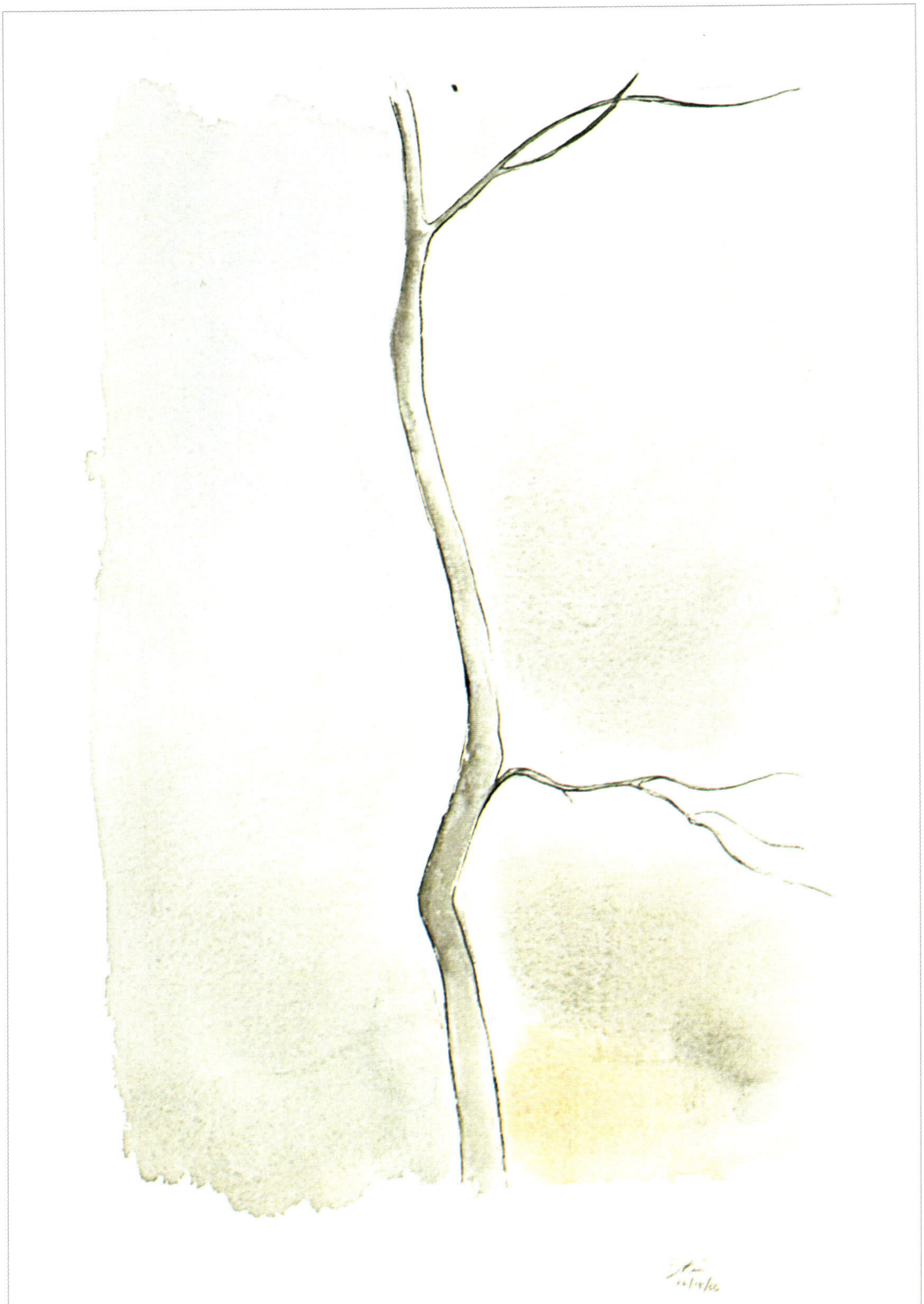

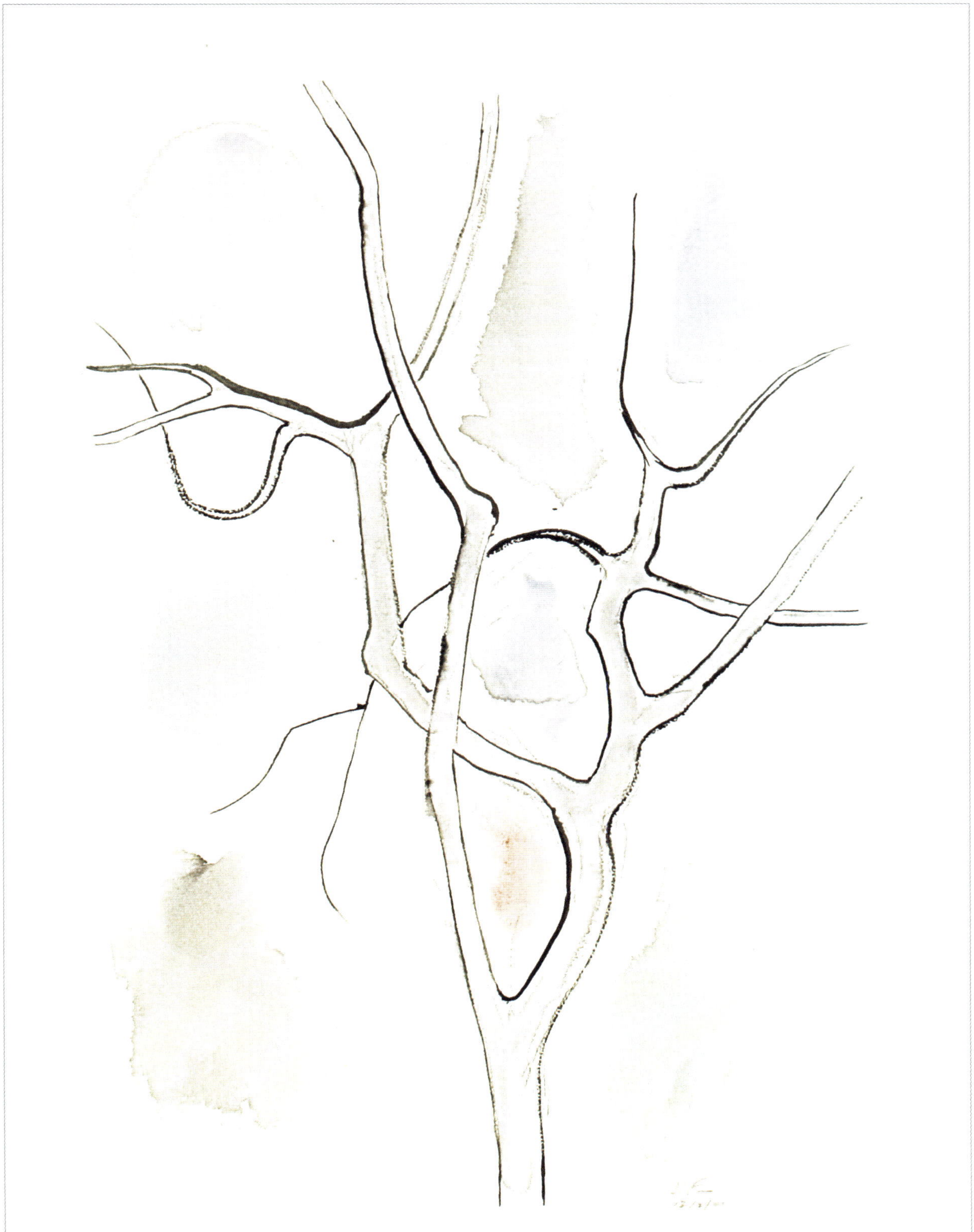

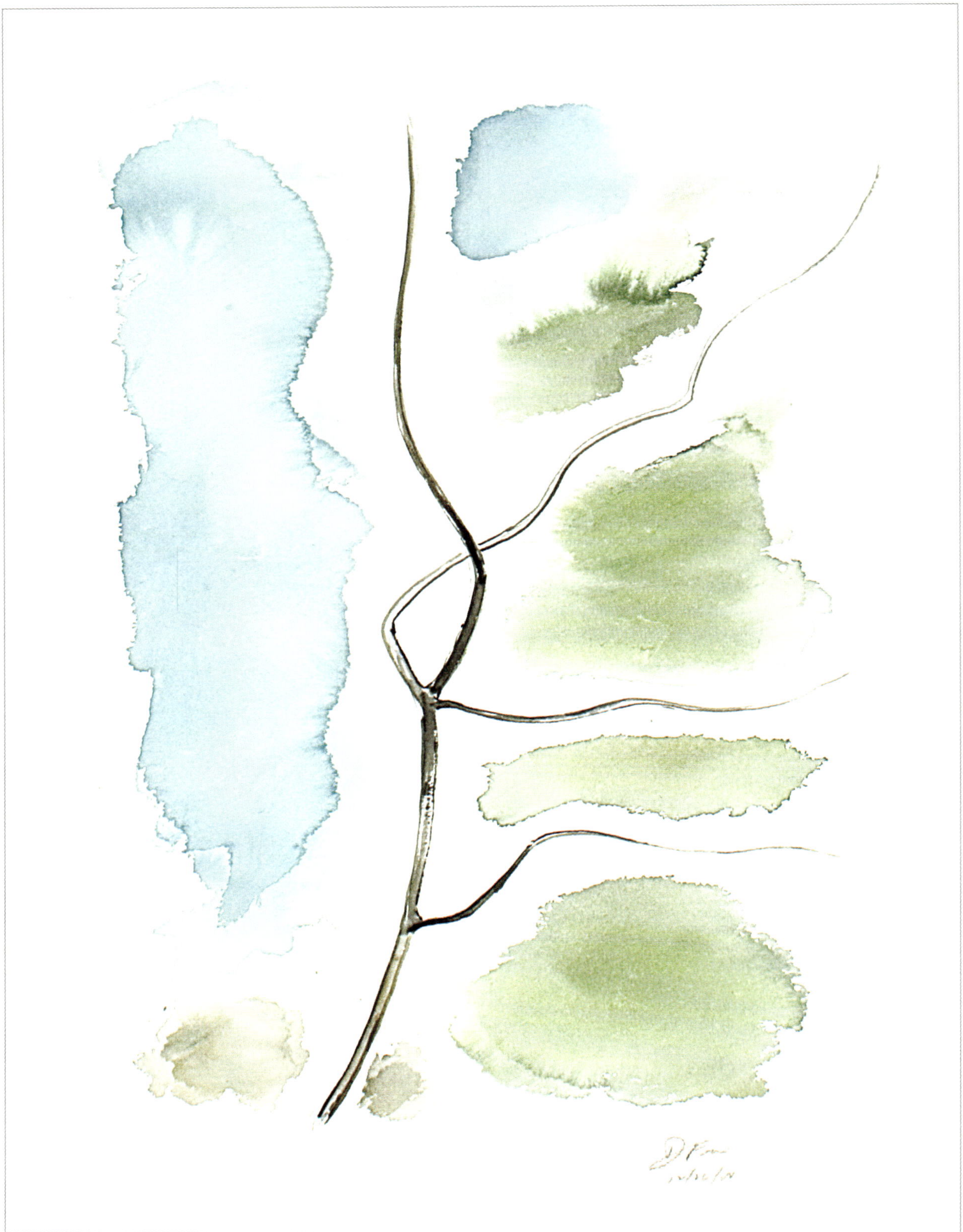

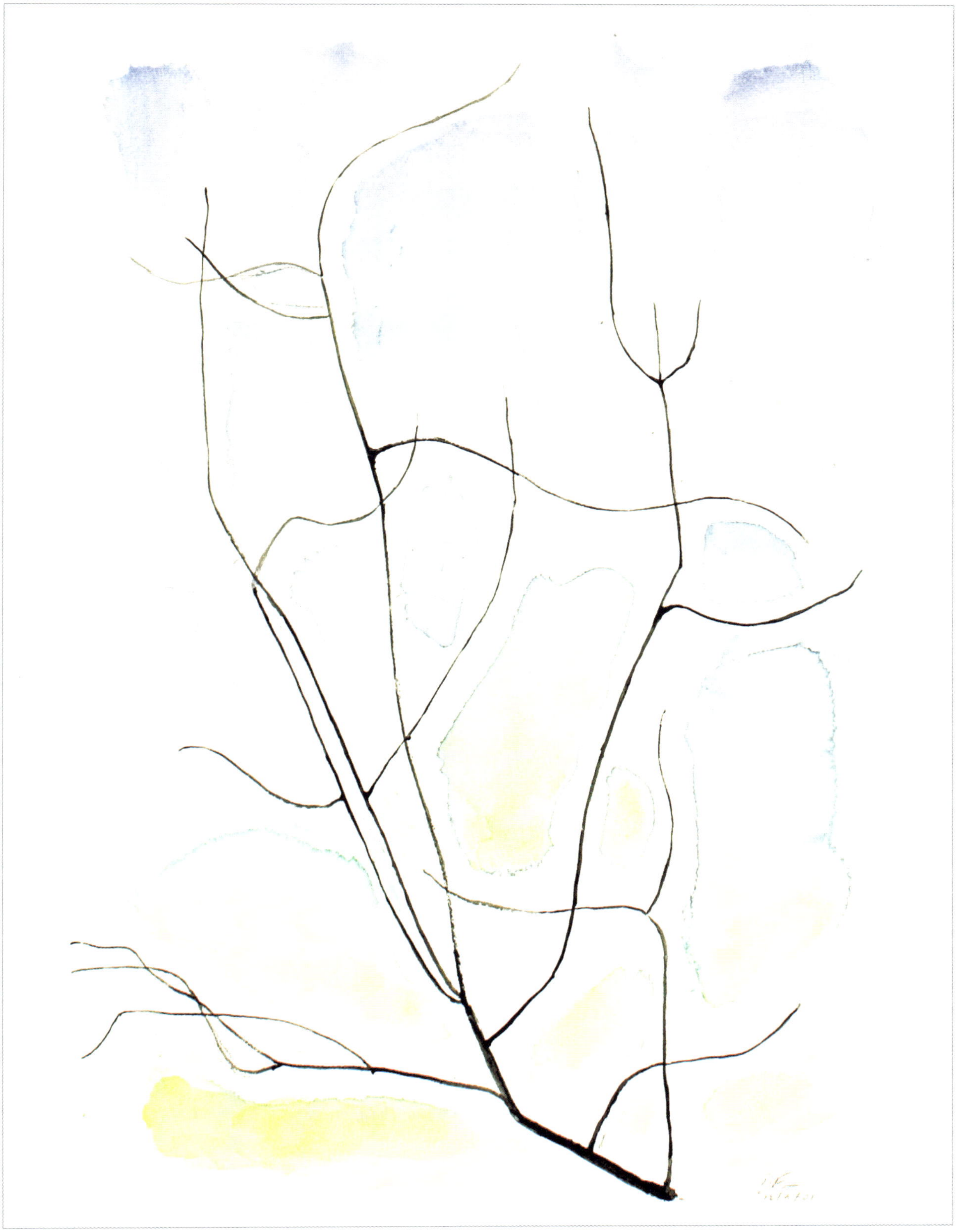

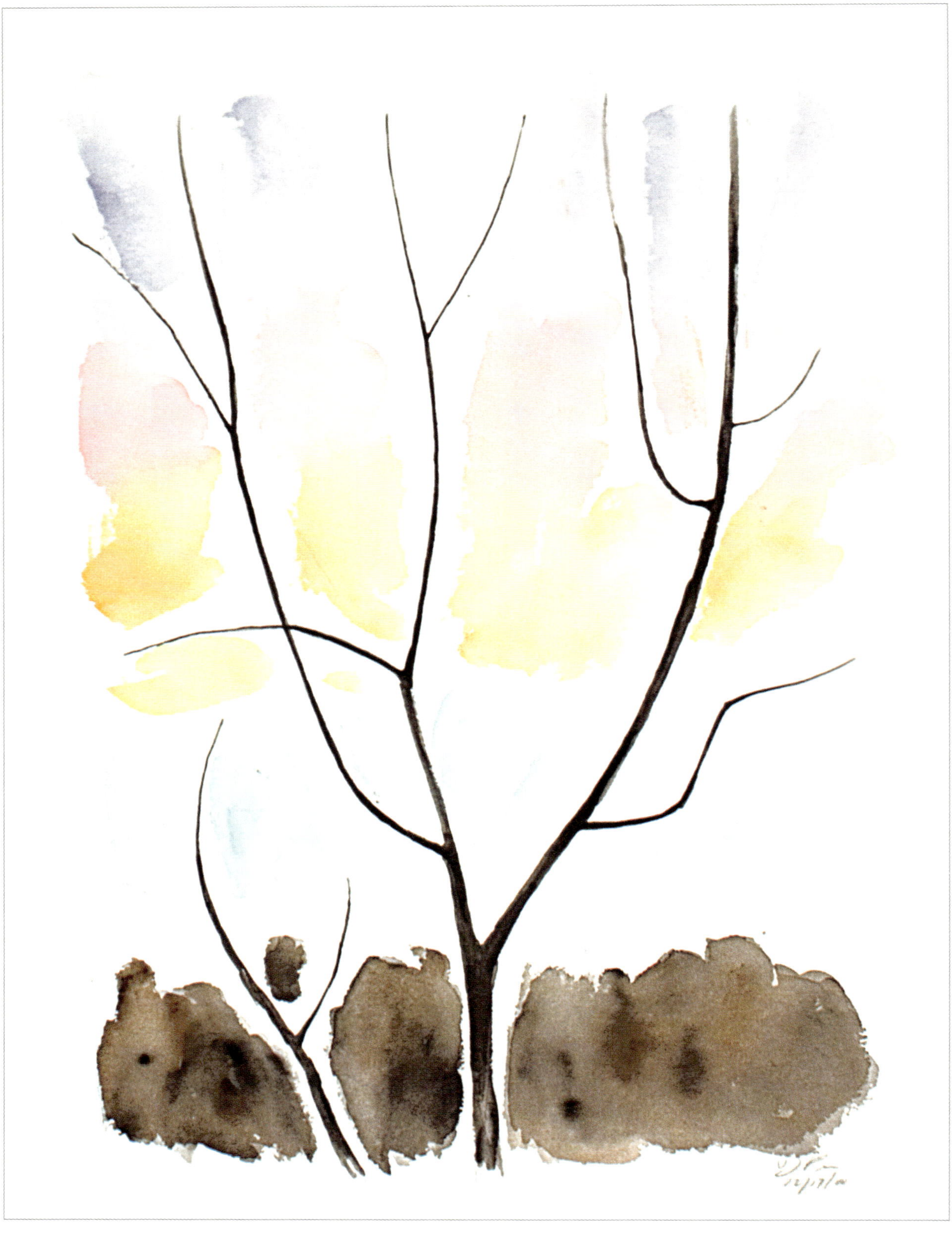

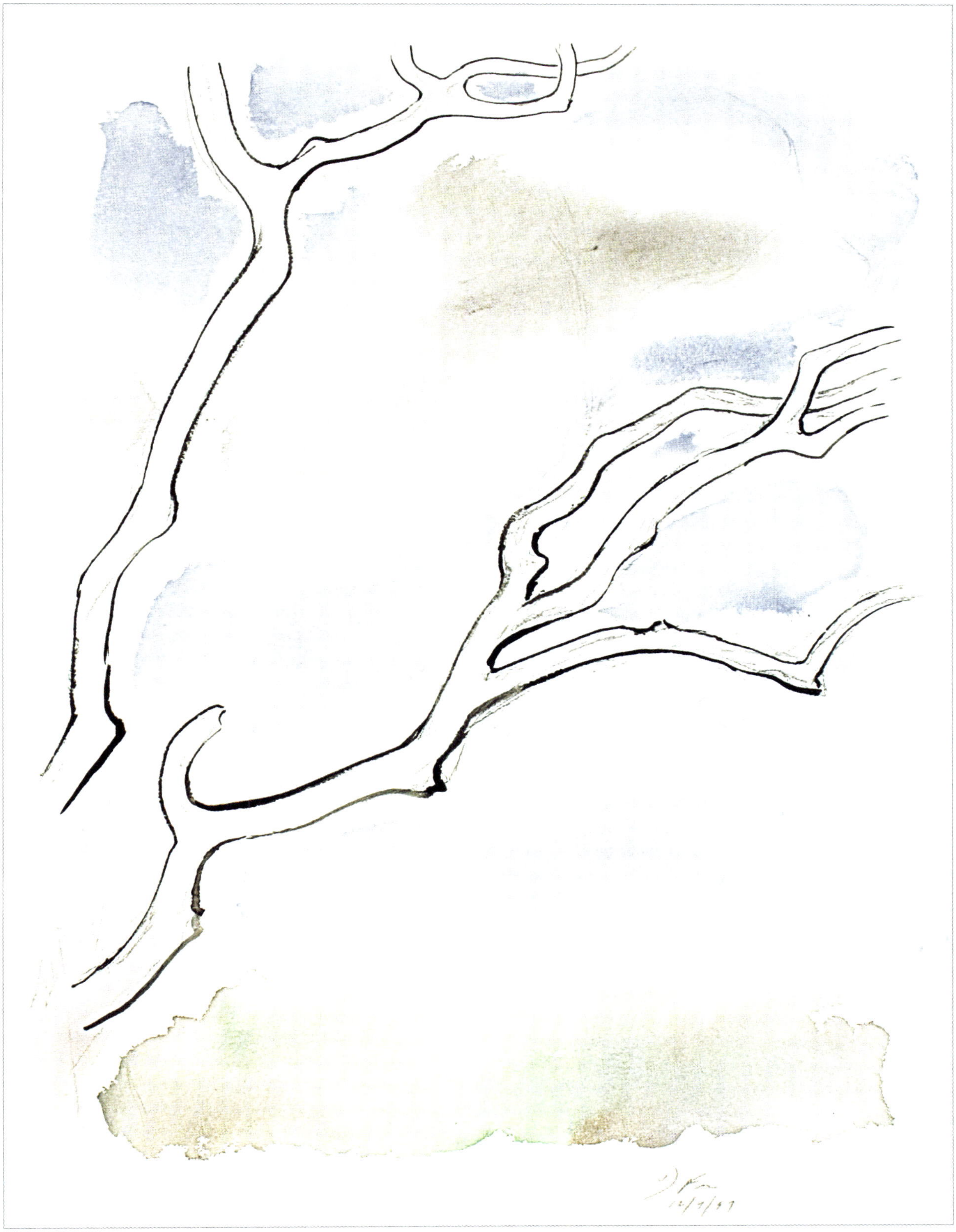

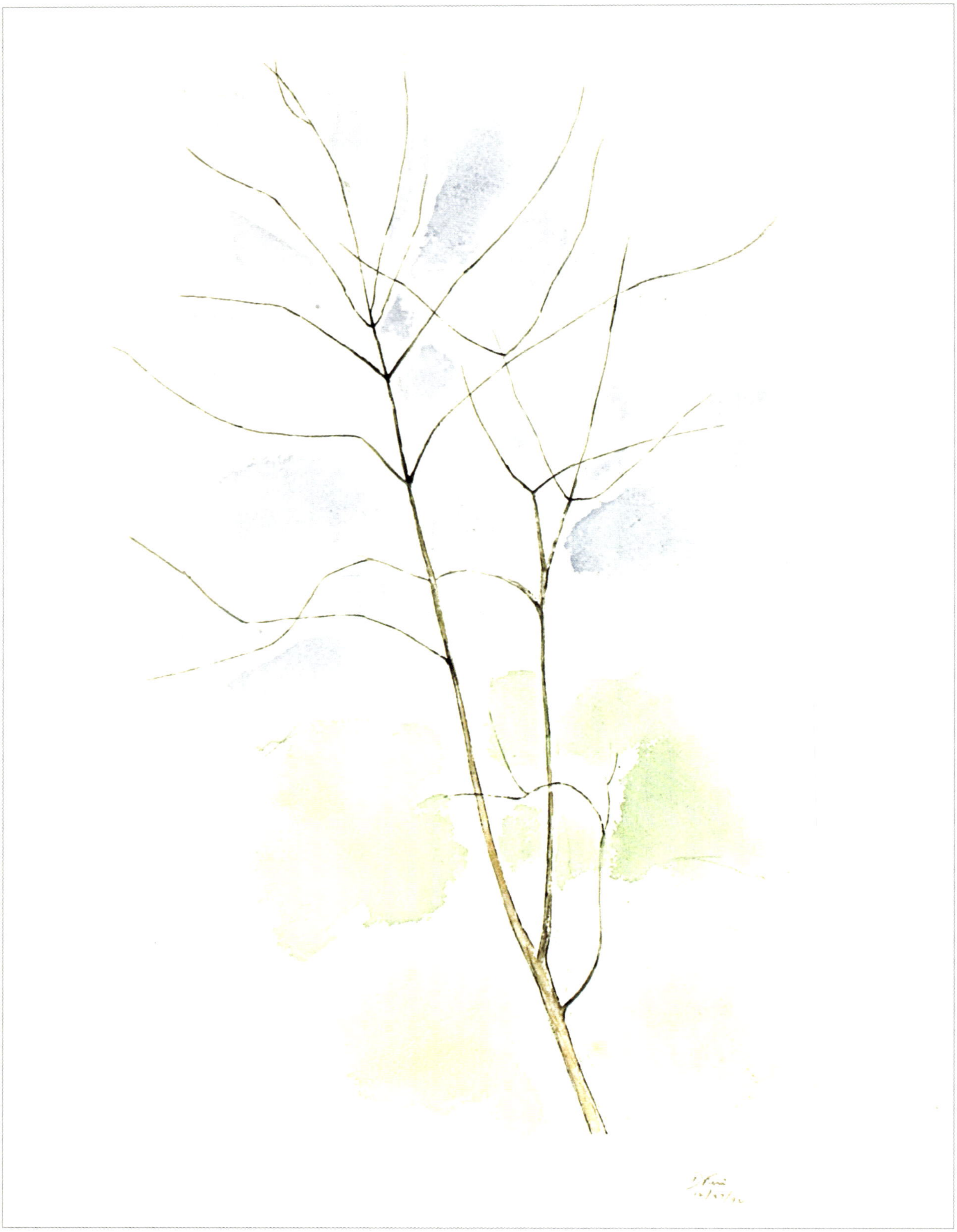

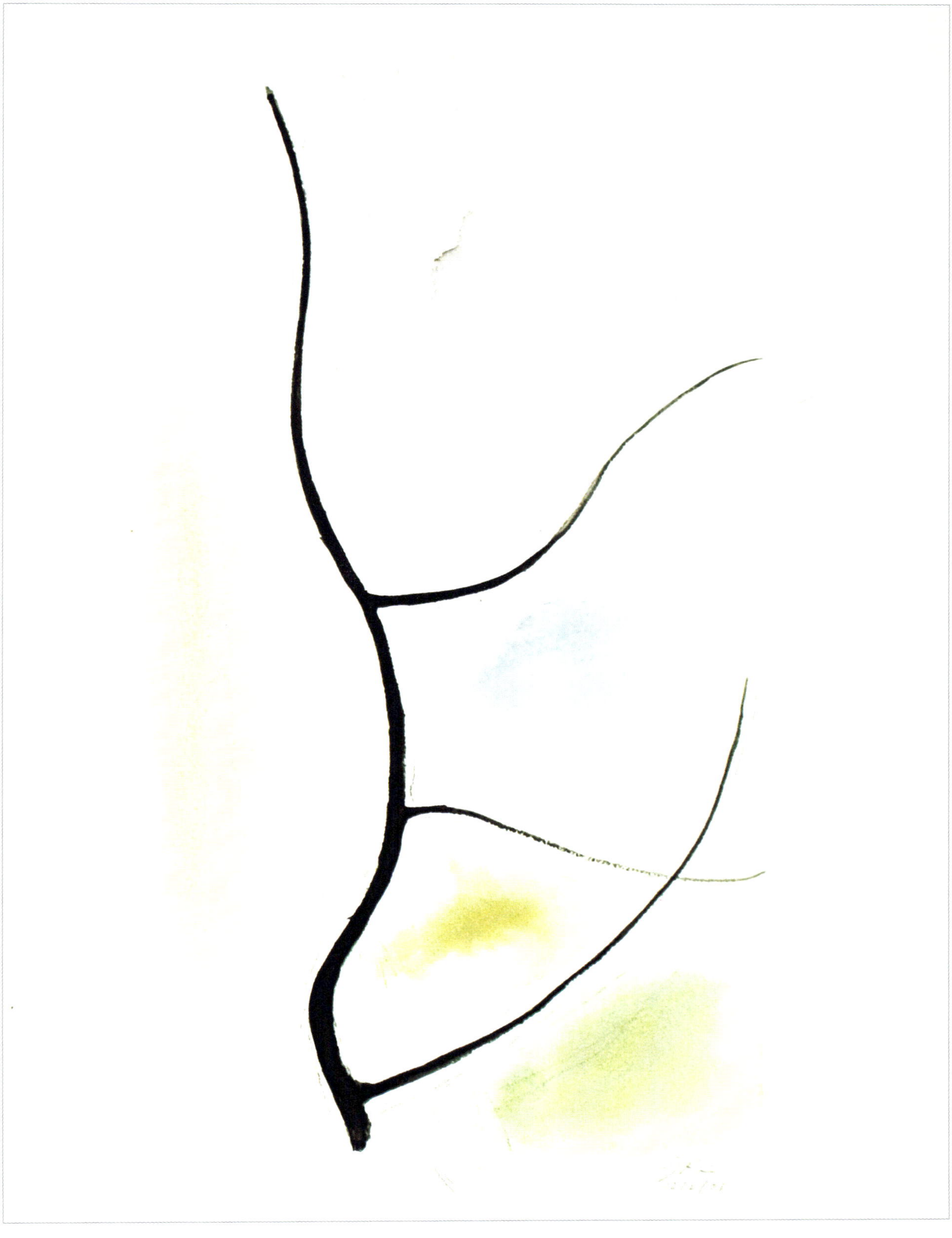

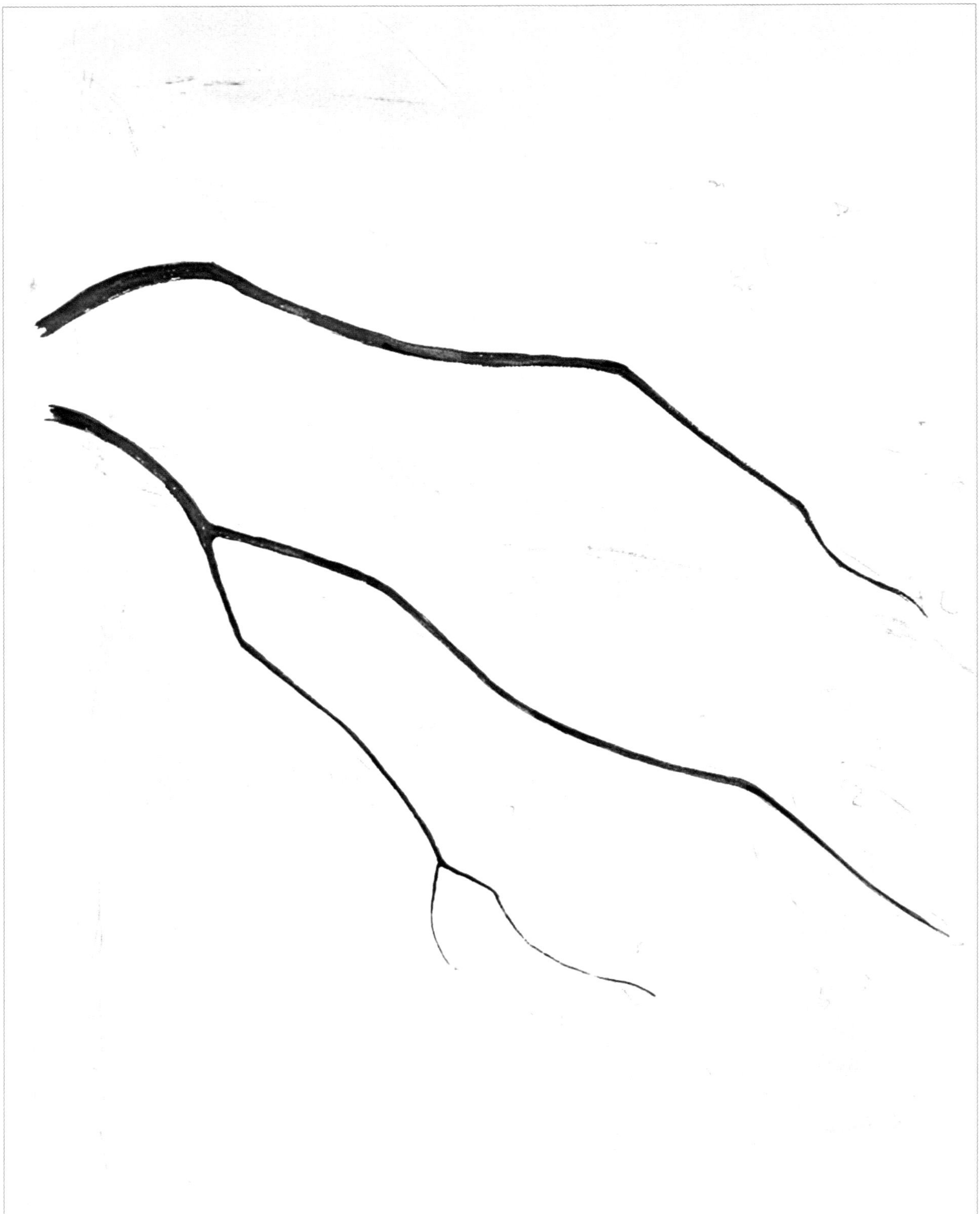

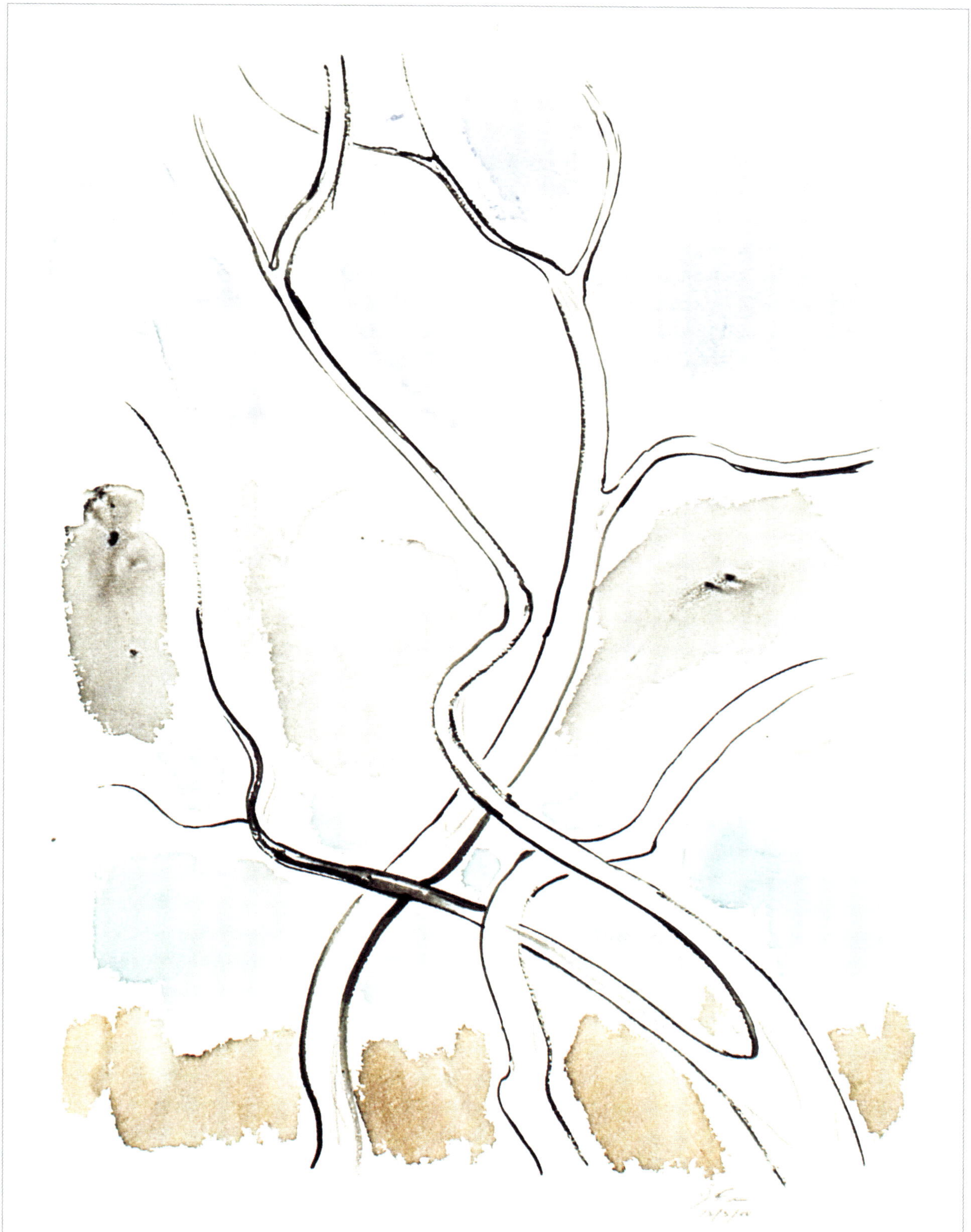